Best wishes of
O. O. McIntyre
New York 1931—

Also by R. Scott Williams

The Forgotten Adventures of Richard Halliburton:
A High-Flying Life from Tennessee to Timbuktu

Odd Words, 1920-1922: An Enhanced
Compilation of Early Columns by Odd McIntyre

How the First Modern Pop Culture
Reporter Conquered New York

by

R. SCOTT
WILLIAMS

An Odd Book:
How the First Modern Pop Culture
Reporter Conquered New York

© 2017 by R. Scott Williams

AnOddBook.com

First published 2017

Manufactured in the United States

ISBN 978-0-9986997-0-7

Cover design by Tom Martin / tommartindesign.com
Cover photo by Blank & Stoller, Inc.

For my friends
(you know who you are)

Acknowledgments

Although writing is usually a solitary experience, a book like this one includes hours of research, so it quickly becomes a group project that includes the fingerprints of many. First, a huge debt of gratitude goes to all my new friends in Odd's hometown of Gallipolis, Ohio. Everyone I had the privilege to meet was anxious to provide artifacts, scrapbooks, photos, stories, and suggestions on where I could possibly find more information. Included in that list of generous Gallipolites is Henny Evans, Randall Fulks, Amber Gillenwater, Julie Howell, Michelle Johnston, Mary Lee Marchi, Jason Riddle, Lora Lynn Snow, Annette Brown Ward, and Dan and Edna Pierce Whiteley.

I'm very grateful to the Esther Allen Greer Museum at the University of Rio Grande, the Gallia County Historical Society, the Gallia County Genealogical Society, the Bossard Memorial Library, and the Ariel-Ann Carson Dater Performing Arts Centre for their help. Many of the photos in the print edition of the book could only be included because of the work of the late Dr. Laura E. Kratz who cared for Maybelle McIntyre's collection and made sure it was located where I would one day be able to find it.

The list of others who helped with the book along the way includes Becky Black, Dorothy Carner, Gary Cox, Greg Daugherty, Jennifer Holt, Donald P. Ranly, Michael Ryan, Sue Schuermann, Rick Shea, and Tim P. Vos. I greatly appreciate Rick Mastroianni who can find just about any book or article that's out there and have it in your hands in hours. Stephanie Castellano, Sharon Shahid, and Edna Pierce Whiteley fixed my typos and grammatical errors and provided suggestions that helped make the book better than it ever could have been without them. My wife, Michelle Williams, read the entire book out loud to me...twice. She provided great edits and suggestions and, without her love and support, I would not have been able to spend so much time and money on this book. My daughters, Alex and Liv, both excellent writers, also provided great ideas and suggestions. I thank my good friend, Tom Martin, for the amazing book cover.

We all owe a huge debt of gratitude to those institutions with the mission of preserving the past and, as it relates to this book, that list includes the Newseum, the Will Rogers Memorial Museums, the University of Missouri, the Library of Congress, the National Archives, the New York Public Library, the New-York Historical Society, and the Museum of the City of New York.

And a standing ovation goes to Odd and Maybelle McIntyre who lived remarkable lives and captured the New York they experienced in decades of columns and articles for the world to enjoy.

Contents

Preface

Photo of Odd McIntyre taken by portrait photographer Pirie MacDonald in the mid-1930s.
The Historical Society of New York Photography Collection

INTRODUCTION

Most of my newspaper days have been consecrated to the study of those fortunates in the passing promenade who have obtained that nebulous quality called celebrity. From the sidelines I have watched the real and the fakes.[1]

O. O. McIntyre

Oscar Odd McIntyre's life is a fascinating story of how a shy high school dropout found fame and fortune writing about pop culture in New York during the Roaring Twenties. It's also a story of camaraderie and friendship between some of the most popular writers, musicians, artists, and entertainers of the first decades of the twentieth century. It's a love story about a married couple who, after years of struggle, made it to the top. It's a story of having the best of everything money can buy, while simultaneously suffering from an undiagnosed illness that resulted in severe physical and mental disabilities. But more than anything, Odd's story is about the power of the written word to, as he put it, "entertain people a little each day." Thanks to the thousands of articles and columns Odd wrote during his lifetime, we have a unique view of pop culture during one of the most exciting times of change and innovation in history. Odd wrote more, made more money, and had more readers than any other columnist in his era. When the world was hungry for newspapers and magazines, and radio and movies were in their infancy, he carefully managed his public persona to become a media superstar.

His rise to stardom is even more remarkable when you learn he was fighting a disease that wasn't yet understood. Trying to hide the symptoms of what was likely pernicious anemia, he struggled with an undiagnosed disorder that caused impaired concentration, great physical weakness, insomnia, severe depression, panic attacks, phobias, and obsessive-compulsive behavior.

Raised by his grandmother in Gallipolis, Ohio after the early death of his mother, he learned to use the deep connection he felt with small-town America, as he wrote about his experiences living a glamorous life of urban sophistication in New York. This allowed him to successfully bridge two profoundly different cultures while working in a period of great innovation in communication, politics, art, and entertainment, as the world was shifting from the Gilded Age to the Progressive Era. New technologies and methods of communication were being quickly adopted around the world, as were new ideas regarding journalism and the role of media in American politics and society. Odd was at the epicenter of communication during the birth of this new modern age.

When differences between traditional values and new urban points of view created a culture war, he was one of the few writers who could bridge both worlds with ease. Later, when the country experienced the disastrous economic depression of the thirties, Odd was there to encourage, to entertain, and to remind readers of the hope that existed all around them, in both the big cities and the small towns.

Odd also personally witnessed and wrote about many of the historic moments and important popular culture movements of that era. He was there with his pad and pencil on a cold, rainy New York day as *Titanic* survivors stepped onto the pier and began sharing their stories of what happened when the "unsinkable" ship struck an iceberg. He was one of the first reporters to interview the Wright brothers when they were a couple of unknown bicycle mechanics trying to build a flying machine. Odd was also there to observe and share the stories of the men and women responsible for creating the music that exploded out of Tin Pan Alley and spread across the world. As Florenz Ziegfeld Jr.'s press agent, he was backstage absorbing—and then sharing—every detail as theater shifted from vaudeville to something completely new and different on

Odd and Maybelle
McIntyre on one of
their frequent trips in
the 1920s. *The Esther
Allen Greer Museum at the
University of Rio Grande*

Broadway. He was the first to write a feature on the stars of *Amos 'n' Andy*, a radio program that became a national sensation. As a close friend of Rudolph Valentino, Charlie Chaplin, and other actors, Odd had a literal front-row seat as moving pictures became nickelodeons, nickelodeons became silent films, and silent films became talkies.

He spent hours in Parisian bars with a group of writers who came to be known as the "Lost Generation," and was there as Ernest Hemingway, Gertrude Stein, T. S. Eliot, and F. Scott Fitzgerald wrote their earliest groundbreaking works.

And through it all, he never stopped thinking of himself as a newspaperman. Working side-by-side with early muckrakers like Ida Tarbell, Lincoln Steffens, and Upton Sinclair, he experienced first-hand the changes that could take place in society when journalists worked to uncover and report the truth in the face of powerful opposition.

His newspaper column, "New York Day by Day," and his thousands of stories in magazines like *Cosmopolitan, Life, McCall's*, and *The Saturday Evening Post* were filled with popular culture references, tales of celebrities out on the town, opinions about modern society, and humorous observations. And what he wrote was remarkably relatable for millions of readers who would never actually get to see New York, Paris, or Hollywood for themselves. Even today, Odd's descriptions of the people he met, places he traveled, and things he experienced provide a unique glimpse into the years when modern entertainment, media, and business were being born.

Despite his popularity with the public, and perhaps largely because of it, his critics were also many. Odd's frequent spelling and grammatical errors were held up for ridicule, and his willingness to stretch the truth for the sake of a good story was eventually used to discredit his work. However, through it all, he remained incredibly popular with the public. Novelist Rupert Hughes wrote, "The fact that he is so popular proves that the public is, as usual, wiser and hungrier for beauty than many believe. His powers of observation and association are astonishing."[2]

Although he created and nurtured an extroverted "man-about-town" image for the world, as he grew older, Odd was plagued by a variety of social anxiety disorders and severe depression. Eventually, he retreated to a life in the shadows, venturing out only at night in his chauffeur-driven Rolls-Royce.

Odd's wife, Maybelle, lived up to her middle name—Hope—and it was she who provided the initial motivation and inspiration for his success. There's no question that Odd's career was a joint venture. Maybelle pushed him forward when he was ready to give up and later managed his career. It was she who negotiated for him some of the most lucrative contracts in the syndication business. Especially toward the end, he could only write if she were in the room, and he would sometimes have a panic attack if she left their building even for a short time.

In assessing the popularity of Odd's column, a writer for *The New York Times* captured the essence of his relationship with readers when he wrote, "His quality of breathless wonder was coupled with an extraordinary ability to make the name of an actress, a crooner or a newspaper rewrite man shimmer in the eyes of the public, who sat on an aisle seat of what for him and them was the greatest show on earth."[3]

The life of Oscar Odd McIntyre is a story of tenacity; of pushing forward despite great obstacles, even when it looks as if there's no possible way to find success. It's a story of what can happen when someone is at the right place, at the right time, with the right talent, and has the good sense to take advantage of it. It's a story of a man who, when no one would give him a chance, created his own way to do what he loved. In the process, he produced an incredible body of work that brings to life one of the most fascinating periods in modern communication and American pop culture.

Part 1:
OHIO

1

A Rough Start

My father weighs in the neighborhood of 250 pounds, has a great shock of white hair and unless he goes out of town never wears a hat. It was not until recently, when he retired to a peaceful cottage on a residential street, that he wore a necktie. Also he eats pie for breakfast.[4]

O. O. McIntyre

Tuberculosis would significantly change the course of Odd McIntyre's life and uproot him not once, but twice during his childhood.

His grandfather, Alexander McIntyre, migrated to America from Kilbarken, Scotland in 1832 at the age of twenty-one, and had settled in Gallipolis, Ohio by 1838. Alex McIntyre met his wife, Mary Joan Jones, when she came to Gallipolis to visit friends. They married in 1847 in her hometown of Walden, West Virginia, located about sixty miles southeast of Gallipolis. The couple first settled in Boyd County, Kentucky, where their son Henry was born in 1854, and their daughter Kate in 1858.

In 1874, Alex and Joan McIntyre joined the hundreds of thousands of settlers who were heading west in the years after the Civil War. They loaded up a wagon and set out for the Nebraska-Missouri border with Henry, their twenty-year-old son who would one day be Odd's father. Henry's sister Kate, however, was not healthy enough for such a journey, so she stayed in Gallipolis.

As their wagon pulled out of town with the other families, the McIntyres couldn't have known they had picked the worst possible year to head West.

The first of the locusts began arriving that summer of 1874, but word had possibly not reached Gallipolis early enough to allow them to postpone their trip. By the time they made it to their destination, it was too late to turn back. In spring of 1875, a nightmare that came to be known as "The Year of the Locust" was unleashed. It was estimated that more than a trillion locusts hatched that year—more than have ever been recorded anytime in history. Professor of entomology Jeffrey Lockwood wrote that the insects streamed overhead for five days. The swarm was 1,800 miles long and at least 110 miles wide, and covered an area equal to that of Connecticut, Delaware, Maine, Maryland, Massachusetts, New Hampshire, New Jersey, New York, Pennsylvania, Rhode Island, and Vermont combined.[5]

Those who witnessed the disaster first-hand later remembered the swarms appeared like a black snowstorm. Their numbers then increased until there were so many they blocked out the sun for days. As they landed in the gardens and fields, they devoured everything from corn, wheat, and flax to the vegetables intended to feed the hard-working settlers and their children. In just a few hours, the locusts could consume an entire cornfield, leaving stalks cut all the way to the ground. One young Nebraska settler later wrote:

Men looked at each other in the face and grew pale. They could have fought bands of Cheyenne or Sioux but these small insects they could not fight. In no time at all, up and down the valley, those honest, brave, patient, hard-working men, women and children were hungry—hopelessly hungry. Families that had been dragging along on a tiny ration of boiled wheat reached the end of that supply.[6]

Having picked the worst possible year to attempt to settle a new farm

Birthplace of Odd McIntyre in Plattsburg, Missouri. *The Gallia County Historical Society*

in the Midwest, Alex McIntyre had little choice but to return to Gallipolis with what little food they had left. Henry was still full of the hope that youth brings, and he liked the area, so he decided not to return to Gallipolis with his parents. Instead, he stayed out West and settled in the town of Plattsburg, Missouri. There, he met Fannie Young. They were married at the home of her parents, John H. and Eliza Tillery Young, on December 1, 1879.

Henry and Fannie became the parents of three young children. Katie was born in 1881 and was named after Henry's sister. Georgia was born in 1882, and the youngest, Oscar Odd, was born in 1884. Fannie selected her son's unusual name in honor of her only living brother, Oscar Odd Young. The actual pronunciation of her brother's name was "Udd."

It had taken a little while for Henry McIntyre, first of his family born in America, to put down roots, but once he did, they grew deep. Understandably, he chose to abandon farming altogether in favor of finding a business with no potential for locust infestation. His skill as a tinsmith, learned from his father, came in handy and provided a way to support his young family. Later, he began managing a hardware store, and then opened a liquor business.

The first blow to Henry and Fannie's young family came in October 1884 when two-year-old Georgia died from tuberculosis. Odd McIntyre was just a baby when his sister died, so he had no memory of her. Sadly, he would also have very little memory of his mother, as she died just three years later of the contagious disease.

Today, we know tuberculosis is spread when an infected person exhales, coughs, or sneezes tiny droplets of infected fluid into the air, which are then inhaled by someone close by. During the late 1800s when McIntyre was born, most still thought of tuberculosis as a hereditary disease rather than something that could be spread from person to person. It wasn't a new disease—by the dawn of the nineteenth century, it had killed one in seven of all the people who had ever lived. However, it wasn't always deadly, and not everyone who was infected was aware they carried the disease.

Tuberculosis continued to spread, and by the end of the same century, more than seventy percent of the U.S. population was infected before they reached the age of twenty. Tuberculosis had become the single most common cause of death.

If a person were unlucky enough to get sick, he or she first began to feel tired and run down. A dry, persistent cough developed, that over time began to dredge up bloody phlegm. Although the most commonly prescribed treatment was rest, fresh air and exposure to sunlight, many individuals who were infected continued working as long as they could force themselves out of bed, having no alternative for supporting their families. They battled a constant low-grade fever, chest pains, and difficulty breathing.

Not just a disease of the lungs, tuberculosis also attacked the spine, kidneys, and other parts of the body. Significant weight loss usually preceded death, and near the end, victims were nothing but skin and bones. The term "consumption" was appropriate, as the disease literally consumed the body. To somehow lessen the horror, it was regarded as "a wasting disease, which produced in its victims a refinement of the body, heightened artistic sensibilities and ennoblement of the soul."[7]

Henry McIntyre, then a heavy drinker with a taste for whiskey, found himself a widower with two small children. The perfect solution to his problem lay just outside Plattsburg at the home of his late wife's parents, John and Eliza Tillery Young. Still living with them was their twenty-year-old daughter, Dora, who agreed to help raise her late sister's children.

The home of his maternal grandparents was where Odd's first memories were made. In later years, he wrote fondly of Grandpa Young,

Rare photo of the lobby of the Laclede Hotel.
Becky Black

calling him "a homespun, lovable and homely old Lincolnian gentleman who chuckled over the pleasantry more than anyone."[8] Odd also joked that when the neighbors looked at him when he was a baby, they thought he was the spitting image of his Grandpa Young. He added that his grandfather "had won a skillet at the county fair for being the ugliest man in Clinton County, Missouri."[9]

Grandma Young was Elizabeth "Eliza" Tillery Young, originally from Woodford, Kentucky. McIntyre remembered her as a "roly poly, laughing, apple dumpling type." The Youngs had married in Woodford on February 27, 1812, and became the parents of eight children. Their home was a happy one, and a safe place for Odd and Katie to spend time after the death of their mother. In addition to raising livestock, Grandpa Young farmed wheat and corn, and often took his grandson with him when he rode out to inspect his livestock. The farm also included herding and

The Laclede Hotel in Plattsburg, Missouri.

Odd McIntyre as a child in
Plattsburg, Missouri.
*The Esther Allen Greer Museum
at the University of Rio Grande*

hunting dogs, and it was there that Odd developed a love for dogs that continued throughout his life.

Around 1890, Henry McIntyre began managing the Laclede Hotel at the corner of Main and Broadway in Plattsburg. Although he visited his children nearly every evening and brought them gifts, bonding with his young son proved difficult for Henry. He had little use for conversation with his children. Odd wrote, "He merely had no capacity to express what emotion he felt…Father rode out in his buggy almost every evening to see us and bring us some trifle but was always awkwardly inarticulate in our presence."[10] Odd later told his editor and biographer Charles Driscoll, "I was always uneasy when alone with him even to the very last time I saw him. I hardly ever smiled when I was with him. I can't remember that he ever kissed any of us children. I felt somehow embarrassed to be in a room with him and I wanted an excuse to get away."[11]

The closest they would ever come to an intimate moment was one evening as the two were walking along a winding creek near the Young's house. Odd wrote that dusk was descending when his father stopped and said, "Son, I miss your mother and always shall." He looked up to see his father's eyes were glistening. Together, they walked back to the farm in silence, and it was the last time Odd ever heard his father speak of his mother.

The children's time living with their maternal grandparents would be cut short when, after just two years, tuberculosis once again touched the family. Early one morning before dawn in December 1888, Grandpa Young woke Odd and Katie and took them to their Aunt Dora's room. Grandma Young sat at the end of Dora's bed crying softly.

"Led by Grandpa, I instinctively tiptoed," Odd wrote. "Aunt Dora opened her eyes, smiled so sweetly and sadly that I began to cry too. It was all strange. This was my first contact with death and it affected me profoundly."[12]

After the death of his sister-in-law, Henry decided it wouldn't be possible for their aging grandparents to continue to raise eight-year-old Katie and five-year-old Odd. The father and his two children boarded a train and headed more than 750 miles east to his hometown of Gallipolis, Ohio, so his young children could live with his mother and sister. It took several days to get from Plattsburg to Gallipolis by train, so Henry was surely aware that he would not be seeing his children very often in the years to come.

Odd remembered his father sitting rigidly staring out the window for most of the trip. The still-grieving father spoke little, but showed he cared for his children the only way he knew how—by giving them presents. One item, a glass revolver filled with colored candies, stood out in Odd's memory for the rest of his life.

Although he was never able to become close with his children, Henry was well-liked in Plattsburg and had a reputation for being both a good businessman and a loyal friend. An article written around 1893 offers a closer look at Odd's father:

> *Mr. McIntyre is the possessor of ability and energy, and is eminently the right man to provide for the various wants of the weary guests who seek shelter beneath his hospitable roof. As a citizen he has during his many years residence in Plattsburg won the esteem and confidence of a large circle of friends, and is now numbered among the prominent and influential busi-nessmen of the city, ever ready to aid the public improvement or assist in any*

*social or benevolent enterprise…a pronounced Democrat, and while not a
politician in the common acceptance of the term, and never an office seeker,
finds special enjoyment in attending the large political gatherings, the State
and National conventions, where the issues of the day are fully discussed.*[13]

Around the time he turned forty, Henry McIntyre decided his heavy
drinking and tobacco use had become a real problem. He locked himself
in one of the rooms of his hotel and arranged for an employee to bring
him food and water, as he suffered the agony of withdrawal for three
days. After he left the hotel room, he never drank or used tobacco again
for the rest of his life.

While the decision to take his young children to live so far away from
Plattsburg was no doubt difficult, Henry must have been comforted to
know they would be surrounded by the love and support of their extended
family and friends in Gallipolis.

After their experience with the locusts, Henry's parents, Alex and Joan
McIntyre, returned to their hometown where Alex set up a tinsmith shop
next to their two-story frame house on Court Street. Alex McIntyre died
in 1882 after an illness that had lasted several years. His obituary in the
Gallipolis Journal read, "Mr. McIntyre was all that could be expected as
a father, friend and citizen. He was a man of correct principles, correct
habits and honest sentiments. He was laid away as he wished and as he
lived, simply, with no show, no glitter."[14]

As Henry McIntyre pulled up to his widowed mother's home with his
children, he knew it was a good place to leave them. In addition to his
mother, the household included his sister, Kate, who now ran a hat shop
around the corner from the house. His youngest brother, George, had
taken over their father's tinsmith shop next door.

Henry McIntyre spent a week at his mother's house before it was time
for him to depart and leave his children behind for good. Of course, it's
impossible to know what he was thinking as he left that morning. Odd
remembered being picked up and silently hugged by their father, and
then standing on his grandmother's front stoop watching as the carriage
carrying him to the train station rolled out of sight. They continued
waving, even though Odd remembered his father never once turned
around to look or wave back.

Odd had a new home.

2

Boyville

No Street—not even Unter den Linden or Champs
Élysées—will ever compare to our Court. It was the
capital of Boyville when the world was corduroyed
and there seemed to be an answer for everything.

O. O. McIntyre

Odd McIntyre had been writing a monthly column for *Cosmopolitan* for sixteen years in the spring of 1929. The magazine's iconic editor, Ray Long, also happened to be one of Odd's best friends, and Long frequently shared manuscripts with him to get his opinion before including them in the magazine. One morning, Odd stopped by the office. As Long rushed off to a meeting, he tossed Odd an early excerpt of *The Autobiography of Calvin Coolidge* to look over until he returned.

President Coolidge had shocked the world two years earlier when, while vacationing in South Dakota, he held a rather unconventional press conference at Rapid City High School. It seemed likely that the president would be announcing his intention to run for a third term in office. As the reporters arrived, they found Coolidge sitting at a teacher's

Second Avenue and the Gallipolis City Park around the time Odd was a boy.

desk. He instructed them to form a single line, and as they filed past the desk, he handed each reporter a slip of paper on which was written, "I do not choose to run for President in nineteen twenty-eight." The demands of his job and the recent deaths of his father and his youngest son had taken a toll on his mental and physical health, and Coolidge was ready for a much-needed break. As the reporters shouted out

Odd (left) with his dog Major around 1895 and (right) as a young man. *Gallia County Historical Society*

questions, "Silent Cal," as he was nicknamed, remained quiet. "There will be nothing more from this office today," he said with a smile and then headed off for some fishing.[15]

Ray Long learned of Coolidge's decision from his friend, Herbert Hoover, while the two were at a party at the Bohemian Grove, the infamous men's-only campground near San Francisco. Even though the club's motto was "Weaving spiders come not here," meaning it is not a place for business, Long was always thinking about his magazine, and he immediately saw an opportunity.

When he returned to New York, he began trying to persuade the president to write the story of his life, which would be excerpted in *Cosmopolitan*. Although Coolidge was hesitant, he was willing to consider the idea. Finally, Long's persistence paid off, and he was invited to the White House to talk it over with the president in person.

When Long arrived, President Coolidge handed him a short, typewritten sample. "If you are not pleased with it, none of the things we've said need bind you," he said.[16] Long was thrilled at the thought of getting the article of the decade in his magazine so, of course, he loved what he read. Coolidge began writing his life story and finished it in three and a half months. Before the manuscript was published as a book, it was to be serialized in *Cosmopolitan*, and Long went to great lengths to make sure no one saw it before it appeared in the magazine.

Odd made himself comfortable in Long's office and read the excerpt that was to be printed in the June 1929 issue with the title "Scenes of My Childhood." President Coolidge wrote about growing up in Plymouth, Vermont, and described a life of New England simplicity. He wrote, "It was all a fine atmosphere in which to raise a boy. As I look back on it I constantly think how clean it all was. There was little about it that was artificial."[17] As Odd read, he began to think about his own childhood in Gallipolis. He wrote in the same *Cosmopolitan* issue:

> *I know that as I sat in the very heartbeat of the greatest city in the world, the years rolled suddenly back and I was a boy...I heard again the melancholy drone of the honeybees and that dolorous ring of the blacksmith's anvil back of McCormack's livery stable. I heard old Mr. Kraus from his seat on the huckster wagon intone, 'Ask your ma does she want any strawberries, bub.' I heard the clatter of the Ohio River Railroad hack moving toward the depot to meet what we knew as 'the noon train.' I heard the flying hoofs of Aaron Frank's black stallion, 'Flaming Arrow' beat against the walls of his stable stall...I saw the cobblestone gutters painted with fresh spring rain, I saw wisps of smoke haze from scattered chimney tops. I saw the West Virginia hills over yonder cowling in dusk and a faint prick of stars in the plush night.*[18]

Odd's columns and articles would frequently include stories of his years growing up in Gallipolis. Some of what he wrote was romanticized in the way memories of the distant past often are, but Odd also wanted to connect with his readers across the country by reminding them of his humble beginnings. Whether they still lived in small towns or had migrated to large cities like Atlanta, Chicago, and New York, most had similar memories of growing up, and they found comfort in his writing about sweeter, simpler times.

Ultimately, it didn't really matter which of the details Odd wrote about his childhood and teenage years were absolute fact. One thing was certain: Gallipolis had been a very good place for Odd and his sister to grow up.

It was different from many of the other small towns and cities in the Ohio River Valley, and from a very early age, every child in Gallipolis was taught about the town's unique history. In 1790, French aristocrats who came to be called "The French 500" settled a tract of land they named the "City of the Gauls." More settlers from France would follow, forced out of their homeland by the economic crisis and social upheaval brought on by the French Revolution.

Around the same time, politicians and land speculators in the United States were looking for ways to help the new nation rise to its feet after the Revolutionary War. In many cases, they were also anxious to grow their own personal fortunes. A group of American businessmen and war patriots, led by Reverend Manasseh Cutler, a minister from Massachusetts, and Winthrop Sargent, a patriot, politician and writer, formed the Ohio Company and petitioned Congress in 1787 for a large tract of land in the Northwest Territory. When William Duer, secretary to the U.S. Board of the Treasury, heard their proposal, he thought he saw an opportunity to get rich quick. He put together a secret deal in which he convinced Congress to accept a reduced price per acre and very liberal credit terms for the land Cutler and Sargent wanted for their operation. What Congress didn't know was that Duer had asked leaders of the Ohio Company to increase the amount of land they requested and give him the option to purchase it later. Duer illegally and secretly obtained the rights to purchase three and a half million acres of Western wilderness at a bargain price. His scheme was "a reckless audacious land gamble of staggering proportions."[19]

Duer opened the Scioto Company and planned to pay for the land by selling chunks of it at greatly increased prices to wealthy American and European investors. Via an agent, he sent brochures to France that described a land with "cotton in great perfection, sugar equal in flavor and whiteness to the best Muscovado, tobacco, superior to that of Virginia and grapes from which a wine may be made preferable to the many wines of Europe."[20]

Those who purchased lots were given fancy engraved scrolls that they understood to be actual deeds to the land they had purchased. Unfortunately, the scrolls were worthless because Duer didn't actually own the land he was selling.

Despite the risky nature of his venture, Duer hired a crew of workmen from Massachusetts to begin carving out a small settlement at a high point on the Ohio River, where the Chickamauga Creek branched out. They cleared the forest, chopping down hundreds of trees, which were then used to build crude houses with dirt floors. They worked through the summer of 1790 and then were paid by the Scioto Company to stay and assist the group of settlers arriving from France.

The French settlers experienced great hardships during their voyage, both on land and at sea. One of the ships on which they traveled, too old for such a demanding trip, nearly sank. Their first stop in America was Alexandria, Virginia, and it was there they discovered the titles to the land they had purchased were worthless. To make matters worse, the settlers in another colony who were supposed to assist the French settlers had spent the winter battling smallpox and starvation and were in no position to help anyone.

On October 17, 1790, the first of the French settlers arrived at what would become the town of Gallipolis. The men, women, and children climbed up the riverbank in anticipation of their first glimpse of their new land. While not quite the paradise they had expected, what they found was likely a relief after their exhausting journey from France and the great disappointment in Alexandria:

> *In the rude clearing they saw four rows of log cabins paralleling the river. Each row was about 300 feet long. At intervals of 100 feet there were open spaces for cross streets. Blockhouses stood at each corner of the cabined area. Nearby was a log stockade enclosing company stores and some larger, finer homes that had been built for the wealthier members. A log breastwork stretched along the crest of the river bank. Surrounding the clearing on three sides was a deep, almost impenetrable forest that looked mysteriously forbidding. The people quietly entered the cabins allotted to them.*[21]

Antoine Saugrain, a physician and chemist, was among the settlers that day as they explored this new town made up of very rustic cabins. He later wrote in his diary, "To the great astonishment of the Americans who had built the huts, we decided to give a ball that same evening. At this first meeting it was decided to call the new town Gallipolis; that is 'the city of the Gauls,' where the virtues of our ancestors could flourish."[22]

Dr. Saugrain would go on to assist Meriwether Lewis and William Clark in gathering the supplies they needed for their famed "Lewis and Clark" expedition.

Of course, the French settlers were not prepared for the hardships this new life presented. Most were not farmers or hunters, but they were able to grow some of their food, and until the Ohio River froze in the winter, they traded with farmers from other towns for extra meat and vegetables. Those who did stop to trade with the French settlers in Gallipolis found the village to be very different from what they were used to.

By 1792, there were still around 400 residents in Gallipolis. While most settlements of this size along the Ohio River were full of rough frontiersmen and women who were farmers and hunters, Gallipolis had a significant number of artisans and craftspeople. The town included goldsmiths, watchmakers, stonecutters, glassblowers, painters, and even a sculptor. One visitor wrote that as he watched, a glassblower made him a thermometer, a barometer, and a glass pipe for tobacco.

Unfortunately, the land the French settlers had "purchased" from the Scioto Company still actually belonged to the Ohio Company. In December 1795, a group of representatives from the town met with agents of the Ohio Company, hoping they would allow them to keep the land on which they had settled. But rather than giving them the land outright, as the group hoped, the agents offered the French an opportunity to legitimately purchase the land for a little over a dollar per acre. Although frustrated, they gave in and purchased 912 acres for $1,140. For some, this was the final blow, and many families began leaving Gallipolis. In March 1795, Congress acknowledged that William Duer and the Scioto Company had swindled the settlers and awarded the 200 or so who remained 24,000 acres of land about fifty miles west of Gallipolis. Many of the original French settlers who remained were too discouraged to continue, so they sold their land and used the money to purchase farms elsewhere. Others chose to stay and settle the property they had been given by the government. By the early 1800s, there were only a few of the original French families remaining in the town.

Perhaps William Duer fully intended to legally purchase the Ohio tract once he had sold enough of the land to the French. Regardless of his intentions, the Scioto Company went bankrupt, and his illegal speculations in land and stocks sent him to prison in 1792, where he died seven years later.

The home of Odd's grandmother in Gallipolis, Ohio in which he spent his childhood.
The Gallia County Historical Society

A little more than 100 years after the first French settlers climbed the bank of the Ohio River at Gallipolis, a young Odd McIntyre was standing on his grandmother's porch waving as a buggy carried his father away. Like the original French settlers, he too was about to begin a new life of adventure.

Much had changed in the century since the town was founded. By the 1880s, when Odd arrived, the 4,500 residents had two banks, eleven churches, and three newspapers. The town had maintained its reputation for craftsmanship, and its prime location on the Ohio River made it a hub of activity as settlers from around the world stopped on their way "out West." Visitors and locals provided plenty of business for the tannery, broom factory, machine shops, and furniture and woodworking factories. There were even two companies that manufactured carriages.

Times were changing rapidly, as many Americans were moving from a life of agriculture to one of living in town and working for a weekly wage in a factory. Industrialization and urbanization were having an impact on the values and ideals from the Victorian Era that had been in place for decades. Although they didn't know it at the time, the scene was being set for the birth of the Progressive Era.

If you were living in Gallipolis on the first day of 1880 and picked up a copy of the *Journal*, you would have read about the activities of a very busy and prosperous town.

Advertisements for local stores filled the front page. Harmison's New York Store offered "Everything Elegant and Cheap that the Heart Could Desire," while Harry Frank's Clothing House offered a "Mammoth Display of Fall and Winter Clothing." If your eye landed in the lower corner of the front page, you would have discovered that the "Great Drug House" of P. A. Sanns & Son "Shines like a Star in comparison with other Establishments in Southern Ohio." Ads for dentists Stafford & Brown and vitapathic physician J. G. Hall were nestled in between ads for a manufacturer of saddles and bridles, Horton's "celebrated" coal, and White Rose fine-cut chewing tobacco.

Communication was evolving, and one article that day mentioned a new technology coming to the community. "One of the consolidated telephone agents was here the other day encouraging the formation of an exchange, and several citizens are now cogitating over the matter,"[23] the article read. The telephone had been a sensation at the 1876 centennial celebration in Philadelphia, but by the beginning of the 1880s, there were only 50,000 in the entire nation. In just twenty years, that number would grow to 1.5 million.

For a town whose success could partially be attributed to its location on a busy river, big changes were also coming in the area of transportation. Another article that morning stated, "The Ohio and West Virginia Railroad, from Logan to Gallipolis on the Ohio River, is fast approaching completion. Track-laying is rapidly progressing from Logan south; a second force of track-layers will be put to work at the Gallipolis end within the next ten days."[24] When trains did finally begin arriving several times each day, they made enough of an impression on Odd to become a feature frequently mentioned in his writing as an adult.

Not everything Odd remembered about Gallipolis was pleasant. Like the French settlers before him, he was unprepared for the new land in which he found himself. Especially in the early years, he was bullied by some of the other boys in town and frequently ended up with a bloody lip or a black eye. To survive, he stayed close to home and played with his sister and her friends where he was sure to be safe.

To make matters more difficult, Odd was growing up without a father consistently in his life. He and his sister would spend a few weeks each year in Plattsburg, and his father would periodically visit them in Gallipolis. In later years, Odd would publicly write affectionately of his father, calling him "one of the truly great Americans."[25] However, long after his father's death, Odd wrote that he remembered his father as a "glum man with a perpetual scowl" or that he was "gruff and uncommunicative."[26]

Henry McIntyre's penchant for giving his children expensive gifts continued throughout Odd's childhood. One of the most memorable was a black horse and carriage that, in Odd's mind, impressed the locals as they drove about the town. He wrote later that riding in the carriage made him feel "regal and grand." His cousin Lucy M. Ritter remembered, "He was always full of fun and excited about some new present his father had sent him…children from blocks around came to see the newest toy."[27] Odd made an impression on her that she never forgot when he proudly paraded down the street with a large box that contained a musical top depicting a circus.

One of his father's early gifts was a Rover safety bicycle. In the mid-1890s, America was undergoing a bicycle boom, and hundreds of manufacturers were going into the bicycle business. Odd practiced until he mastered tricks on his bike like climbing through the frame while the bike was in motion, and riding with the handlebars completely removed. When he was ten, he attended a gathering of the Gallia County Chapter of the League of American Wheelmen, a group that advocated for paved roads for bicycles. He won first place as "champion trick bicycle rider." The fact that he was the only competitor didn't dampen the memories of his enthusiastic performance:

> *I was attired in a red sweater, a baggy pair of green knickerbockers and white knee-length hose, purloined from my sister, Kate. A space was cleared on the bicycle track, a hillbilly band played 'Over the Waves,' and I pedaled into the arena. I rode tiptoe on one pedal, hopping over to the other, crawled through the frame, reared on one wheel and executed a circle, stopped dead still and folded my hands serenely over my breast, and as a thrilling climax rode with one foot on the seat and the other on the handlebars. With my cap held aloft…Anyway, I was called to the judges stand and presented with an appropriately engraved gold medal which, incidentally, turned green before I could get home again to show Grandma.[28]*

Odd eventually became friends with a group of boys whose names would appear periodically in his future articles and columns, including Harry Maddy, Earl Mauck, George Bovie, Ned Deletombe, Alfred Resener, Henry Cherrington, Ernest Shivley, Merrill Kerr, and Morris Small. There were others, like Sam Riff, whom he called "a sort of Huck Finn of the river," and Shine Bell, with whom he was arrested for skinny-dipping in Chickamauga Creek on a Sunday.

As teenagers, Odd and some of the boys created a club called The F.S.G.A., the meaning of which has been lost to history. They booked venues for dances, which were then decorated with banners. On the wall of a smoking room, they once hung a lithograph of vaudeville actress Della Fox wearing tights and seductively smoking a cigarette.

Despite living in a close-knit community and having a family that supported and loved him, things were not perfect in the young man's world. While he occasionally shoplifted and charged things he didn't really need to one of his father's accounts, Odd's biggest problem was his inability to focus on traditional schoolwork and conform his behavior to the standard of the day. The education system at the turn of the century was unable to adapt to a bright student with Odd's special needs. He wrote:

To this day, I have an unreasonable hatred for schools. To me they are hideous symbols of restraint. I never spent a single happy hour inside a schoolhouse. One of the reasons I have not been back to my beloved hometown for more than twenty years is that dolorous chimes of the public-school bells transport me into a fit of absolute unconquerable melancholia. I often awaken, bathed in a cold dew, over a nightmare that the truant officer is dragging me back to school.[29]

In retrospect, Odd's difficulty fitting in as a student and his extreme anxiety over school seem to indicate something other than normal adolescent rebellion. He had a combination of extreme creativity and high sensitivity, and was beginning to display symptoms of the illness he would have as an adult. His frustrations could still be felt in his writing decades after he left school:

I was once humiliated in school, too, a humiliation beyond anything I have since known and it has left a scar. Following an impertinence to my teacher, the principal of the school was called in to see what could be done. He heard her story and without asking me a single question charged at me in the manner of an infuriated bull. He yanked me from my seat, dragged me to the teacher's platform and thrashed me soundly with a switch before the entire school. I was gamer than now; despite the pain, I was determined not to cry. That increased his fury. When he finally quit I was near the fainting point. That principal is one of the few people I have never forgiven. Some years ago I was guest of honor at a luncheon at which he was among those who came around to shake hands with me. He was unctuous and beaming but he got an arctic reception. Refusing to accept the hand he extended, I declared, 'You know why and if I were not a guest here I would sock you in the jaw.'[30]

Throughout Odd's life, there were certain individuals who could discern a kind of brilliance in him that others could not. One of the first was a woman Odd called Aunt Annie. Annie Vanden Adams was the wife of Charles Adams, a family friend and former border in the McIntyre home. She was born to James and Margaret Vanden in a house at 425 Third Street in Gallipolis. Her ancestors were among the original settlers of the town, having migrated from Holland. They joined the French settlers in 1792. According to family stories, Aunt Annie's great-grandfather, Martinius Vanden Bemden, was said to have hunted with Daniel Boone during the years that Boone lived in nearby Point Pleasant, West Virginia. While working as a teacher, Annie met and married Charles who was living with the McIntyre family. She and Odd's Aunt Kate also became close friends.

When Odd was a boy, Charles and Annie Adams lived just a few blocks away from the McIntyre home, above the Adams Furniture Store, which Charles ran. Their home became a place of creative refuge for Odd. Annie Adams was one of the few people in his life at the time who shared his growing interest in popular culture, politics, and the world outside their small town. It didn't hurt that she always had a platter of fresh-baked cookies in the parlor. It was there that he was first exposed to magazines like *Puck* and *Judge*, and he was able to explore stack after stack of back issues of magazines and newspapers.

Before television and radio, magazines were the primary mass medium for exploring contemporary culture and entertainment. Some also did important investigative journalism, exposing corruption and illegal practices in government and industries like railroad, oil, and food

Cover of *Puck* from September 12, 1900 featuring a political cartoon of Theodore Roosevelt by Udo J. Keppler in which the Republican vice-presidential nominee was portrayed as part untamed stallion and part gunslinger. *HarpWeek.com*

production.

One of Odd's favorites, *Puck*, was the first humor magazine published in the United States and was understandably seductive for a boy with a creative mind like Odd's. By the time he was sixteen, the nation's most popular satirical journal had been shaking things up for nearly thirty years.

With a name inspired by a character in Shakespeare's *A Midsummer Night's Dream*, *Puck* was the first magazine to include illustrated advertising and the first to successfully use full-color lithography printing in a weekly publication. It addition to being one of the most graphic and visually-pleasing magazines of its time, it was also one of the most powerful. One historian noted, "It is hard to overestimate the political influence of *Puck* during the last two decades of the 19th Century. It was greater than all newspapers combined."[31] By the 1900s, around the time Odd began reading back issues of the magazine at Aunt Annie's, *Puck* had shifted its focus slightly and began to include color illustrations of fashionable women by artist Charles Gibson.

Judge, another satirical magazine, had been started by a group of artists who left *Puck* to go out on their own. Similar to *Puck*, it used cartoons and humor to address issues relating to politics, religion and business, but it was different in that it took a decidedly Republican slant and targeted subjects considered off-limits by the editors at *Puck*.

Odd took such an interest in the back issues of the magazines and old newspapers that Aunt Annie bought him a large scrapbook and taught him how to make glue using flour and water. Together they clipped out the images and articles that he liked and glued them into the scrapbook. When many others gave up on Odd, she nurtured the spark she saw in him, helping to flame it into a passion. Odd never forgot her kindness.

After he signed his first syndicate contract, one of the first letters he sent was to Aunt Annie. He wrote, "I know you and Uncle Charlie will be pleased to know that the little boy who used to have so much fun at your house—which is me—has just signed a three year contract with the McNaught Syndicate."[32]

In addition to magazines and newspapers, Odd loved to read the dime novels of the day. Around the turn of the century, improved printing technology and rail distribution contributed to the increase in the production of novels aimed at a young working-class audience, especially males. Sold at newsstands and general stores, they featured the men and women of the Wild West, murder-solving detectives, and tales of

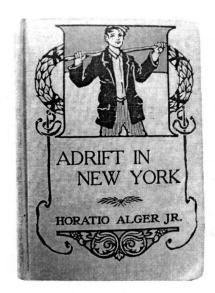

Horatio Alger Jr.'s *Adrift in New York*, published in 1903, featured a young protagonist trying to find success while living on the streets of New York.

romance. Rather than spending time doing homework—or schoolwork, for that matter—Odd preferred to read about Frank Merriwell, a character who appeared in more than two hundred dime novels. The hero of the series solved mysteries and righted wrongs while excelling at football, baseball, basketball, crew, and track at Yale. Reading another of his favorite dime novel writers, Horatio Alger Jr., perhaps contributed to Odd's dreams of success.

Most of Alger's stories followed the same "rags to riches" formula and featured poor children, usually in New York, who struggled with a variety of challenges. By the end of the stories, with the help of a mentor and by applying the values of honesty, integrity, and hard work, they find a place in society where they are accepted. In the years to come, Odd would have his own struggles in New York, and the boys of Alger's novels surely came to his mind.

Of all the elements that contributed to Odd's "alternative education," newspapers were what seemed to most capture his attention. One teacher, Alice Bradbury, noticed Odd had become more interested in creating a newspaper than in doing his actual schoolwork. Even if handed a math worksheet, Odd would draw out a newspaper and write stories about his classmates.[33]

Another incident relating to his education stands out because of the sheer nerve—or desperation—it took to pull off. It's easy to skip a class or a day of classes, or even a week of school. That was nothing to Odd; he skipped an entire term. After telling his grandmother goodbye and leaving for school, he would stash his books in a hiding place he created at the lumberyard on Back Street, and then make his way to Chickamauga Creek where he enjoyed what he called a "Huck Finn life." The truth

Odd's grandmother Mary Joan
Jones McIntyre. (left) *Courtesy
Edna Pierce Whiteley* (top) *Courtesy
The Esther Allen Greer Museum at the
University of Rio Grande*

finally came out at the end of the term after a chance encounter between
his grandmother and a teacher from the school. As he stood in front of
his grandmother, expecting her to be angry, she instead broke into tears:

> *At last she started to say something, but suddenly her voice quavered and she
> bent over in a paroxysm of sobbing, rocking back and to and fro and twisting
> her handkerchief into an anguished ball...All through the night—I slept in a
> cot in her room—I could hear her toss and moan, and though she never referred
> to the escapade or rebuked me, she went about for several days as one who had
> just recovered from a frightful seizure.*[34]

About six weeks before the end of his third year in high school, the
principal had had enough. After yet another infraction, he slammed Odd
down into a chair in his office, and through deep breaths said, "You are
through, right now. When you go home, don't ever come back. Mark
my words. You will never come to any good." He leaned forward and
angrily continued, "You will be a bitter disappointment to yourself and
anyone who cares about you."[35]

Obviously, the principal was wrong about Odd, and he eventually made his family proud. In 1911, Odd was living in Cincinnati and had taken the train back home because his grandmother was very ill. At twenty-seven, he was already an assistant editor of *The Cincinnati Post* and would soon be departing for New York and a job with *Hampton's Magazine*. Sadly, his grandmother couldn't comprehend any good news or career updates. Her mind was failing, and she was confused during his visit, and called him "Odd Georgie," which was the name she had used for her late son, Odd's Uncle George. Odd later wrote:

> *With a suffocating lump in my throat, I sat beside her chair, holding her gnarled, withered hand and trying to touch off a spark of memory that would make her recall the boy she had 'raised.' It was hopelessly futile. She just rocked gently and clung to my hand…the depot hack pulled up at the door and I had to leave. I stooped over and kissed her dry, bloodless lips and she gave me a quick, convulsive hug accompanied by a sudden faint and startled cry. I should like to think that for a brief second in that embrace the cry was an echo of recognition rumbling down the haunting corridors of memory, but I fear it is not so…it was the nearest my heart ever came to breaking. I was never to see her again in this world.[36]*

3

Della and Maybelle

This morning traded Harry Maxon three Julia Arthurs for one Della Fox.

O. O. McIntyre

Entertainer Della Fox found 1900 to be a very tough year. Odd's "first stage love," as he later called her, was drinking herself to death. In June, her family had her committed to a sanitarium, and the newspapers went wild. All over the country, readers shook their heads as they read of her problems, that were attributed to "an excessive use of stimulants" and deemed "the penalty of high living." The final incident had taken place just a few weeks earlier at Proctor's Twenty-Third Street Theatre in New York, where she was booked in a series of performances singing songs from the comic operas that had made her famous. A few minutes into the first performance, it was clear she was in no shape to sing, and her contract at Proctor's was canceled. Afterward, she moved into the Parker House Hotel at Thirty-Ninth Street and Broadway, where bills for wine "made even the bell boys—veterans though they were of hotel life in the Tenderloin—open their eyes and gasp."[37]

Entertainer Della Fox showing off the "Little Della Fox Curl" that swept the country and triggered a national sensation among teenage girls.

When she began hallucinating and accused friends and family members of trying to steal her jewelry and money, her brother decided it was time to get her some help, and Della was moved to a sanitarium.

Della May Fox was born October 13, 1870, in St. Louis, Missouri. Her father, Andrew Fox, was a photographer who specialized in photographing stage actors and actresses. Della's early exposure to the American theater was through her father, and the positive response from audiences to her childhood theatrical performances resulted in a young woman determined to make it in show business. By the time she was nineteen, she was singing and acting in a variety of theaters in New York, including Niblo's Garden on Broadway. It was said that while there were many other singers and actresses with much more talent, Fox became a star because of the sheer magnetism she exuded on stage. Physically, she was very small and plump, and became known for her curly hair and "childlike" persona.

"Little Della Fox," as she was called, created a sensation with her signature hairdo, in which one curl dangled over her forehead. Suddenly, teenage girls around the nation could be seen sporting the "Little Della Fox Curl."

As Odd later wrote, "The feminine figure had not yet attained its whiplike grace. Beauty was somewhat elephantine. And to my amateur eyes, the plump Della was the loveliest creature I ever beheld." Fox was propelled to superstardom after she joined DeWolf Hopper and his opera company, and began appearing with Hopper in performances both in New York and on the road. Soon, her face and ample figure began appearing frequently in magazines and newspapers and on a variety of products, including cigarette cards.

Della Fox cigarette card.

It was for his collection of Della Fox cigarette cards that Odd was most famous among his peers in Gallipolis. Innovations in advertising at the end of the nineteenth century had introduced the concept of celebrity images on collectible items. Tobacco companies began including small cards with images of celebrities such as athletes and performers in their cigarette packs. To get the money to buy cigarettes, Odd wrote he and his friends "scoured the backyards for old bottles, salvaged tidbits from junk heaps, mowed the lawn and otherwise slaved in the cause of the Great Art."[38] Odd was proud of his collection of Della Fox cards, that included her in "fourteen different poses" including in "tights kittenishly arching a bow, standing imperiously with a shepherd's crook, reclining on a stage

(top) Promotional poster for *Wang* staring
DeWolf Hopper and Della Fox, *Library of Congress
Prints and Photographs Division*

(left) Actor DeWolf Hopper, *Wake Forest University
ZSR Library Theater Actor Prints and Photographs Collection*

rock, in a Spanish laced bodice daintily holding her skirt edges at arm's length, in glittering black jet looking over her shoulder and holding a silk hat aloft, and in many other postures."[39]

His testosterone-fueled dreams came true when Odd first laid eyes on a poster in front of the Ariel Opera House. Gallipolis had been included in Della Fox and DeWolf Hopper's tour of the country performing their hit comic opera *Wang*. Only five years old in 1900, the theater was creating a great deal of controversy in Gallipolis because of the "risqué" nature of some of the productions. Articles in the local papers around this time criticized the sexual undertones of the shows, and called for the firing of the manager who was responsible for booking such "scandalous" content.

While *Wang* was tame, even by 1900 standards, it stirred up controversy with scenes in which Fox, playing the role of a male prince, wore tights that allowed the audience to see more of her legs than would usually be considered appropriate for a young lady. The play, set in Siam, featured a mixture of musical performances, comedy, and burlesque.

This was Odd's chance to meet the girl of his dreams in person. Fortunately, he had a friend, Bert France, who worked backstage at the Ariel.

France agreed to sneak Odd backstage if he would be quiet and stay out of the way. Odd anticipated the big night for weeks and did all he could do to prepare. He wrote that in the days leading up to her visit to Gallipolis, he thought of Della Fox during the day and dreamed of her every night. When the evening finally came, he dressed especially nicely and used a little extra "hair slick." After coming up with a good excuse and getting permission from his grandmother for staying out late, Odd headed down Second Street to the Ariel. France sneaked him in, and Odd staked out a hidden corner in the wings, feeling much older than his sixteen years. Then it happened. Odd wrote:

A dressing-room door opened and there SHE stood, gorgeously arrayed in pink flesh tights, her bare neck and arms powdered to a snowy whiteness. In her hand was a lighted cigarette—the one she puffed while singing about 'a summer night, a babbling brook.' Remember? My heart executed several loop-the-loops and stood still. She was moving toward me for her entrance. Through the blur it struck me her expression had somehow lost its photographic sweetness. She appeared to halt right at my side and I heard what I always imagined was a mellifluous voice thunder at the stage manager, 'What is this brat doing in the wings?' How easily the careless word or the heedless gesture may break a tender heart! I crept back to the little frame house on Court Street—a stricken, bruised and disillusioned thing, refusing the usual slice of sugared bread and glass of fresh milk before retiring.[40]

While Odd's brief "love affair" with Della Fox ended poorly, fortunately, she was not the only young lady who captured his heart in those early years. He knew his secret was out when he overheard his grandmother yell over the back fence to Aunt Amelia Stark, "I think he's girling."[41]

Maybelle Hope Small as a young girl. *The Esther Allen Greer Museum at the University of Rio Grande*

Maybelle Hope Small lived just a block away from Odd, and he had had a crush on her for almost as long as he could remember. Maybelle was born in Gallipolis on February 9, 1884, to Charles Richard Small and Catherine "Kate" Gatewood Small. The Smalls were married on October 26, 1880, at the home of her parents, Captain James and Elizabeth Gatewood. Captain Gatewood was a prominent timberman in Gallipolis and one of the founders of the Gatewood-Fuller Furniture Company.

When they married, Charles Small was managing Small's Landing, his father's coal mine. He was a widower with two young children; Nellie was six and Homer was four. Maybelle likely got much of her ambition from her father, as he was a man of many talents. After working for his father's coal mine, he later became a Gallia County sheriff, then for many years he was both wharf master and steamboat master of Gallipolis.

Odd and Maybelle knew each other for so long, they were never really certain exactly when and where they first laid eyes on each other. Odd wrote a few different stories about the moment he first noticed Maybelle. He referenced one meeting at a Sunday school social and another when the grade school was having a group photo taken and their hands accidentally touched. She apparently made an impression

Maybelle Hope Small as young woman around the time she and Odd began dating. *The Esther Allen Greer Museum at the University of Rio Grande*

when he saw her skipping rope in front of a large red brick house that he would eventually purchase for her as a twenty-fifth wedding anniversary present. He wrote, "The first time I cast sheep's eyes at Maybelle Hope Small…she was in gingham and spring-heeled shoes, with two braids down her back the color of pulled taffy…we were in kindergarten and I was five years old and in kilts."[42]

Already struggling with the extreme shyness he would deal with throughout his life, there is no doubt that working up the courage to talk to her as they grew older was a long, painful process. From riding past her house on his bike and showing off his latest tricks, to waiting until he saw her enter the soda shop to decide he was hungry for ice cream, their courtship was helped along by proximity and persistence.

In one story they would frequently tell in later years, Odd drew Maybelle's name as a partner for a Sunday school fundraiser and picnic. The boys each had to pay for the lunch that was prepared by the girls whose name they had drawn. Fate intervened, and Odd drew Maybelle's name—but then it came time to give her the money. Tortured for days with anxiety and fear, Odd finally rode up to the Small family's home on his bike, knocked on the door, and waited. When it finally opened, he stammered, "Are you Maybelle's mother? Um, here's the money for her lunch." He thrust the coins in her hand, turned bright red, ran for his bike, and rode off before Kate Small had time to look down at the coins she now held.

On the night of the annual moonlight hayride to George's Creek, to Odd's great relief, there was an open seat in the hay next to Maybelle. At least for Odd, that was the real beginning of their courtship. From then on, everyone knew that Odd always carried Maybelle's books home from school.

Odd was never shy about sharing his feelings regarding his wife in his columns. He once wrote:

> *Life has splattered my path with many exciting and memorable footprints. I have stood where Lindberg landed in France, lighted the Prince of Wales' cigarette from the end of my own while waiting at the hat-checker's in a London night club, spent a ghastly night in a cutthroat water-front hotel in Antwerp, waved to the Kaiser at his Doorn exile and stood ankle-deep in water that flooded a top-deck cabin on a supposedly sinking Atlantic liner. Yet the emotional wallop that stands out most vividly is that late afternoon when I, a stone-bruised lad, hobbled along carrying Her books home from school!*[43]

Although Odd became, as he called it, "a one-woman man," he did see his first love, Della Fox, one last time. In his early years as a theater critic in New York, he was sent to interview the actress in a rundown, shabby hotel frequented by "down-on-their-luck" entertainers. Of course, she didn't remember being in Gallipolis or calling Odd a brat, but he wrote that after the interview, he left "terrifically conscious of the mustiness and emptiness of a dead passion."[44]

4

Printer's Ink

Since my earliest recollection I wanted to be a newspaper reporter and I cannot tell you why.[45]

O. O. McIntyre

It's impossible to know if the letter actually came from Arthur Brisbane of the New York *Evening Journal* or if someone on his staff wrote it on his behalf. But it was postmarked "Genesco, New York," which was the location of Brisbane's summer home, so it was certainly possible it had come from the man himself.

Receiving a letter from one of the most famous editors in the country made young Odd McIntyre a celebrity for a few weeks in Gallipolis. An inspiration to Odd, Brisbane had become a reporter at nineteen for *The Sun* in 1883 while Charles A. Dana was editor. By the time he was twenty-five, Brisbane himself had become the editor of the influential newspaper. From there, he went to work at *The World* under Joseph Pulitzer, until William Randolph Hearst recruited him to the *New York Journal*. Brisbane was a major player in a remarkable revolution that occurred in newspaper publishing during the last two decades of the nineteenth century. Previously, newspapers had been read primarily by

Newspaper editor Arthur Brisbane (left) and media tycoon William Randolph Hearst (right). *Library of Congress Prints and Photographs Division*

the educated upper class, and debates between political parties usually dictated the content. Newspapers like Pulitzer's *World* and Hearst's *Journal* were among the first "urban tabloids," which helped introduce the idea that news could also be entertaining. They discovered that large headlines shouting out the sensational news of the day grabbed the attention of city-dwellers; and the more sensation, the more sales. Stories were made shorter and easier to read for the uneducated and immigrants and entire articles could be completed during a city commute to an office or factory. No longer just a sea of tiny letters floating on page after page of newsprint, these newspapers also included illustrations and cartoons and launched a whole industry of talented writers and artists, that seemed to spring up overnight.

Suddenly, there was a growing need for comic strips, women's columns, theater reviews, fashion advice, and sports news. With editors owning newspapers in multiple cities around the nation, it became cost-efficient to use some of the same content in all their newspapers. Edward Willis Scripps started with *The Penny Press* in Cleveland in 1878, and by 1909 he owned thirty-four newspapers in fifteen states. More than half the material in his papers was made up of content from his own news service and feature syndicate.

The economics of the newspaper business was evolving quickly, and in 1898, there was a major shift when the National Biscuit Company—

which later became Nabisco—launched the first million-dollar advertising campaign. The price of newspapers was kept low and advertising revenue was expected to help pay for the costs and generate profits. The higher the circulation, the more advertising they could sell, thus creating even more profit for the owners.

This great potential for revenue generated intense competition between newspapers for readers. Around the mid-1890s, the term "yellow journalism" was used to describe the rise of sensational stories that frequently contained exaggerations or intentional misrepresentations of the truth. The name was inspired by a character from *Hogan's Alley*, a comic strip that was originally a popular feature in Joseph Pulitzer's New York *World*.

Created by Richard Outcault, who later illustrated Buster Brown, the strip featured the adventures of a young boy named Mickey Dugan who came to be known as "The Yellow Dugan Kid." The character was bald, had large ears, and always wore an oversized yellow shirt. The strip was so successful for the *World*, William Randolph Hearst paid Outcault a substantial amount of money to move it to his *New York Journal*. Pulitzer wasn't about to give up a property that was generating so much revenue, so

Hogan's Alley from the March 15, 1896 issue of Pulitzer's *World. The San Francisco Academy of Comic Art Collection, The Ohio State University Cartoon Research Library.*

he hired a cartoonist to draw a similar comic strip that featured many of the same elements, including the yellow shirt. As the competition between the two newspapers grew, they each began increasing the amount of space dedicated to running the cartoon, and "The Yellow Kid" became a symbol of the decline of journalistic integrity.

At the time, few editors embraced yellow journalism more than Arthur Brisbane, who became one of the most powerful editors in the country:

> *He had cut his teeth in Charles Dana's London bureau, where he had the good fortune, for a journalist at least, of being present when Jack the Ripper was terrorizing Whitechapel. Brisbane devoted himself to the Ripper tale, often sending back reports so exaggerated and colorful that his New York editors considered them stomach-turning. As Brisbane himself once noted, he knew that "murder, mayhem, and mystery" sold newspapers. When Pulitzer, his second major employer, complained that his precious journal was turning into a Victorian scandal sheet, Brisbane retaliated by trotting out the circulation figures and the increased advertising revenues.* [46]

Odd was happy to pull his personal letter from Brisbane out of the blue envelope for anyone who asked. It read, "There is nothing open

The Ariel Opera House in Gallipolis, Ohio. *Lora Lynn Snow*

at the present." However, it offered great hope in Odd's young mind because it continued with, "But I'll keep your name on file." It was even exciting for Odd to think his name would be in Brisbane's file. Almost as impressive as the signature were the words printed in red ink at the top, "Dictated to the Phonograph."[47]

At the turn of the century, Odd was a young man trying to figure out his place in the world. Although he dreamed of becoming a reporter, he knew his father would never approve. Henry McIntyre was still running the Laclede Hotel in Plattsburg, and when it was clear Odd would not finish high school, his father pressured him to leave Gallipolis and go to work for him. When Odd took a job as night manager at the Park Central Hotel in Gallipolis, it was likely a sort of compromise. He was able to join the "family business" and do something that would gain his father's approval, while still being able to stay close to home, his friends, and Maybelle. One can imagine, after all the struggles with her young grandson, Grandma McIntyre was relieved to mail Odd's father a July 1901 clipping from the *Gallipolis Daily Tribune* that read, "Mr. Odd McIntyre, one of our most accommodating and clever young men, is now night clerk at the Park Central."[48]

The hotel, adjacent to the Ariel Opera House, was considered the finest hotel in the region. Opened on New Year's Eve in 1883, it included modern conveniences like hot water, electric lights, and steam heat. There was even a tunnel that ran underground from the theater to the hotel that made it especially convenient for the traveling entertainers who came to Gallipolis. The performers and others from New York and Chicago were the guests who most interested seventeen-year-old Odd. He loved hearing about how they lived, worked, and played in the big cities, and it was his first opportunity to experience in real life some of the ideas and images from the scrapbooks Annie Adams had helped him assemble or that he had read about in the books by Horatio Alger.

Although he was finally headed in a direction that his father could appreciate by working in a hotel, Odd still spent his spare time either at the offices of the *Gallipolis Daily Journal* or on the heels of the newspaper's young editor, James T. Johnson.

While large city newspapers relied on sensational stories and attention-getting graphics to maximize readership, the weeklies and dailies in towns like Gallipolis featured reports about the lives of regular folks who lived in the community. Sometimes referred to as the "rural press" or "grassroots journalism," they avoided sensationalism and gossip, and reported on births, deaths, marriages, and gatherings of business and society clubs. News from the local churches, schools, and libraries were included, and the residents of the towns often functioned as reporters themselves, providing articles, letters, poems, and other content that was enjoyed by their neighbors. Newspapers in small towns usually emphasized the positive and pleasant things that happened, leaving out anything that would reflect poorly on the residents of the community.

Because of the lack of television and radio, and with so many niche communities, there was enough business for multiple newspapers in one town to thrive, if managed properly. Many also generated additional revenue by using their presses for printing flyers, brochures, and other items for community businesses.

Around the time Odd was working as a night manager at the Park Central Hotel, there were five locally produced newspapers in Gallipolis: the *Daily Tribune*, the *Daily News*, the *Journal*, the *Bulletin* and the *Times*.[49]

Fortunately, the *Journal's* editor, James T. Johnson, or Jimmy, as the residents of Gallipolis called him, took an interest in Odd. Like Annie Adams, Johnson saw something in Odd that he thought was worth nurturing. His mentorship made an impression on Odd that would last for the rest of his life. Odd wrote, "I admired him more than the reigning United States president. I used to follow him around from store to store where he gathered the news of the day. I finally became his messenger boy and carried his news. He wrote every item as it was collected and took it to the newspaper office completed."[50] Also a correspondent for *The Cincinnati Enquirer*, Johnson was popular in town and prominent in the social, political, and business affairs of Gallipolis. Most days, he collected his stories on a bicycle with a pencil and pad in hand. He frequently pedaled up to groups gathered in the park and asked, "Any items for the paper today?" His marriage in 1889 to Pearl Kerns should have brought Johnson much happiness, but she died soon after they were married.

Pearl's death devastated the young reporter and he never really recovered. He confided to the editor of another local paper that he would be glad when the end came, so he could finally "lay down the burden of his life and be with Pearl once again."[51]

Despite his grief, he continued teaching Odd what it took to produce a newspaper. Johnson and the *Journal's* owner, Peter McMullen, took advantage of Odd's enthusiasm and put the budding reporter to work.

Maybelle Hope Small and Odd McIntyre before they were married. *The Esther Allen Greer Museum at the University of Rio Grande*

Odd set type, washed off the forms for the old bed press, and cleaned the office. Eventually, Johnson let him write his own stories. The first item Odd wrote appeared in the "Personal Notes" section. He later said that the moment he saw his words, "J. B. Rothgab was a visitor from Cheshire today," in print, he decided then and there he would become a newspaperman.[52]

All the training came in handy in the spring of 1902, when Johnson was unable to work because of an injured index finger. McMullen handed Odd a notebook and pencil and told him to "rustle up" some news. The January 8, 1902, *Tribune* included the item, "Mr. J. T. Johnson, city reporter for the Journal, is laid up from a wounded index finger and Mr. Odd McIntyre is doing his work for him."[53] He certainly had the time then, because he was no longer night manager of the Park Central Hotel. He had been fired for falling asleep on the job and causing some of the guests to miss their train. His heart was clearly never going to be in the hotel business.

McMullen began paying Odd two dollars per week to fill in for Johnson, and he was also earning extra money ushering at the Ariel Opera House, a job that allowed him to see all the shows that came into town. Years later, Odd remembered, "I trotted up and down the main street gathering local items…after doing the reportorial chores, I helped turn the big press wheel, wrapped the papers to be mailed and carried them down in a clothes basket to the post office. Then I returned and distributed type until supper time."[54]

Around this time, Maybelle was thinking about her future, as well. She had been traveling out of town to attend finishing school, and had discovered there was a world outside of Gallipolis. But knowing about it and experiencing it were two different things. In 1900, women were still not allowed to vote, serve on juries, or hold elected positions. Their place in society was tied very closely to the men they married. According to the Supreme Court at the time, they were not "persons" under the Fourteenth Amendment to the Constitution, that guarantees equal protection under the law. For Maybelle and other young women like her, this was not acceptable. They wanted something more out of life than running a household in a small town and having no control over their own destinies. Odd wrote, "One night—a starry night with crickets chirping—we sat in a hammock at her house and she told me I should break away from my hometown…she saw no future."[55]

Meanwhile, Jimmy Johnson was not getting better. He had a fever that gradually worsened and he suffered from intense weakness and headaches. Eventually, he couldn't even get out of bed. The doctor diagnosed him with typhoid fever that then worsened to pneumonia. Johnson died at 10:15 a.m. on March 27, 1902, at the age of twenty-seven.

McMullen gave Odd a small raise, and named him the editor of the *Daily Journal*. Already a fan of entertainment of all kinds, Odd was thrilled to discover that reporters could get free admission to entertainment venues like Prince's Floating Opera and the Ariel Opera House, with the expectation they would write about the shows there.

Odd had been reporting for the *Gallipolis Journal* for about a year when his father came home for one of his yearly visits. There was more tension than usual between father and son during this visit, as his father had arranged for Odd to take a test to attend West Point. For once, Odd stood up to his father and refused. But as Odd discovered as soon as his father left, Henry McIntyre still had no intention of letting his son become a newspaper reporter.

After his father said goodbye to the family and left for Plattsburg, Grandma McIntyre and Odd's sister, Kate, shared the bad news. His father had enrolled Odd at the Bartlett Commercial College in Cincinnati. Henry fully expected Odd to quit his job and obey, with no questions asked and no discussion. And he did. It's natural to wonder why Odd didn't refuse to go to Cincinnati, just like he refused to go to West Point. He had a job, and his grandmother certainly wouldn't have kicked him out.

Although he would hate leaving his newspaper job, the opportunity to live in a big city like Cincinnati must have been enticing for a young man like Odd. And of course, as Maybelle pointed out, the two of them weren't going to find the kind of future they wanted by staying in Gallipolis. Odd packed his single bag and bid his *Gallipolis Journal* readers farewell. His comments, saved in Maybelle's scrapbook, reflect Odd's love of journalism and his understanding of its importance to a democratic society:

> *With this issue of the Journal its reportorial duties pass within the control of a new man…I discontinue reportorial work with regret. The profession is one among the noblest…Next to the pulpit the press stands preeminent as the exponent of that which is highest and best. Conscientiously edited and conducted it appeals to a wide congregation. To have a part among the splendid fellowship which is laboring for the betterment of humanity is a high public privilege and I trust I appreciate its value.[56]*

In addition to paying Odd's tuition to the business college, Odd's father had arranged for Odd and his sister Kate, who accompanied him, to live with a family friend on West Seventh Street in Cincinnati. He also sent money to Kate each month for the siblings' expenses. Henry McIntyre's plan for his son was that he would spend six months at the business college, gain some basic office skills, and then go to work for a Missouri friend of his who was a congressman in Washington, D.C. Odd would need to quickly learn bookkeeping, stenography, and how to use the typewriter.

Around this time, Odd received his last piece of advice from his Grandpa Young, with whom he had remained close. After a visit, Odd departed his grandparent's home for the train station. Grandpa Young said, "Just be yourself and don't ever try to put on airs." Many years later, Odd wrote, "It didn't sound so hot then—merely the mutterings of a doddering old gentleman. Yet today I am not so sure it is not about the best advice possible for a young man standing on the threshold of his career."[57]

Bartlett's Commercial College and School of Business was established by Robert M. Bartlett in 1834 in Philadelphia, and is considered to be the first business college in the world. He opened another school in Pittsburgh and then one in Cincinnati, which Odd attended. Located at Main and Fourth Streets, the school was where "young accountants are regularly and systematically, and thoroughly trained to the theory and practice of book-keeping, and having passed through the course are examined, and if found duly proficient, receive regular diplomas."[58] By the time Odd arrived, the founder had been dead many years, and the name of the school had been shortened to the Bartlett Commercial College. Run by Robert Bartlett's son, C. M. Bartlett, the school focused on teaching skills that would be of use as potential office workers were moving from small towns to big cities, and from farming and agriculture to business and professional jobs. An ad in the Hamilton, Ohio *Journal* in 1901 explained the college's curriculum:

The fall term of the Bartlett Commercial College offers unequal advantages to persons desiring a thorough, practical course in either bookkeeping or shorthand. In the bookkeeping department students are taught ten-systems of accounting in use at the present time in the largest business establishments. They also receive a thorough training in commercial arithmetic, commercial law, essentials of English, business correspondence, punctuation and spelling. We have exclusive right to teach Gregg shorthand in this section of the country, a system that holds the world's record for speed with legibility, and which can be learned in from one-half to one-third of the time required by the Pitutanic systems. In this department the students receive instruction in touch typewriting...our graduates are in demand. More than seventy firms applied to us during the month of August for bookkeepers and stenographers.[59]

From the very beginning, Odd was more interested in what was going on at the Cincinnati newspapers than what was happening in the shorthand classes at Bartlett College. While he failed every single area of business

A an early view of Cincinnati's Over-the-Rhine neighborhood.

study at the school, touch typing was the one skill at which he excelled. He was attending school in the city where just fourteen years earlier the first typing contest had been held, pitting Frank McGurrin of Salt Lake City against Louis Traub of Cincinnati. McGurrin used a QWERTY-style typewriter with a shift bar and the touch-typing technique, while Traub used a typewriter with double rows of keys and typed while looking at the keyboard. McGurrin won the competition, setting a new speed standard of ninety-eight words per minute. The QWERTY keyboard and touch technique were then embraced by the industry and are still used today.

While other students were learning shorthand and math, Odd daydreamed, skipped class, or looked for opportunities to practice typing.

Sometimes he slipped out and explored the neighborhoods where large newspaper offices and plants where turning out daily and weekly newspapers and other publications. In addition to large daily papers like *The Cincinnati Times-Star, The Cincinnati Enquirer,* and *The Cincinnati Post,* immigrants could get their news from one of many non-English newspapers. For example, by 1900, more than 200,000 native-born Germans lived in Ohio, and many were faithful subscribers to Cincinnati's *Tägliches Cincinnatier Volksblatt,* that was published in German six days a week.

Many of the German immigrants, who brought with them a tradition and knowledge of brewing beer, began setting up on the outskirts of town in an area that came to be called Over-the-Rhine. By the end of the 1800s, Cincinnati had become the "Beer Capital of the World," and many breweries, bootleggers, and saloons could be found there. Over-the-Rhine was a tempting neighborhood for a young man living away from home and with time to kill. Odd wrote, "It was a phase of life that from the sidelines interested me more than bookkeeping or stenography but was a bad place for a youth with no parental restraint."[60]

His constant failures at Bartlett College were made worse by his loneliness and a period of what he referred to as melancholy, but which was very likely the symptom of an illness that would plague him in later years.

By the ninth month of the six-month program, it was obvious to Henry that Odd was wasting both time and money. Kate opened the mail one day to find two train tickets. She was to return home to Gallipolis, while Odd was instructed to go to Plattsburg where he would work at his father's hotel. As he sat alone on the train headed to Plattsburg, he felt like a complete failure. For the first and only time, he considered suicide. He wrote:

> *In the end I went to Plattsburg. On that long and lonely ride to Missouri I had the first realization that I had already become what the world knows as a failure. Nothing is so utterly blighting to a young man. It inspired the only thought of suicide I ever had. The only thing encouraging about my life were the letters in a firm round hand from Maybelle Hope Small. She for no reason at all had a little faith in me.*[61]

5

Dayton

I think I miss as much as anything the barn-like, drafty and cavernous structures that housed so many of the best newspapers in the land. There was rare music in the squeak of the rickety stairs, romance in the antiquated desks and a Dickensy flavor in the cobwebby ceilings.[62]

O. O. McIntyre

The years after leaving Cincinnati and the business college were tough ones for Odd. He worked for his father at the Laclede Hotel for part of the time, but when he was there, it was clear he was somewhere he didn't want to be, doing something for which he had no passion. Odd had developed a taste for beer in Cincinnati, and he spent more time at the local saloons and pubs than working in the hotel. At one point, he left Plattsburg for a short stint in another small Ohio town after receiving a telegram from Earl Mauck, a friend from Gallipolis. Mauck was returning home and recommended Odd for his job at the *Morning Tribune* located in the pottery town of East Liverpool, Ohio.

The area was perfect for making pottery, with a great amount of clay in the soil, natural gas to fuel the kilns, and the Ohio River for transportation. More than fifty percent of the nation's ceramics were produced in the town, and millions of bowls, plates, cups, and saucers made their way from Liverpool to homes around the country. About ninety percent of the town's population was employed in low-paying production jobs at one of the nearly thirty potteries in the area. Odd observed many residents working long hours in spaces that were nearly unbearable. The extremely hot and dirty conditions resulted in a community plagued by pneumonia, bronchitis, and lead poisoning. He certainly couldn't see a future for himself and Maybelle in East Liverpool.

The prodigal son returned to his father's home in Missouri to once again try his hand at the hotel business, but he quickly fell back into his old ways. When not working at the hotel, Odd could be found in the saloons, drinking beer and playing cards. Despite his worry, Henry McIntyre still had difficulty communicating with his only son, and the two barely spoke. Henry surely shook his head in frustration when thinking back to his own struggles to survive the locust plague that summer in 1874. He remembered looking into the faces of the starving families, and had hoped the things he had done for Odd would keep him from ever being in the same position. After five months of watching Odd waste his life, Henry finally had enough. Odd wrote:

> One night I came home after midnight a little tipsy. All lights went out in the town at 12 o' clock. Stumbling through the dark hallway, I heard my father call, 'Son, I want to talk to you.' I went in his room. He lighted a lamp and sat on the side of the bed in his nightclothes—his gray shock of hair was tousled and his expression one of a sore-footed bear. He had spent many sleepless nights in his anxiety for sure. 'You have disappointed me,' he said. 'And I want you to clear out of this town by tomorrow night.' And he fairly flung a $20 bill at my feet. I walked away without picking it up, although I hadn't a penny. [63]

In the morning, Odd headed to the telegraph office, where he sent requests to ten randomly selected newspapers. His telegrams begged for a job as a newspaper reporter and requested a quick reply. The editors who received the telegrams could surely smell more than a hint of desperation in the young reporter's plea. He checked in at the office periodically throughout the morning, but by noon, no reply had come.

It appeared he was finally broke, without even enough money to buy dinner. Finally, at the end of the day, a fourteen-word reply from the *Dayton Herald* in Dayton, Ohio changed the direction of Odd McIntyre's life forever and set him on the course to becoming the highest-paid reporter in the world. The telegram read, "Can place you at twelve dollars a week if you can come at once."

He packed what few belongings he could carry, shoved seven borrowed dollars into his pocket, and grabbed the first train out of town without saying goodbye to his father. Plattsburg and his failures were behind him, and this time he planned to keep it that way. He had had enough of the shame of failure, the steady disapproval from his father, and the frequent pull of anxiety and depression. He was ready to start fresh in Dayton, save enough money for an engagement ring, and finally marry Maybelle.

The *Dayton Herald* had begun in January 1887. Two years later, Herbert H. Weakley, a prominent Dayton civic leader, banker, and lawyer, bought nearly all the stock, becoming the newspaper's primary owner. Weakley increased the *Herald's* size from four to eight pages and remodeled a building on the southwest corner of Second and Jefferson as the newspaper's headquarters. Under his leadership and management of every area of the business, including writing and editing, the *Herald* increased circulation and became the most-read newspaper in Dayton. By the turn of the century, it was also the only politically independent newspaper in town, and was referred to as "The Paper of the People." Like other cities and small towns, Dayton was growing rapidly. In 1870, the population had been 30,500, but by 1900, there were more than 85,000 who called Dayton home. Not only was it a good place to live during the Progressive Era, it was also a good place to work. A key group of leaders, including Weakley, saw to it that the city was at the top of the list for manufacturers looking for a place to settle with some of the cheapest electricity that could be bought. Others in the country used the "Dayton Model" as an example of a successful, progressive city, based on its education and training for workers, company gardens, and modern lunchrooms.

Weakley didn't grow his successful newspaper alone. By the time Odd showed up in Dayton, Charles J. Geyer had been working for Weakley for more than twenty years, and was instrumental in managing every aspect of the newspaper. Geyer was only in his late thirties, and Weakley, in his seventies, depended on Geyer's youthful energy and his wise counsel for all major decisions.

Newspapers were continuing to change rapidly, and Weakley and Geyer were well aware they were going to have to change with the times. It was no longer enough to provide readers with just the facts. They now expected to be entertained, as well.

Odd's train finally pulled into the station at Dayton. He was covered in cinders and was dressed in the rumpled suit he had been wearing for several days. His appearance was important to Odd, so he quickly found a hotel close to the newspaper so he could clean up and look as presentable as possible for his first day. As he checked in, he paused before he wrote "Plattsburg" on the line that asked for his hometown. He looked at the hotel clerk, then back down at the registry, and wrote "Kansas City." He didn't want the clerk to think he was a hick.

Odd arrived at the newspaper and found himself immediately intimidated by Weakley, whom he described as "a white-haired, little tittupy man with a querulous voice."[64] As Odd entered, the old man was pounding his rolltop desk and yelling at some reporter who saw Odd's entrance as a good excuse to make a quick exit. Weakley looked up and down at the pitiful creature who had just arrived in his office and couldn't imagine what he was doing there. When Odd finally introduced himself, and Weakley realized this was the desperate reporter he had hired by telegram, he pushed himself out of his chair and walked over to Charles Geyer. Weakley and Geyer whispered, looked back at Odd, and then Weakley shook his head. Years later, Weakley confessed that he had not liked the way Odd looked when he arrived at the newspaper that day. Weakley said, "I'm sorry young man, that job has been filled. Anyway, I thought you were older. I'll take your name and address in case anything else opens up."

Odd nervously replied, "Is there something I could do around here… anything?" Weakley told Odd there were no jobs available, and the two newspapermen watched as Odd slunk from their office and into the streets of Dayton.

Rejected once again, Odd reached in his pocket and felt the four dollars remaining. He had come all this way for nothing. Since he now owed the hotel two dollars, he had only two dollars left. He returned to his hotel and sat on the side of the bed with his head pressed into his hands. A maid came in to clean his room, and after observing him for a moment asked, "Are you ill sir?" All he could manage to squeak out was, "No,

I'm fine," without even looking up.

After several hours, Weakley called the hotel and asked Odd to come to the newspaper at five that evening. He arrived feeling hopeful, but Weakley, feeling guilty about the way things were handled, just wanted to give him the train fare to make it back home. Odd paused for a minute. Where was home? He couldn't return to Gallipolis and prove right the principal who predicted he would bitterly disappoint his loved ones. Going back to Plattsburg and his father's house was also out of the question. Finally, Odd asked for a ticket to Cincinnati and implored Weakley to wire him should any jobs open up. He let him know he would be at a hotel on Walnut Street.

Something about the whole situation didn't seem right to Charles Geyer. It nagged at him that they had agreed to hire Odd, had him travel two days to Dayton, and then didn't even give him a chance. He couldn't shake the memory of Odd's face when they told him they weren't going to give him a job.

After Odd arrived at the hotel in Cincinnati, he checked in using the

The *Dayton Herald*, June 3, 1904.

Orville Wright and Wilbur Wright on the front porch of their home at 7 Hawthorne Street in Dayton, Ohio in 1909. *Library of Congress Prints and Photographs Division*

last of his money and went to bed hungry. He was now completely broke. Lying in bed, looking at the ceiling, he had no idea where to turn next or how he was going to make it out of this situation.

The answer came the next morning when a telegram appeared under his door. It was from Geyer. His conscience had gotten the better of him, and he offered Odd a two-week trial as a reporter back at the *Herald*. He had also arranged for train fare. Odd left Cincinnati and headed back to Dayton without a penny in his pocket, and as he watched the streets of the city pass by from his seat on the train, he vowed he would never be broke again. The horrible feeling of being completely hopeless had planted itself deeply in his spirit. Although he would eventually find fame and financial security, a fear of failure and being without money would stick with him for the rest of his life. He was eager to begin his new job as a reporter in Dayton and, as fate would have it, what would eventually become one of the stories of the century was right under his nose.

Odd was checking out the style of writing in *The Cincinnati Enquirer* when a noticed a small feature story about two brothers living in Dayton who were working on a flying machine. He decided to pay a visit to the Wright brothers himself to see if they were interesting enough for a story for the *Herald*. Odd watched first one brother and then the other observing him through a peephole in the door of their workshop on West Third Street. After no response from his first knock, he knocked again. The door opened slightly, and as Orville Wright cautiously squeezed through, Odd was able to get a peek into the room where Orville and his brother, Wilbur, were attempting to create the first flying machine.

Odd found the brothers to be secretive and not at all interested in sharing information about their project with anyone from the press. Before the Wright brothers turned their attention to flying machines they had worked with printing presses and bicycles, so they certainly had mutual interests with the young reporter standing in front of them. While engaged in small talk, Odd likely figured out a way to mention his notoriety as a champion trick bicycle rider in Gallipolis. Despite very little cooperation from the inventors, Odd wrote what he could for "time copy," to be used anytime there was extra space that needed to be filled in the newspaper. There really wasn't much interest from the public in what Orville and Wilbur were doing in their bicycle workshop at the time, but Odd's story added a bit of humor, and after it ran, the *Herald* received a few letters complimenting the article and its young writer.

Later, when the Wrights' brother, Lorin, excitedly showed the editor of the Dayton *Journal* the December 17, 1903 telegram announcing "SUCCESS FOUR FLIGHTS THURSDAY MORNING ... LONGEST 57 SECONDS," it still wasn't seen as worthy of more than a small mention. There were many amateur and professional inventors claiming their inventions were going to get people in the air, and fifty-seven seconds didn't seem newsworthy. After another telegram, this one sent by the brothers to their father, Bishop Milton Wright, the *Herald* included a small story in the December 18, 1903, issue:

Dayton Boys Solve Problem
Wilbur and Orville Wright Successfully Operate a Flying Machine in North Carolina.
Bishop Milton Wright of this city has received a telegram from his sons Wilbur and Orville Wright, who are at Kitty Hawk, N.C., their fourth autumn, experimenting in gliding through the air on aeroplanes of their own make, and regulated by devices of their own invention, saying that they have

had gratifying success with their true flying machine...[65]

It would be awhile before the Wright brothers would become a sensation in newspapers and magazines, so with his early story about the brothers, Odd was ahead of his time.

At the *Herald*, he finally found the success that had eluded him for so long. He worked harder and longer than the other reporters, often sleeping at his desk. Assigned to cover City Hall, Odd made friends with the police officers and reporters from competing papers. As he watched, listened, and learned how it was done, he even began getting tips from some of those working at City Hall. Still afraid of old Mr. Weakley, who observed the comings and goings of everyone at his paper, Odd would run past his office out of fear of being stopped and fired. In his mind, as long as he kept running, Weakley would have to catch him before he could fire him. His fear quickly paid off.

One day, during Odd's trial period, Weakley asked Charles Geyer, "Who's that quick-stepping boy that's always in a hurry?" One thing Weakley appreciated was speed in his employees, and Odd seemed to be a reporter always rushing to get his work done.

Now earning twelve dollars each week, he was able to send letters to Maybelle that were upbeat and enthusiastic. He had dated other girls during the last few years, but later claimed he always knew he would eventually marry Maybelle.

Odd was finally at the right place, at the right time, and with the right skills. The price of a newspaper had been made affordable for the masses by steam engine-powered presses, the manufacture of cheaper paper, and vastly improved transportation systems. Many Americans, especially those living in larger cities, were reading multiple newspapers each day. The use of the telegraph as a tool for gathering details about a story and getting it quickly back to the newspaper was contributing to an entirely different style of reporting. Although the telegraph was fast, it was also expensive since companies like Western Union charged by the word. To save money and increase the speed of telegraphing stories back to the newspaper, reporters out in the field abbreviated and left out unnecessary words, and telegraph reporters back at the newspaper rewrote the stories before they were printed. A common affliction among telegraph operators of the day was called "glass arm" that was caused by strain on the muscles of the wrist and arm due to the repetitive action it took to send code quickly.

The necessity for brevity resulted in a change from long articles with lots of detail to shorter stories with the most important facts listed at the beginning of the article. In the first decade of the twentieth century, newspapers were at their most powerful, and the new style of reporting suited Odd's abilities. His writing, that was more personable and easy to read, was suddenly what newspaper consumers wanted.

Odd survived his two-week trial, but after the third week, he arrived at work early one morning and was horrified to find Weakley standing at the entrance of the newspaper waiting for him. It was the only way Weakley could catch him. The old man asked Odd to walk with him. Odd assumed his worst nightmare was about to come true—he was going to be fired again. He would be a failure, and his father and the principal would be proven right.

Odd had recently written several letters to his father to try to make peace, but had torn them up before he put them in the mail. Now, he was glad he hadn't mailed them. His heart was beating fast and he was so distraught he could barely hear what Weakley was saying. Finally, he caught enough of his words to realize he wasn't getting bad news after all. The fact that Odd was the first to arrive in the morning and the last to leave in the evening had not been lost on the old man. Odd's youth and enthusiasm were apparent in the articles he was writing, and Weakley liked what he was reading and wanted to see more of it in his paper. Instead of firing Odd, he was promoting him to city editor, a position that included the management of four other reporters. As Odd wrote many years later, "I was improving the paper. There was the brighter touch that youth's enthusiasm will always bring."[66]

After his promotion, Odd made many changes at the newspaper and even began a daily column he called "Just for Fun." It featured short blurbs of news about locals separated with three dots: Ted Smith has a new bicycle…Banker Wintergreen has put a new cupola on his house… Bill and Nancy Sullivan just returned from a trip to Toledo. He noticed the newspaper's customers enjoyed reading about their neighbors and, just like in Gallipolis, everyone in Dayton loved seeing their own name in print. Understanding that idea would contribute greatly to his success in the future.

Herbert H. Weakley died suddenly at his home on July 30, 1906, after a heart attack at seventy-two. Odd's role at the newspaper continued to grow, as he was needed to fill some of the void left by Weakley's death.

One morning in 1906, Odd answered his phone and the receptionist asked if he had time to meet with the editor of *The Cincinnati Post*, Ray Long. Little did Odd know just how that meeting would change the trajectory of his life and career.

That day, Odd and Ray Long would discover they had much in common. Long was born on March 23, 1878, into a poor family in Lebanon, Indiana, a small town in the Midwest similar to Gallipolis. His mother supported Long and his siblings by working, as did Odd's sister Kate, in a millinery shop. At thirteen, Long quit school and became a telegraph messenger boy for *The Indianapolis News*. Like Odd, Long struggled with grammar and spelling, and wrote and edited "by ear." Blessed with a fun, outgoing personality, Long showed an interest in politics and developed a keen sense of salesmanship at an early age. He worked as a page in the Ohio state legislature and became a precinct captain at seventeen. By the time he was twenty-two, he was working as a reporter at the *News*.

Odd was shocked when he saw just how young Long actually looked. He had heard that E. W. Scripps hired young and paid poorly, but he had assumed an editor of *The Cincinnati Post* would at least have a beard. The two had lunch at the Dayton Elks Club and immediately hit it off. Both were very young men working in the trenches of the newspaper business during a time when it was rapidly changing. Both had worked hard to get where they were, and both had big plans for the future. Odd also found Long's lack of arrogance appealing. As Long told it, he had "wormed" his way into a job at *The Cleveland Press* then "drifted" over to the *Post*. Soon after he arrived at the *Post*, there was a "shake up," and when it was over, Long humbly claimed he was the only one who knew his way around the building, so they made him managing editor.

Odd later wrote that on that day a friendship began that endured through fair and foul weather for decades. Odd gave Long the credit for his success and noted that "while he has bawled me out unmercifully, and I have said things to him that would not look well in print, it was never done save for what we believed to be the other's good."

In 1930, Long provided the introduction to *Twenty-Five Selected Stories of O. O. McIntyre*, writing, "To me, Odd shares more in a few words than any other writer I know. To me each of his words is greatly worthwhile."[67] On another occasion, Long wrote, "No one in the world can irritate me so much as O. O. McIntyre. He's been one of my closest friends for twenty-five years, but in that twenty-five years, I've vowed at least fifty times to never speak to him again. Yet I not only speak to him; I welcome his company as I do that of few men."[68]

Back on the first day of that friendship in 1906, during lunch at the Dayton Elks Club, Long was intent on recruiting Odd to work for him at *The Cincinnati Post*. He liked the short, clear, and direct writing he'd seen coming out of the *Herald*, and he knew much of it was due to Odd's changes to the style of the articles and other content he was creating.

Even though the position of telegraph editor making twenty-five dollars per-week was a raise for Odd, the position was less prestigious than his job in Dayton. And as with anything new, there was an element of risk. Now that Odd had finally tasted success, changing jobs wouldn't be easy. Long was persistent and wouldn't take no for an answer. When Odd finally went to talk to Geyer about leaving, he received a counter offer of thirty dollars and the position of managing editor. He had a tough decision to make.

In the end, it was one of his mentors at the *Herald*—ironically, a telegraph editor—who convinced him to go by saying, "You're young and need seasoning. Take my advice. Skip."[69]

Before he accepted, Odd's insecurities began nagging at him, and he convinced himself he was not worthy of this new opportunity. He worried someone was playing a trick on him by impersonating Ray Long. He wrote to a friend who lived in Cincinnati and had him visit the *Post*, find Long, and write back a detailed physical description. His friend complied, and Long's identity was confirmed. He accepted the offer.

Odd's time in Dayton ended much like it had begun. Maybelle later shared that once he made his decision to leave for Cincinnati, Odd sat on the edge of his bed with his head in his hands and cried.[70]

6

The Cincinnati Post

Out of the free and easy camaraderie of the old Post days grew some of the finest contacts I have ever known. There isn't—to be mawkish for the moment—an old Post man who wouldn't, in the Broadway vernacular, 'go the route for a pal.' Those of us who survive are constantly in touch with one another. There is in our lives an experience that has come to only a few.[71]

O. O. McIntyre

When Odd McIntyre arrived at Edward Willis Scripps's Cincinnati newspaper in 1906, the *Post* was at war against the city's boss, George B. Cox. Since 1886, Boss Cox's power had grown steadily until he ultimately controlled every area of the "Queen City." As a writer for *The Saturday Evening Post* explained:

Cox bossed Cincinnati for a good many years and grew rich and powerful, and ramified until he directed absolutely all the municipal machinery of that big city. Elections went as Cox directed. The votes were cast as Cox said.

He ran things, elected mayors and councilmen and judges and law officers, and sat in a room above a saloon in the daytime and issued orders. At night he shifted to a table in a beer hall and issued his orders from that throne.[72]

Eventually, no mayor, judge, or congressman was elected without Cox's endorsement.

In the last half of the nineteenth century, explosive urban growth and an influx of immigrants resulted in many large cities around the nation becoming a breeding ground for unethical and dishonest leadership. These "bosses" and their cronies were more interested in building personal fortunes and power bases than in pursuing interests beneficial to their communities. Memphis had Boss Crump, Louisiana had Boss Huey Long, New York had Boss Tweed, and the list went on and on. These leaders were often able to build power by controlling the outcomes of city elections and creating indebted elected officials. Those officials then did as they were instructed to retain their power and influence. They could also be counted on to look the other way when the boss made choices that weren't in the best interest of the community or were, in many cases, illegal. Often, newspaper owners, editors, and reporters were either closely tied to the bosses or too afraid of lost advertising to write critically of the corruption that was rampant in their own cities.

Although it led with "The Stage Memories of Clara Morris," the January 1903 issue of *McClure's Magazine* is considered the starting point for an investigative style of journalism that came to be known as "muckraking." A popular literary periodical, *McClure's* published the work of leading writers like Rudyard Kipling, Jack London, and Arthur Conan Doyle. The January 1903 issue contained three important stories that exposed corruption and exploitation: Ida Tarbell's second installment of "The

The January 1903 issue of *McClure's Magazine.*

Odd (far right) at work with other reporters at *The Cincinnati Post.*

History of the Standard Oil Company," Lincoln Steffens' "The Shame of Minneapolis," and Ray Stannard Baker's "The Right to Work." From that point on, newspaper and magazine journalists significantly increased their efforts at writing stories that laid bare the unscrupulous tactics of powerful individuals and organizations who victimized those they were charged with serving.

These Progressive Era journalists were nicknamed "muckrakers" by President Theodore Roosevelt, who borrowed the term from John Bunyan's *The Pilgrim's Progress* that referenced a rake that was used to dislodge filth and muck. In addition to unearthing corruption, these young, idealistic reporters sought to write stories that would result in positive actions like the creation of local parks and playgrounds, closure of red-light districts, and improved education for local citizens. At *The Cincinnati Post*, their efforts centered on bringing down Cox's highly corrupt political machine and replacing it with a more just city government.

Most of the young *Post* reporters, many of them recruited by Ray Long, played as hard as they worked. Days were spent at what Odd called a "ramshackle newspaper office that seemed on the verge of collapse,"[73] while nights were frequently spent on Vine Street and in the famed beer gardens, concert halls, and burlesque houses of Over-the-Rhine. From his months of skipping classes at business school, Odd was already very familiar with the neighborhood bars. At the time, it was called the "Paris of America," and the sounds of singing waiters, three-piece bands, and full orchestras filled the streets. Odors of wienerwurst, steamed dumplings, potato pancakes, and sauerbraten wafted through the neighborhood, and a hungry customer could easily find the best German cuisine at prices even young muckrakers could afford. In the November 1925 issue of *Cosmopolitan*, Odd reflected on the area he remembered as "a Barbary Coast, Coney Island, and Broadway all rolled into one."[74] He wrote:

> *Vine Street was the haupt Strasse (the main street), narrow, cobblestoned and roaring with life...Huge dray horses sweated along with the ponderous loads of beer for the Queen City was always thirsty. Young men drank beer and burst into song. Older men puffed at their long pipes and "sat over" a glass of beer all evening. Mothers patiently knitted. Almost every other building housed a saloon, hotel, gambling house or concert hall, and the concert halls on Vine Street were the best in the land. Over-the-Rhine should be remembered for its culture as well as its beer.*[75]

With his move to Cincinnati, some of the best popular entertainment in the United States was now easily accessible to Odd. At the People's Theater at Vine and Thirteenth Streets, he was frequently in the audience to see comedy acts, live theater, and lots of burlesque.

While nights were spent at the theaters and saloons, long days were spent at the *Post*. Its location on Longworth Street, in the vice district, made it easy to observe comings and goings from "unsavory activities," since it was a common practice for the prostitutes to have their names painted on the doors of their rooms. Physically, the newspaper office was much like the ones Odd would write about many years later:

> *There was rare music in the squeak of the rickety stairs, romance in the antiquated desks and a Dickensy flavor in the cobwebby ceilings. Newspaper work is a rough-and-tumble affair and no occupation for sissies. Duding it up is a major crime against the Fourth Estate that loves it. The newspaper office, true to its healthy tradition, should have sawdust, cockroaches, spittoons and buzzard-gagging paste pots, and the fetid air should turn blue now and then with lusty oaths...they have been shorn of those jousting*

telegraph operators whose terrific hangovers vanished magically with the first click of their keys. The tramp printer, too, here today and gone tomorrow, who despite the dissolute tendencies turned out expert work and cheered the whole craft by a philosophy worthy of Epictetus himself.[76]

Edward Willis Scripps, the *Post's* owner, was a man of many contradictions. While he championed the causes of the poor, his newspapers were notorious for paying low wages. He was physically a large man who instilled fear in others, but was sick for much of his life with chronic bronchitis. He crusaded for liberal causes around the country and wanted to see power in the hands of the common man, yet he controlled every single detail in the lives of his own wife and children.

Scripps's introduction to the newspaper business had come at the age of eighteen when he joined Ellen, his favorite sister, and other family members working for his half brothers, James and Will, at the *Advertiser and Tribune* in Detroit. James Scripps later started *The Evening News* in Detroit, and gave Edward Scripps a newspaper route, that he managed so well, it contributed greatly to the newspaper's overall success.

While he rose through the ranks of his brothers' newspaper business, Edward also became well known for his drinking and womanizing. By 1881, his lifestyle was impacting his health; his weight dropped, and he began coughing up blood. His alarmed sister took him to Europe, where he spent several years recovering.

Meanwhile, James Scripps began purchasing newspapers throughout the Midwest.

E. W. Scripps at his desk in the 1880s. *Mahn Center, Ohio University Libraries*

Once he returned to the United States in the summer of 1883, Edward Scripps decided it was time to settle down, get married, and focus on work. He first acquired the controlling interest in the *Penny Post* in Cincinnati, then turned his attention to finding a suitable wife. In 1885, he attended a church social and met Nackie Holtsinger, the nineteen-year-old daughter of the minister. Although she was sixteen years his junior, in four months they were married and his womanizing days were officially over.

During the next two decades, Scripps's life consisted of managing his growing family, building his newspaper business, and constructing a huge estate near San Diego, California, called Miramar Ranch.

In 1902, Scripps started the Newspaper Enterprise Association, that provided illustrations, cartoons, and articles for his newspapers around the country. By paying a fee, newspaper editors were given access to content they never would have been able to afford otherwise. The model was so successful, he expanded the service to include other newspapers, and one of the earliest modern syndication services was born.

The *Cincinnati Post*, like all of Scripps's newspapers, was written with the working class in mind, and production costs were kept low to allow the newspapers to be sold more cheaply than those of many of their competitors. While most newspapers during the time supported specific political parties and let their affiliation dictate their content, Scripps's newspapers had no such affiliation and supported efforts around the country to improve working and living conditions for laborers. He expressed his editorial policy in an early issue of the *Penny Post*:

> *We have no politics in the sense of the word as commonly used. We are not Republicans, not Democrats, not Greenback and not Prohibitionists. We simply intend to support good men and condemn bad ones, no matter what party they belong to. We shall tell no lies about persons for love, malice or money. It is no part of a newspapers business to array itself on the side of this or that party, or fight, lie or wrangle for it.*[77]

Scripps figured out a model for running a newspaper that ultimately made him and his family very wealthy. He would find a city with a population of 50,000 to 100,000 that had a successful conservative newspaper. He then selected a young editor and someone to run the business side of the newspaper and advanced them a small amount of money to start a new newspaper primarily for working-class residents. If the newspaper was successful, he continued to support it, and provided the editor and business manager with stock. If it were not, he withdrew his support, and the newspaper would close. Scripps wrote, "We employ only very young men, men who have not elsewhere, under other employment, earned a right to prestige. Young men have practically been working for us at apprentice wages while they are doing their best work."[78]

One of Scripps's associates sarcastically explained the business model in a slightly different light. He wrote, "He would hire a shed down by the railroad station, put in a press that Gutenberg had scrapped and some linotype machines held together with bailing wire, then put in a kid for twelve dollars a week to be editor and promise him one percent of the profits as soon as circulation hit a million."[79]

Muckraker Lincoln Steffens was a huge fan of Scripps. When he found out sculptor Jo Davidson had been commissioned for a bust of the publisher, he sent the artist a letter in which he wrote, "You must do a great thing with Scripps. He is a great man and an individual. There is no other like him: energy, vision, courage, wisdom. He thinks his own thoughts absolutely. He sees straight. He sees the line he is on and his thinking sticks to that. I regard Scripps as one of the two or three great

Newsboys selling the *Cincinnati Times Star* in 1908. *Library of Congress Prints and Photographs Division*

Odd (far right) at work with other reporters at *The Cincinnati Post.*

men of my day."[80]

By 1906, when Odd was brought on, the *Post* had been a voice against political corruption in Cincinnati for many years. However, Scripps found that when the newspaper aggressively exposed wrongdoing, Boss Cox would force businesses to withdraw advertising. In Scripps's words, the *Post* had been "compelled to a course of persistent compromise" and had "kept its hands off of enough to still enjoy a large amount of advertising."[81]

As muckraking journalism grew more popular with readers, Scripps saw an opportunity to solve the Boss Cox problem once and for all. He encouraged the young editors and reporters at the *Post* to go after the city's boss.

During the years Odd was at the *Post*, he worked side-by-side with some of the most talented writers, journalists, and artists ever brought together to work on one newspaper at one time. He witnessed first-hand the power of a group of young people working for a common cause, using journalism as a tool to right some very egregious wrongs. He had loved the newspaper business before he arrived in Cincinnati, but during his years at the *Post*, he developed a deep appreciation and admiration for newspaper men and women that would last for the rest of his life. The group Ray Long helped assemble in those early years was full of, as Odd described it, "journalistic fledglings, with pin feathers just sprouting."

John Vandercook, barely thirty, was the newspaper's quiet, unassuming general manager and editor. "Van," as his friends called him, began his newspaper work as a reporter for the *Cleveland Press* in 1891. In 1898, he was sent to London, where he established himself as a talented correspondent. Vandercook was the first to report the death of Queen Victoria, one of the biggest scoops of the century. As Odd told it, Vandercook "sat on a fast horse, a half-mile away, watching a window, and when a signal was flashed from the window he galloped to a cable office."[82]

Vandercook was described by one associate as being "of slight and delicate physique, with a diffident and somewhat hesitating manner."[83] Even more importantly to his role as editor, it was said he "loved honor, loved the truth, loved justice and he loved to fight for them."[84] Years later, when Odd was being heavily criticized, he remembered the many times Vandercook reminded the team that "the penalty of excellence is criticism."[85]

Ray Long, who was responsible for bringing Odd to Cincinnati, already had the title of managing editor, and he was still in his early twenties. He and Odd had already discovered they had a lot in common from their childhoods, and they soon found out they also both had an appreciation for bold fashion choices. As a young man, Long noticed one of the sports editors at the *Indianapolis News* was wearing a checkered suit and carrying a cane. He knew right then and there how he wanted to spend the rest of his life. He worked his way up from copy boy to reporter before joining *The Cincinnati Post*, covering the police beat, in 1904. Long's talent was quickly realized, and he was promoted to managing editor after just thirteen months.

Long brought his friend, Roy Howard, from St. Louis to Cincinnati to work as the *Post's* assistant telegraph editor. The two had worked together in 1902 at the *News* and became lifelong friends. Small in stature but not in style, Howard gained his work ethic early, helping to support his family with money earned delivering newspapers, ushering at the local theater, mowing lawns, and delivering beer in a horse-drawn wagon. As a junior in high school, he began writing articles for the *Indianapolis News*. He was working for Joseph Pulitzer's *Post-Dispatch* in St. Louis when Long recruited him to the *Post*. Howard's first day on the job was on his twenty-second birthday.

"THE BOSS"

Newspaper artist Elmer Bushnell's illustration of Boss George B. Cox.

The always well-dressed William Phillip Simms was the newspaper's handsome drama critic. After graduating from the University of Georgia, he spent a few years at *The Atlanta Journal* before coming to the *Post* at age twenty-four. Odd remembered Simms was the only one in the group to own a silk hat and an opera coat and together, he and Odd enjoyed many of Cincinnati's theaters and concert halls. Before he was married, Odd lived at the Gerdes Hotel where, in addition to being inexpensive enough to allow him to save for a wedding ring, it was also where many of those who worked in the entertainment business stayed while in Cincinnati. This provided Odd with an opportunity to gain an insider's knowledge of how the turn-of-the-century entertainment business worked—information that would soon come in very handy.

Slightly older than the others at thirty-two, Eugene Walter worked the police beat and wrote about Cincinnati's underworld. A veteran of the Spanish American War, Walter was an aspiring playwright and married a beautiful Broadway actress, Charlotte Walter.

Reporter Russ Wilson was quick with a practical joke and was always trying to make the others laugh. He attended Princeton and received a law degree from the University of Cincinnati before joining the *Post*.

Born in Lithuania, Alfred Segal studied to be a rabbi but later decided to pursue journalism. Odd later wrote that Segal was, in his opinion, the best reporter in America and could do more with a story than anyone he ever knew. Segal wrote articles that focused on the underdogs of the city, fighting for justice for many who would otherwise have no voice.

Odd even got to work with one of the earliest female reporters, Jessie M. Partlon. A staunch progressive and an advocate for women's equality, Partlon strongly favored women's equality and wasn't afraid to write about it. Though women were unable to vote, she encouraged them to pay attention to elections with an article that featured the headline, "Jessie Partlon Declares That a Woman's Brain was Given Her to

Boss George B. Cox. *Library of Congress Prints and Photographs Division*

Use." Avoiding the typical "women's stories," Partlon wrote on everything from coal strikes and murder trials to city corruption and the plight of Cincinnati's poor.

The art department of the paper was also overflowing with young talent. Elmer Bushnell, Homer Davenport, Ray Rohn, Harry Graff, H. T. Webster, and R. M. Brinkerhoff were just a few of the cartoonists and illustrators with whom Odd developed close friendships in those years. They would all go on to make a significant impact in editorial cartooning, illustration, and design.

One *Post* reporter Odd didn't get to work with at the time, humorist Irvin S. Cobb, was fired from the newspaper after only a month. He returned home to Kentucky, where a few weeks later, he received a telegram offering him another job at the paper. He wired back and told them they could "go to hell." He later became one of Odd's closest friends.

What Odd called "the rowdiest, the youngest and the most talented group of reporters ever gathered together at one newspaper" had their hands full with Boss Cox. No one is the villain of his own story, and Cox was certainly no different. Toward the end of his life he told a reporter, "I am the Boss of Cincinnati. I never dodged that statement in my life. I've got the best system of government in the country. If I didn't think this system was the best, I would consider that I was a failure in life."[86]

Cox's life began right there in Cincinnati on April 29, 1853. His father had immigrated to the United States from England, and the family was already struggling financially when he died. It was during the Civil War that eight-year-old Cox dropped out of school and began working a variety of jobs at butcher shops, newspapers, riverboats, grocery stores, and other places. Eventually, he went to work for his brother-in-law, a gambler, running his keno room. He then tended bar and later purchased a West End bar located at Central Avenue and Longworth Street, or "Dead Man's Corner," as it was nicknamed. Cox later claimed the frequent police raids of his bar were due not to the nightly illegal gambling or frequent murders, but to the fact that he was a Republican in a city run by Democrats. He had developed a number of powerful connections and was popular in his neighborhood, so when he ran for city council, he won his one and only election. The leaders of the Republican party of Hamilton County saw that Cox was a talented, popular politician, so they made him chairman. With that position came the right to appoint workers for more than two thousand jobs. Through his many relationships and political maneuvering, he was eventually able to control more than twenty-five thousand votes through the appointments he made. His influence extended to those who worked in the courts, clerks, janitors, street cleaners, secretaries, and many others. The son of one of those employees explained, "My father is a janitor of one of the public school buildings. They demand of him that he control my vote and those of the two young men who board with us. We are carefully watched when we go to the polls."[87]

Cox also paid voters from other towns to vote in Cincinnati elections and made sure to keep the large immigrant population happy. Eventually, no business could succeed in Cincinnati without the approval and support of Cox and his cronies.

Business associates arrived at his office at the Cincinnati Trust Company hat in hand, but his real "throne" was at a table in Wielert's Café and Pavilion on Vine Street. It was the largest and finest saloon in Cincinnati. With the slogan "Known to Every Business Man Throughout the Country," the saloon featured the largest outdoor beer garden, and as a special nod to the owner's heritage, had busts of German composers and authors lining the perimeter.

In 1895, Cox built a stunning 10,000 square-foot mansion at the corner of Brookline and Jefferson Avenues in the Clifton neighborhood. It was designed by Cincinnati's leading architect, Samuel Hannaford, and featured a three-story turret, several round rooms and a number of secret passageways. With details like stained glass windows, hand-carved mantles, and beautiful imported chandeliers, it was the finest home in the area at the time.

Odd wrote many years later, "Cox made mayors and judges, but he could never make society. He built a suburban mansion where his wife, who had come up with him in the world, waited in green and yellow silks—like poisonous wallpaper—for guests that never came."[88]

For many immigrants, Cox seemed like a benevolent leader and someone who looked after their interests. Famed muckraker Lincoln Steffens wrote, "The bums get free soup; the petty criminals 'get off' in court; the plain people or their relatives get jobs or a picnic or a friendly greeting and the Germans get their beer whenever they want."[89]

During his research of the municipal government of Cincinnati under Boss Cox's rule, Steffens found very few willing to risk talking with him:

> *Cox can punish; he does punish, not with physical cruelty, as a Czar may, but by petty annoyances and 'trouble,' and political and business ostracism. The reign of Cox is a reign of fear. The experience that made my visits there a personal humiliation was the spectacle I saw of men who were being punished; who wanted to cry out; who sent for me to tell me the facts that they knew and suffered and hated; and these men, after leading me into their back offices and closing the door, dared not speak. It was rumored that I was shadowed, and that made them afraid.*[90]

After many rejections, Boss Cox finally met with Steffens in person. After he agreed with Steffens that he was the boss of Cincinnati, Steffens added, "Of course, you have a mayor, a council and elected judges also,

Lincoln Steffens in 1914. *Library of Congress Prints and Photographs Division*

no?" Cox nodded in the affirmative and arrogantly replied with a slight smile, "I have, but I have a telephone too."

By the first decade of the twentieth century, Cox's version of municipal government had been causing significant harm to the city for years. The bookkeeping system hadn't been updated in decades, the quality of the public schools was way below that of cities of similar size, and the park system was nonexistent. Even worse, the equipment and procedures used by the health department were so old, the death rate was higher than it should have been. Water wasn't being properly treated, and there were more deaths from tuberculosis and other diseases than in other cities of similar size. New businesses were discouraged, to keep businesses that supported Cox from having competition. Developments in transportation were also limited. Because of the significant amount of payoff Boss Cox's machine demanded of those working in the transportation industry, modern trolleys, essential to residents of urban centers, weren't available to the residents of Cincinnati.

In 1905, Scripps and the *Post* allied with Lincoln Steffens, who was by then making a name for himself. Steffens' article in that July 1905 issue of *McClure's Magazine* was titled "Ohio: A Tale of Two Cities." He pointed out the corruption in Cincinnati and called its residents "craven cowards."[91] Steffens compared Cleveland, "the best-governed city in the United States," with Cincinnati, which he called "the worst."

Although the *Post* was a great place for Odd to learn about journalism and the production of a quality newspaper, he continued to struggle with grammar and punctuation, and hated spending so much time in an office. He felt he was writing more headlines than articles. While Odd did receive a promotion to city editor, he really hoped to be promoted to managing editor. Unfortunately, he was forced to sit by and watch as several of his peers were promoted to the role instead. Odd later admitted he would not have been very effective as a managing editor because what he really enjoyed was the process of producing a newspaper. He loved the organizing, the building, and the pulling smaller pieces together to make a whole.

During his time at the *Post*, Odd and his father began to reconcile. In November 1907, the Laclede Hotel was destroyed in a spectacular fire that burned throughout the night. A few weeks later, at age fifty-three, Henry McIntyre married Sultana Duncan, a woman he had been seeing for a while. They moved to Richmond, Missouri, where Henry ran the

Richmond Hotel for two years while the Laclede was being rebuilt. He visited Odd in Cincinnati but never showed much enthusiasm for his son's work.

Odd finally saved enough money to buy Maybelle an engagement ring. They were married on February 18, 1908, Odd's twenty-fourth birthday. He didn't tell anyone at the *Post* that he was getting married because he liked to keep his personal life private. He didn't feel that he should ask for time off, so the wedding took place at the home of James and Florence Smith White, rather than back home in Gallipolis. Florence White was a friend of Maybelle's, and the Whites lived in nearby Newport, Kentucky, just across the Ohio River from Cincinnati.

One morning, shortly after they were married, Odd stopped at the front door and asked Maybelle if she needed him to give her any money. He wrote that at that moment, she let him have "both barrels of her philosophy." With a tone in her voice he had never heard before, she replied, "As long as I am married to you, I shall never ask for one cent of money. …I have never asked my parents for a penny and I shall never ask you."[92] From then on, every Saturday, Odd gave Maybelle his entire salary. She paid the bills and then each of them got five dollars.

Henry T. Hunt around 1912, *Library of Congress Prints and Photographs Division*

The men and women of *The Cincinnati Post* continued the fight against the Cox machine. They reported the news, wrote editorials, and drew cartoons. Occasionally, reform candidates would win an election, but for the most part, Cox retained his power. It would take many years, hundreds of hours of investigation and writing by many talented journalists, and several court cases before Cox finally fell from his throne and even longer for the machine he built to grind to a halt.

They found an important ally in Yale graduate Henry T. Hunt, who was elected prosecuting attorney in 1908. Hunt became so popular in Cincinnati he won the election for city mayor in 1911. During his two-year

An article Odd wrote for *The Cincinnati Post* in 1930 about his memories of working for the newspaper. *The Public Library of Cincinnati and Hamilton County*

term, Hunt introduced the inspections of tenement houses, appointed school nurses, provided food inspection and dental services for school children, closed illegal gambling halls, introduced a plan to improve city sewers, introduced the regulation of loan sharks who preyed on the poor, and settled several strikes.

One of the *Post's* stories reported on suspicious aspects of Cox's management of the city's money. It ultimately resulted in an investigation in which Cox lied under oath and, in the spring of 1911, Hunt indicted him for perjury. The January 1912 issue of *Collier's* magazine described the scene that day as Boss Cox arrived in the courtroom:

> *His obsequious henchmen filled the benches, the lobby, and the corridor. Men guarded every entrance to prevent the photographers from recording his disgrace. He moved into the courtroom like a king—a massive, somewhat pursy man, twin brother in physical make-up to John L. Sullivan as Sullivan looks today. While the clerk read the charge, he sat with his hands on his outspread knees and glared defiance from that dull but powerful eye of his. But as the long arguments went on, his face and manner changed. He began to swallow often, to moisten his lips now and then, and presently I noticed that his complexion, which seemed so florid when he entered the room, had gone pasty and sallow.*[93]

Although the charges were later dropped after a series of "legal moves," Cox's career in politics was essentially over. He was removed from his position as president of the local bank, and he retired from politics to manage his theaters and a movie production company he had started

By 1911, it had been a great five years for Odd, but things were changing quickly at the newspaper; and where Odd was concerned, not for the better. Ray Long left the *Post* and moved to Cleveland to become managing editor of Scripps's *Cleveland Press*. Victor Morgan, Odd's last boss at the *Post*, was very different from those he had worked with previously. While Ray Long and John Vandercook had become Odd's personal friends and mentors, he believed Morgan was a bully who would rather shout and harass his staff than go out for drinks after work. Odd remembered, "For some reason, I became his pet aversion. At morning conferences he would embarrass me before my staff of reporters and heckled me in other ways." Dealing with a problem like this was not something Odd handled well, possibly because of the relationship with his father. He added, " I had not then nor have I now, the capacity to fight back. People I don't like, I avoid. But I could not avoid him. I began to have spells of insomnia, my work suffered and I lost weight…I think the staff on the Post had begun to pity me. My voice had lost its authority."[94]

Finally, Morgan demoted Odd to assistant managing editor. Odd knew his days at the *Post* were numbered, but he felt trapped. A way out finally came in the form of a telegram from Ray Long who had recently accepted the position of managing editor of *Hampton's Magazine* in New York. When the telegram arrived, Odd read the words that would bring an end to his suffering: "I have a $65 a week job for you on *Hampton's Magazine*. Can you come?"

Normally, such a drastic change would have filled Odd with fear, but his hate for Morgan far outweighed any other emotion in the moment. He called Maybelle to let her know, then he walked into Morgan's office and happily quit. The couple had saved a little money, and both had always hoped to one day live in New York. Their dreams were about to come true, but in ways they never could have imagined.

In an article for the *Post* almost twenty years after he had left the newspaper, Odd wrote, "I have watched, with pardonable pride, many of that old gang go like a shot to the highest editorial posts in the world, become famous playwrights, noted European correspondents, successful merchants, mayors and publishers and not a single one of them ever acquired that psychological pomposity called the 'big head.'"

John Vandercook left Cincinnati and headed to New York, where in 1907, Scripps made him president of the United Press Associations. In the spring of 1908, he was on his way from New York to Chicago when he had an appendicitis attack. He died two weeks later. His obituary read, "His death removes a strong figure from the newspaper field and causes a bereavement keenly felt by a host of personal friends."[95]

Roy Howard was made president of United Press after the death of his friend John Vandercook. In 1925 he was appointed co-director of what became the Scripps-Howard chain and then served as president until 1952. Considered one of the most influential American newspapermen in the twentieth century, he was featured on the cover of *Time* magazine in 1931.

William Phillip Simms became a well-respected war correspondent. Always impeccably dressed, he was noted for both his wardrobe and his interviews with leaders around the world.

Not everyone left the *Post* permanently. Alfred Segal went to *The World* in the 1920s to cover the famous Ruth Snyder murder trial. He was offered a full-time position on the newspaper but turned it down to return to Cincinnati. He wrote, "I like my front porch in Cincinnati better than anything I ever saw in New York."[96] In 1921, he began writing a column called "Cincinnatus" and continued writing it until his death at age 84 in 1968. It was the longest-running column ever produced by a single writer. Through his writing, Segal was credited with being one of the major champions of reform in the city.

Eugene Walter left Cincinnati in 1907 to pursue his dream of becoming a playwright. He wrote numerous plays for stage and screen that became hits, including "Paid in Full," "The Easiest Way," and "The Wolf." Always in love with show business, he married three times and each wife was an actress.

Walter wasn't the only one of Odd's Post friends to leave the newspaper business. Russ Wilson, the reporter known for his sense of humor, continued the fight against corruption in Cincinnati but from the other side of the newspaper. In 1930, he was elected mayor and served Cincinnati in that capacity until 1937. He then spent sixteen years on the city council. Wilson focused on creating jobs and construction during the economic depression of the 1930s when so many were desperate for work. He was celebrated for his writing and oration skills, but he was best known for his unique sense of humor and wit. Because of what he had experienced while reporting on Boss Cox's machine, he became a champion for good urban planning and city development.

On February 29, 1916, Boss Cox and his wife went to the Walnut Street Theater then returned home for a late dinner. He first mentioned he had a headache, and then complained that his arm felt numb. An hour later, the man whose words had ruled a city could only speak gibberish. His doctor was called, but a stroke caused Cox to slip into a coma from which he would never recover. He succumbed to pneumonia on May 20, 1916.

The king was dead.

Almost a century later, *The Cincinnati Post* died, too. Both readership and advertising declined dramatically in the first decade of the twenty-first century as more and more readers turned to online sources for their news and information. The newspaper was 126 years old when it published its final print edition on December 31, 2007.

In a fitting tribute to the men and women who had contributed so much in the past, the front page that sad day featured a giant "–30–" as the headline. That was the symbol historically used by print journalists and telegraphers to signify "the end."

Part 2:

NEW YORK

7

The New Yorker

As a country town boy my first impression of what I regarded as the successful New Yorker came when I beheld a traveling optician who came to our town every few years to fit Grandma's glasses. He added the magic flourish "New York" after his name on the Park Central Hotel register.[97]

O. O. McIntyre

A s their train pulled into Pennsylvania Station on an early July morning in 1911, not even one of the deadliest heat waves in history could dampen Odd and Maybelle McIntyre's excitement at finally arriving in New York City. The young couple was popular, and their Cincinnati friends and associates at the *Post* had sent them off in style. *Post* editor Harry Brown, a New Yorker by birth and one of the couple's best friends in Cincinnati, held a dinner at which he presented Odd with a small silver knife engraved with Odd's name, suggesting that he should use it to "cut his way through Broadway."

On the day of their departure, a large group of friends showed up at the train station to bid them farewell, and Brown presented Maybelle with a bouquet of flowers. Odd wore his favorite checkered suit and, although Maybelle talked him out of the red tie he had intended to wear, his bamboo cane allowed him make a strong fashion statement.

Like his grandparents and father unknowingly heading west into the locust plague in 1874, Odd and Maybelle waved good-bye to their friends not knowing they were headed toward a deadly natural disaster of their own. As they traveled more than 600 miles east, it became noticeably hotter and more uncomfortable on the train. Not only was it too hot to rest, the excitement of what was ahead made Odd both thrilled and terrified at the same time. He had loved Cincinnati and the business of putting together a daily newspaper and, had it not been for Victor Morgan, he likely could have stayed at the *Post* for the rest of his life and been happy.

He tried to hide it from Maybelle, but anxiety began to wear on Odd the closer they got to New York. More and more frequently, he had been plagued with what he referred to as "melancholia," but what was likely depression brought on by undiagnosed pernicious anemia. It was a great relief when they finally arrived and found a familiar face waiting for them in the crowd. Ray Long welcomed the young couple and helped them get on the right bus heading to their new home, before going back to the *Hampton's Magazine* office. Odd later noted that, while his own checkered suit may have turned a few heads, Long wasn't exactly dressed like an undertaker that day.

The fare on the other buses in the Fifth Avenue Coach Company line was a dime, but it was worth it to Odd to pay twice as much to ride on the upper deck of the famed Fifth Avenue double-decker bus, which, in addition to a slight breeze, provided the best possible view of their new hometown.

In 1885, a railroad was planned for Fifth Avenue, going from Canal Street through Washington Square and all the way to Fifty-Ninth Street. To the wealthy residents who lived and worked along the avenue, this was an outrage. Property owners like Cornelius Vanderbilt, Darius Odgen Mills, William Waldorf Astor, and John Jacob Astor banded together and organized the Association for the Protection of the Fifth Avenue Thoroughfare. The group announced it would "resist this attempt to steal the avenue with all its means in [its] power." It took several years, a great amount of money and significant legal maneuvering, but eventually the group won. Horse-drawn stagecoaches carried passengers up and

The streets of New York around the time Odd and Maybelle arrived for their first ride down Fifth Avenue on a double-decker bus. *Library of Congress Prints and Photographs Division*

down Fifth Avenue for several years but, by 1897, another change was looming. On August 21 of that year an article appeared in *The New York Times* about the Fifth Avenue Coach Company's decision to abandon horse-drawn stagecoaches in favor of horseless transportation:

> *One of the officers of the company, speaking of the proposed change yesterday, said, 'When the first horseless carriage rolled down Broadway it became evident to the principal stockholders of our company that only a short time would elapse before the Fifth Avenue line would have to do away with its horses not only for the sake and comfort of its patrons but also as a matter of economy. At present the market is flooded with all kinds of patents and inventions providing for horseless carriages.*[98]

Just a decade later, in August 1907, the company auctioned off all its horses, stages, and harnesses and replaced them with motorized buses. One era ended and another began. It didn't take long before the city determined the only solution to the increasing amount of traffic from horse-drawn carriages, buses, automobiles, and pedestrians was to widen Fifth Avenue by fifteen feet. It was a controversial project, as business owners and residents were each financially responsible for altering the front of their structures and removing any encroachments like steps, porticos, and gardens. As *The New York Times* reported:

> *Probably no local improvement made by the city at nominal cost to the municipal treasury was ever received by the people most directly affected with so much regret as the widening of Fifth Avenue, now in progress. While it is generally admitted that the usefulness and beauty of the avenue as a driveway and as a channel for general traffic, will be greatly increased by adding fifteen feet to the roadway, the property owners along the avenue do not appreciate the amount of money that it is costing them to remove their encroachments outward from the building line on to the sidewalk.*[99]

The Marble Collegiate Church at Twenty-Ninth Street tore out its beautiful courtyard, while the front of the Church of the Heavenly Rest on the east side, at Forty-Sixth Street, had to be completely remodeled. Many of the old brownstones along Fifth Avenue had been built with large steps leading up to a front door, which presented an interesting architectural challenge. Once the steps were removed and a new doorway installed at sidewalk level, what had been doors were turned into large ornamental windows.

The Marshall Field estate between Thirtieth and Thirty-First Streets had to remove a sixteen-foot stoop, while titans like William Waldorf Astor, John Jacob Astor, and Frederick W. Vanderbilt had to demolish gardens, porticos and doorways.

Although the widening of Fifth Avenue was poorly received by many of those who had to make significant changes to their homes and office buildings, it did ease the traffic problems and helped make it one of the most well-known destinations in the United States.

When reflecting on those first moments riding on top of a double-decker Fifth Avenue bus, Odd wrote, "There was a typical country boy thrill in mounting the circular staircase to the upper deck. I shall never forget it. I seemed on the top of the world. What a city; and there is not a day it does not stir my pulse...There was another thrill when we turned from 34th Street into the Avenue. It seemed to me then the most beautiful street in the world...it has an indefinable dignity—a majesty."[100] In later years, the story of that first ride would grow, in typical McIntyre style, to include the sights of his favorite restaurants, with a few celebrities thrown in for good measure. He wrote, "The excitement of that ride up the avenue of avenues atop a swaying green bus...they were lunching at the flower-boxed windows of the great Waldorf. Near the library I saw Caruso in an ensemble of green. In front of Delmonico's a cavalier was helping Norma Bayes—no less—into a hansom. On the portico of the old Savoy I saw silver champagne buckets flashing at the tableside. Here I was on the top of the world."[101]

At the time, Fifth Avenue may have actually been the most beautiful street in the world. The impressive building designed to be the main branch of the New York Public Library had opened just two months earlier in a ceremony that included remarks made by president William Howard Taft. Whether or not Caruso was out front "in an ensemble of green," it was an amazing sight. At the time, the Beaux-Arts building was the largest marble structure in the world and included more than seventy-five miles of shelves.

It was right at home with the other impressive structures on the street, including Saint Patrick's Cathedral, the Waldorf-Astoria, and the Metropolitan Museum of Art. Many of America's wealthiest families built their mansions on Fifth Avenue, and as Odd and Maybelle traveled

Article about the "new" Fifth Avenue in New York, June 27, 1909. *The New York Times*

down the street, they admired the homes of Cornelius Vanderbilt, Andrew Carnegie, John Jacob Astor, Solomon Guggenheim, and many others. Eventually, Odd and Maybelle would have money to spend in the many upscale shops they passed, but on their first day in New York, it was enough just to see stores like FAO Schwarz, Tiffany & Co., and Brentano's in person.

Even if they had the money to spend, shopping wasn't on their minds. They were excited to get to their new home, a brownstone boarding house on West Seventy-Second Street they found through friends in Cincinnati.

Young New Yorkers try to beat the heat of the 1911 heat wave. *Library of Congress Prints and Photographs Division*

Room and board at Mrs. McFadden's boarding house was twenty-five dollars a week. As Odd and Maybelle headed up three flights of stairs to their tiny room in the back of the house, the heat became more intense with each step. The air was stifling when they finally entered, as the room only had one window and any breeze was blocked by the rear of another house, only twenty feet away. Odd and Maybelle McIntyre's arrival coincided with the beginning of an eleven-day heat wave that crippled eastern North America. While those who had the means to leave New York City headed for the seashore, many were forced to stay and suffer.

On July 7, a *New York Tribune* article featured the dramatic headline "HEAT'S SCYTH MOWS DOWN 56 ON FIFTH DAY."[102] The thermometer on the Times Building, baking in the sun, registered as high as 103 degrees, and the humidity made the high temperatures even more oppressive. By the time the heat wave had broken on July 13, *The New York Times* reported more than 230 deaths in New York and thousands who were severely ill from the heat, some even being declared temporarily insane. Babies suffocated in their cribs, children drowned trying to find relief in any body of water, and the elderly, unable to leave their beds, died baking in their own homes. In several instances, deaths were from suicide.

One New Yorker, crazed by the heat, ran out of his house carrying a meat cleaver. Before being subdued, he severed the fingers of a policeman responding to the scene. Another, a well-educated engineer, who had been "perfectly normal" until the heat wave, was taken into custody for behaving erratically. He then proceeded to bless each of the policemen with a crucifix, telling them he was "a successor to the Lord," and that his fame would soon be worldwide. Family members said, because of the heat, he had not slept in ten days.

A seventy-year-old man known in his New York neighborhood as "the Hermit" because he rarely left his house, was discovered dead, "stretched out on the torn, old mattress of his dilapidated wooden bed."[103]

This was one time when the old adage "The show must go on" did not apply. On Broadway, the cast of Gilbert and Sullivan's *Pinafore*, including DeWolf Hopper, convinced management to cancel shows until the heat wave passed. The Russian Ballet at the Winter Garden and New York's *Folies Bergère* also closed.

Horses were crucial to the transportation and delivery of merchandise, including much-needed ice. During the three worst days of the heat wave, more than 450 horses died. While some were carried off and disposed of, many others were left in the streets where they began rotting in the intense heat. Eventually more than 600 horses died in New York City alone.

At night, Odd and Maybelle stayed up and took turns fanning each other, so sleep was difficult at best. Although Mother Nature had not provided a fitting welcome for Odd's arrival in New York, a complete stranger did. After washing up and changing into fresh clothes the first night in their new home, Odd stepped out into the street to explore and buy a pack of cigarettes. As he stood on the corner examining his new neighborhood, a well-dressed lady stopped and asked him for directions. Odd wrote, "I could not tell her, but she will never know how pleasing it was. She had taken me for a New Yorker."[104]

Odd McIntyre around the time he moved to New York to work at *Hampton's Magazine*.

8

Hampton's Magazine

Broadway numerically has more publications than Manhattan proper. A dozen or more periodicals screech of its wonders, shams, laughs and tears... the most successful of the daily newspapers for Broadway is the Morning Telegraph. It is said the chorus girl's breakfast is 'a cigarette and the Morning Telegraph.'[105]

O. O. McIntyre

After a very sleepless first night in New York, Odd headed out into the hot, humid morning and boarded the elevated train, or the "El" as the locals called it, and headed in for his first day of magazine work. In Manhattan, the El ran along Greenwich Street and Ninth Avenue on tracks towering three stories above the city streets. Electric trains had replaced the earlier ones that had been driven by steam. Most New Yorkers lived ten minutes or so from the El and, although it blocked the sun and was annoyingly loud and dirty, it provided a way for residents to live in one neighborhood and get quickly to another for work and leisure.

The *Hampton's Magazine* offices were at the new Marbridge Building at 1328 Broadway between Thirty-Fourth and Thirty-Fifth Streets, on the east side of Herald Square. The first thing Odd discovered was that the hours of a magazine were very different from those of a newspaper. He was the first to arrive that morning, so he had to talk the cleaning lady into letting him wait in Ray Long's office. As he timidly looked around, he realized the different hours weren't the only adjustment he was going to have to make. Odd was used to what he called "the roar, hullabaloo and disorder" of a messy newspaper office. By the time Odd arrived in 1911, Hampton's had a circulation of around 450,000 and its pages were filled with articles by some of the most popular writers in the business. *Hampton's* sophisticated offices reflected its important position in the publishing world. There were glass-topped desks, expensive rugs, and bookcases filled with collectible first-edition books.

Finally, Ray Long arrived and, after a bit of small talk, he showed Odd to his new office. Odd was surprised to see that, thanks to Long, "O. O. McIntyre" was already applied to the door in gold leaf. The moment Long left his office, Odd picked up the phone and called Maybelle to describe the office and excitedly tell her about his name on the door. That somehow made it official. He really was an editor on a New York City magazine. They had come a long way from Gallipolis.

The magazine itself had also come a long way since George A. Sherin and Roland Hennessy launched it as the ten-cent *Broadway Magazine* in 1898. It featured provocative stories and gossip about the New York stage world, along with illustrations of girls in turn-of-the-century swimsuits, burlesque actresses in tights and reproductions of famous art featuring female nudes.

The magazine changed hands several times through the early years. In 1905, Theodore Dreiser, who had been working for various New York magazines for more than a decade, applied for the position of editor. He submitted a plan to the owners that would allow him to add more respectable articles and better quality illustrations and photography. He was hired for the job with the warning that the position would not likely last long because the magazine was again for sale.

Later that year, the sale was completed and Benjamin B. Hampton became the new owner of what he renamed *Hampton's Broadway Magazine,* and then later shortened to *Hampton's Magazine.*

"B. B.," as his close friends and family called him, was born to a respected newspaper family on March 8, 1875 in Macomb, Illinois. His grandfather owned and operated the weekly *Macomb Journal* and his father and grandfather were founders of the *Illinois By-stander*. In 1895, Hampton and his father purchased the *Galesburg Evening Mail*, where young Hampton began applying some of the new ideas that were changing the newspaper landscape around the turn of the century.

He immediately added the telegraph as a tool for quickly getting news from the street to the newspaper office, and he championed a more creative style of writing for his reporters. As the newspaper's circulation increased, Hampton began selling and creating more advertising until he finally discovered he was enjoying that part of the business more than producing the newspaper. He purchased a printing press that produced posters and flyers for plays and musical performances, which led him to managing vaudeville acts and promoting street fairs. Hampton had a knack for understanding how printed words and images could not only inform the public, but could inspire them to action—like buying a product or a ticket to a vaudeville performance.

In 1898, Hampton and his wife moved to New York and he went to work with writer and advertising pioneer, Charles Austin Bates, and quickly became well-known in the growing New York advertising scene. After the success of a booklet he produced for his client, the American Tobacco Company, titled "How to Make the Cigar Stand Support the Drug Store," Hampton opened his own advertising agency. A 1907 article in *Printers' Ink*, a trade journal for the advertising business, applauded Hampton's management style:

> *B. B. is what the Spaniards call "suave." He is smooth. There is probably no man in New York who is so good at explanation. Some men have tact, others have diplomacy, others a bull-dog resistance that can't be beat down. But B. B. is just suave. His speech has a homely flavor and pungency that probably survives from Macomb... This faculty also enables B. B. to take a half-dozen men, each with a valuable little talent, and so explain them to one another that they all go work in sweetness and light to produce a whole.*[106]

Hampton's ability to get others to "work in sweetness and light" came in handy when he decided to buy the struggling *Broadway Magazine*, take a year to improve its quality, increase the advertising sales, then sell the magazine for a large profit. However, once he and Theodore Dreiser, who stayed on as editor, began the work of producing a magazine each month, Hampton discovered he loved the way the magazine business combined journalism, entertainment, and advertising—all areas in which he excelled.

In the short time he had worked for the magazine, Dreiser had turned it into a legitimate national news and political journal, featuring articles by some of the nation's best-known muckrakers. Hampton later wrote of Dreiser, "The minute I set eyes on him, I figured the man was a genius."[107]

Although Dreiser certainly appreciated Hampton's money keeping the magazine afloat, he didn't appreciate Hampton's input on the editorial direction and content. Dreiser wrote that he considered Hampton "a small, energetic, vibrant, and colorful soul, all egotism and middle-class conviction."[108] By 1907, the magazine's circulation had risen to a respectable 100,000, but Hampton needed it to be much more if the magazine were to be profitable. And to get there, it would need to reflect Hampton's vision, not Dreiser's. Dreiser finally left the magazine and eventually became a celebrated best-selling novelist who was nominated for a Noble Prize for literature in 1930.

With Dreiser gone and Hampton serving as editor himself, he needed

Benjamin B. Hampton, *George Grantham Bain Collection, Library of Congress Prints and Photographs Division*

help. The crusade Ray Long had led against Boss Cox at *The Cincinnati Post* was just the type of writing Hampton was anxious to see in his magazine, so he recruited the editor to New York. He knew Long would be just as eager as he to publish stories about current events and progressive middle-class society that included enough sensation to keep readers coming back for more. In fact, when Ray Long joined the magazine they were in the midst of just such a story.

In 1909, two American explorers, Dr. Frederick A. Cook and Robert E. Peary both claimed to be the first American to reach the North Pole. Cook, a medical doctor from New York, declared he and two Inuit companions had reached the North Pole on April 21, 1908. Robert E. Peary, a civil engineer and a commander in the U.S. Navy, claimed he and his long-time associate, Matthew Henson, had reached the North Pole on April 6, 1909.

At the time of the controversy, both were well-respected explorers with good reputations who had once been friends and research companions. On an expedition to North Greenland in 1891, Peary fractured his leg in an accident and Cook had treated him so well, Perry made him his second in command. Later, after they had gone their separate ways, Cook came to the rescue once again when Peary was lost in the Arctic. Cook joined the search party and then, after Peary was rescued, he nursed him back to health. The two remained friends until their very public dispute, after which they became bitter enemies.

Cook seemed, by all accounts, initially willing to share the media attention, but Peary quickly declared Cook was a fraud and that his claims of reaching the North Pole were lies. Their claims and counter-claims were made publicly, and trying to determine which of the two really made it to the North Pole first became a national pastime. Peary, who was a better self-promoter and knew how to work the media, eventually won in the court of public opinion. *Hampton's Magazine* certainly played a part by casting Peary as hero and Cook as villain in order to sell magazines. The cover of the January 1910 issue featured a dramatic photo of Peary, credited to Benjamin Hampton, that showed the haggard explorer's face and beard encircled by a caribou fur-lined parka. Underneath was the headline "Peary's Own Story of the Discovery of the North Pole."

The contents of the article left no doubt that Peary was the first man to reach the pole. A photo of an American flag atop a mound of snow was described as "The first photograph taken at the North Pole" and

Photo of explorer Robert E. Peary selected by Benjamin Hampton for the cover of the January 1910 issue of *Hampton's Magazine*.

the article began with grandiose sentiment, supposedly written by Peary, that was sure to inspire any patriotic American:

> *I have always been proud that I was born an American, but never so proud as when on that biting, sunlit Arctic day I saw the Stars and Stripes waving at the apex of the earth, and told myself that an American had set "Old Glory" there. As I watched it fluttering in the crisp air of the Pole,*

I thought of the twenty-three years of my own life which had been spent in laboring toward that goal, and realized that at last I had made good; that I could now lay at the feet of my country a trophy which the greatest nations of the world had been struggling to attain for nearly four hundred years.[109]

Those may or may not have been Peary's actual feelings, but they were definitely not his words. Hampton had been eager to get Peary's story in his magazine as quickly as possible, so he sent T. Everette Harré, novelist and member of the editorial staff at Hampton's, on an exploratory mission of his own. Harré was to track down Peary and secure the rights to his story, no matter what it took. What it took was forty thousand dollars. Harré then worked with another Hampton's writer, poet, and short story author, Elsa Barker, to ghostwrite a first-person account of Peary's adventure. The series ran through the year, with the dramatic climax planned for the August 1910 issue. To boost sales, promotions for the issue included the promise that Peary would provide "definitive proof" that it was he who had made it to the North Pole first, not Cook. However, Barker, trying her best to use information provided by Peary, found little proof and more than a few inconsistencies in Peary's accounts.

Historian Lyle Dick found that notes on the galleys and proofs of the articles do confirm that Hampton knew how to create a story that would entertain his magazine's readers. After one particularly detailed segment, Dick notes that Hampton wrote in the margin, "I would throw away hundreds of words of technical travel detail and get in some good, live description and explanation."[110]

The American public was hungry for more about the discovery and the competition between Peary and Cook. Merchandise like books, toys, collectible medallions, and postcards couldn't be produced fast enough, and the controversy became the first "story of the century."

Hampton was now eager to get Cook's account in his magazine before someone else got to him, so in the summer of 1910, he once again turned to T. Everette Harré. Harré negotiated an agreement with Cook's brother and finally departed for Europe for his first meeting with the explorer. While he was gone, Harré leased his New York apartment to Ray Long and his new wife, Pearl Dillow Schou, who had just arrived in the city from their European honeymoon. Long's second marriage occurred shortly after his divorce from his first wife, Florence. The wedding took place on July 25 at the home of New York Congressman

Ray Long and his second wife, Pearl Dillow Schou, shortly after their marriage in 1910.

William Sulzer, and Roy Howard and his wife served as attendants. Long's new wife, a graduate of Vassar, was very familiar with the newspaper business, having worked as a journalist for several newspapers using the pen name Dorothy Dale. In later years, she would become an editor for the *Red Book* and *Photoplay* magazines.

Harré's meetings with Cook went well and he brought the explorer back to America and hid him from other journalists in New York. According to writer and Odd McIntyre biographer, Charles B. Driscoll, Hampton and Long were hopeful they could convince Cook to confess to being a fraud to help them sell more magazines. Driscoll wrote, "Long tried to induce

The January 1911 issue of *Hampton's Magazine* that featured the story of explorer Cooks "confession."

Cook to write a dramatic story of how storms and the Arctic wastes had caused him, in a delirium, to imagine he had discovered the pole, when he actually had not. Cook refused, saying that would not be true."[111]

The story, for which Cook was only paid a thousand dollars compared to the forty thousand dollars paid to Peary, was published in the January 1911 issue with the title "Dr. Cook's Own Story." Cook approved the article and the layout and signed each page, so he was more than a little shocked when he stood at a newsstand and saw the cover featuring the teaser:

> *Dr. Cook's Confession. Did I get to the North Pole? I confess that I do not know absolutely. Fully, freely and frankly I shall tell you everything. Dr. Cook's own story in this issue.*[112]

It was Hampton and Long who made slight changes to the article and inserted "Dr. Cook's Confession" into the cover art at the last minute. To make sure they sold as many issues of the magazine as possible, Hampton sent out a press release about Cook's confession and plea of "insanity." Rather than the patriotic salute that began Peary's article, the article on Cook begins with an editor's note that immediately casts doubt on his claims:

Since the sudden and mysterious disappearance of Dr. Frederick A. Cook, in November 1909, until the publication of this series, no word has been received from this man...Why did Dr. Cook disappear? Was not this a tacit admission that he had presented a fraudulent claim to the discovery of the North Pole?[113]

While Cook actually "confesses" to nothing in the article, he does admit it's very difficult to know for sure whether the North Pole has been reached or not. While Cook announced publicly that the magazine article was "a sensation-provoking lie," the article and news coverage surrounding it did a great deal of harm to his reputation. After the article, most people decided it was Peary who had discovered the pole and that Cook really was a fraud.

Ironically, T. Everette Harré, who had been so instrumental in the Hampton's Magazine stories about both Peary and Cook, became a strong supporter of Cook and even quit the magazine to work with Cook on his book, *My Attainment of the Pole*. Charles Driscoll wrote in 1938 that he believed what Hampton and Long had done in "unjustly stigmatizing a great explorer as an impostor was deliberate misrepresentation and chicanery" and was "the most dastardly deed in the history of journalism."[114]

As it turned out, casting Dr. Cook's claim as fraudulent may not have been the dastardly deed Driscoll alleged. In his book, *Cook & Peary: The Polar Controversy, Resolved*, Robert M. Bryce, a historical researcher who spent twenty years studying the controversy, contends that neither explorer actually made it to the pole and that both knew they were lying when they claimed they did. "The evidence points to both claims as frauds, and knowing fraud," Bryce wrote, "not self-deception, but purposeful."[115]

Odd had joined a magazine with writers who were accustomed to controversy, and an editor eager to use it to sell magazines. While Ray Long fit right in from the beginning, Odd struggled on his first day and never fully recovered. Around ten that first morning, an office boy came by to let Odd know he was wanted in Benjamin Hampton's office for an editorial meeting. Odd wrote, "My throat immediately became as dry as an Arizona River bed and goose pimples chased each other up and down my spine."[116]

As Odd entered the office, he saw a group of men sitting around

Hampton's desk. Ray Long greeted Odd and introduced him to others on the editorial team. However, rather than sit in one of the chairs in the circle, Odd grabbed one in the back corner of the office—as far away from Hampton as he could get. Odd looked down and tried not to make eye contact with anyone. He didn't say a word and barely even understood much of what was being discussed in the meeting. Finally, Hampton looked past those in the circle and noticed Odd just sitting there.

"What do you think, Mr. McIntyre?" he asked.

Odd realized every eye in the room was on him. He turned bright red and, although he tried to speak, words wouldn't come out of his mouth. He sat there frozen and the silence seemed to drag on forever. The others in the room began to look at each other and smile. Then, everyone looked at Ray Long. Hampton wasn't impressed. He added to Odd's misery by saying, "We expect men on this magazine to have ideas and to be able to express them."

The rest of his first day, Odd wandered around the office trying to look busy. He was perplexed as to why Long had even hired him. Suddenly, he was homesick for Cincinnati and deeply regretted making the move to New York. Long had disappeared from the office and Odd incorrectly assumed it was because he was so disappointed in his new assistant. Odd later decided it was actually Long's loneliness that had prompted him to send that one-way ticket to New York. He simply wanted someone he knew and trusted close by. In fact, it was more than that. Long actually liked the way Odd wrote and edited and thought he had a good "ear" for what people wanted to read.

Although things did improve some in the weeks ahead, Odd never really thrived at the magazine. He had assumed he would be doing at least some writing, but he spent most days reading manuscripts written by others. There was a new energy among those in the newspaper and magazine industries, and the writing was quickly changing to meet the needs of a society undergoing a rapid evolution. Odd was there evaluating and offering suggestions as the magazine tackled ideas like women's suffrage, environmental protection, access to healthcare for all Americans, and civil rights. They were revealing social injustices, pointing out when unregulated big businesses were willing to harm consumers to make a profit, and looking for abuses of power everywhere from Washington, D.C. to courthouses across America.

Odd was once again in a place where he could learn from and

befriend some of the best writers, journalists, artists and photographers in the business. His new friends included Sam Blythe, a political satirist who would become a regular contributor to the *Saturday Evening Post*; Rex Beach, an American novelist, playwright, and Olympic water polo player; Ellis Parker Butler, a celebrated author; Sophie Irene Loeb, a well-respected journalist and social welfare advocate; and Ida M. Tarbell, the author and journalist who pioneered the muckraking movement.

In that first week, Odd was also befriended by Harris Merton Lyon, a New York journalist and short story writer whose work appeared in many of the most-read magazines of the day. In 1908 Lyon had published his first collection of short stories, *Sardonics*, and it had been considered moderately successful.

Odd and Lyon, who had previously worked for *The Houston Post* and *The Kansas City Star*, had a lot in common; they were both, in Odd's words, "square-toed country boys." They were around the same age, and they both grew up in small Midwestern towns—Odd in Ohio and Lyon in Missouri. It was actually Theodore Dreiser who first saw genius in young Lyon's writing and hired him as a consulting editor back when Hampton's was still called *Broadway Magazine*. In his book, *Twelve Men*, Dreiser wrote a portrait of a young writer who was based on Lyon. Dreiser wrote, "He dawned on me in the spring of 1906, a stocky, sturdy, penetrative temperament of not more than twenty-four or -five years of age; steady of eye, rather aloof and yet pervasive and bristling; a devouring type."[117]

While Odd was in Cincinnati learning the newspaper business at the *Post*, Lyon had been in New York writing short stories. Dreiser wrote that Lyon "had a style as clear as water, as simple as rain; color, romance, humor; and if a little too much of vanity and self-importance, still one could forgive him for they were rather well-based."

The friendship of Lyon and Odd developed around a mutual dislike of where their careers were at the moment and their desire to find success in an era when everything was changing so rapidly. Lyon showed Odd the city and

Writer Harris Merton Lyon,
University of Missouri Digital Library

101

introduced him to many of the restaurants in New York that had more charm than class. Lyon preferred to eat at "shabby little quick-lunch rooms where the characters were more important than the food."[118] This greatly appealed to Odd who had begun a love affair with the restaurants of New York that lasted for the rest of his life.

Lyon's advice to Odd was to quit magazine work and write. While Odd didn't have the courage to quit, Lyon did; at least for a while. He released his second book of short stories, *Graphics*, in 1913. Writers like H. L. Mencken, Willa Cather, and Carl Sandburg were fans of his writing and recognized his talent publicly, but newspaper critics, not used to the new "realistic" style of writing, were not as receptive. Although Lyon was not commercially successful, he was greatly respected in literary circles and, as writer O. Henry lay dying, it was Lyon he asked to complete his last unfinished short story, "The Snow Man."

Despite his talent, after becoming ill with Bright's disease, Lyon was forced to do any writing he could to support his growing family. Once, he and Odd were dining together and someone remarked to Lyon that someday he would be remembered with the likes of O. Henry. He smiled and said cynically, "That will be comforting news to the worms."[119] Odd last spoke with Lyon in 1914, when they ran into each other in front of a New York advertising agency where Lyon was working. Odd was saddened to see the writer whom many considered a literary genius reduced to turning out "snappy phrases for lead pencils, canned soup and such rubbish." Odd later told Maybelle that Lyon had seemed disillusioned, discouraged, and broken.

Lyon died in June 1916 at the age of thirty-three. After his death, Odd wrote a tribute to his friend:

Like Stephen Crane and Frank Morris, his genius burned briefly—and he died neglected. He was among the first men I met in New York and, for a time, we worked side by side on a magazine...He died from overwork— leaving a realistic novel unfinished. His 'Sardonics' and book of short stories, 'Graphics,' are among the finest pieces of American short-story writing. The last time I saw him was in front of an advertising office where he worked. They had assigned him—one of the few literary geniuses America has produced—to writing ads for tobacco. He was not bitter. Just disillusioned. Even now, Lyon ranks with O. Henry and his earthly reward was a series of acrid disappointments.[120]

Odd always felt recognition for Lyon would come eventually. In an undated letter to Lyon's widow, he wrote, "I have often sung his praises in print and in several speeches. He will be remembered long after Dreiser is forgotten, although it seems a pity to me it should not come sooner. It will burst like a bombshell any day—those things do. Mark my prediction."[121]

While Odd knew *Hampton's Magazine* was financially struggling when he accepted the position, he didn't know just how close to the edge of disaster it teetered. After owning the magazine only a few months, Hampton offered reader's stock in the new and improved publication. He raised and quickly spent one hundred thousand dollars. In future years, he raised another six hundred thousand dollars the same way. Despite the revenue from selling shares in the magazine, advertising, subscriptions, and newsstand sales, by the time Odd arrived in the summer of 1911, the magazine was broke again and in need of several thousand dollars to continue. Stinging articles directed at Wall Street and big business had left Hampton with few friends willing to invest, and he himself had no more money to keep it going. He was nearing a physical and emotional breakdown, so Hampton left New York while his brother took on the challenge of selling the financially struggling magazine.

The eventual buyer was Frank Orff, a publisher from St. Louis. He quickly combined the magazine with one of his other publications and renamed it the *Hampton-Columbian Magazine*. Suddenly, Odd noticed many of those he had seen regularly for the two months he had been at the magazine began disappearing, and individuals loyal to Orff began taking their place. Odd was no fan of Orff and described him as "a church deacon type, unctuous, given to soaping his hands."[122] Odd was especially offended by Orff's bad toupee, which always seemed to Odd to be "slightly askew." He didn't have to be offended for very long. Odd remembered:

> One noon, Mr. Orff dropped into my domain, shook hands and asked me how long I had been employed there, spoke in his whinnying voice of his love for his fellow man and then went to his own office and in true Christian spirit sent me the following note a half hour later: Your services on the 'Hampton-Columbian Magazine' are no longer needed after today. I was fired. While expected, it of course came as a jolt. It always does. Two weeks

salary was due but I had been doing nothing and I did not have the heart to ask for it. I took my few belongings and went home.

Two days later Odd got a call from Long letting him know he was once again needed at the magazine. As it turned out, with Hampton gone, Orff needed Ray Long more than he didn't need Odd. When Long found out Orff had fired Odd, he threatened to quit unless Odd were re-hired immediately. Although Long's act of friendship was appreciated by Odd and Maybelle, no one would be working for the magazine much longer.

Like Hampton, Orff also sold stock to help finance his magazines and, soon after Odd's departure, Orff was accused of misrepresenting his company's finances and the circulation of his magazine to make more money. Although he and others in his organization were acquitted in a lengthy court battle, the magazine didn't survive the blow.

After a brief period in which he and Odd searched for newspaper jobs together, Ray Long became editor of a set of magazines called *Red Book*, *Green Book* and *Blue Book* and moved to Chicago, where he continued his rise to the top of the magazine publishing business.

Benjamin Hampton worked for several years as a vice president of the American Tobacco Company but, always excited by the "next big thing," he saw great potential in the budding movie industry. He became the president of the General Film Company, that distributed silent movies, then started his own production company. Hampton was the first to turn the novels of Zane Grey into movies. After the death of his first wife, he married silent screen actress Claire Adams, who had appeared in many of his films.

Toward the end of his life, Hampton wrote *A History of the Movies*, in which he shared both a first-hand and historical account of the earliest years of the movie business. He died at the age of fifty-eight in 1932.

After being fired from *Hampton's Magazine* twice, Odd decided producing a daily newspaper was more to his liking than the magazine business. It was time for the shy reporter who hated meeting strangers to hit the streets of Park Row and find a newspaper job.

9

Titanic

It was a night of howling wind and rain and a drenched city turned out to welcome survivors. For the early morning edition I assembled facts turned in by others and wrote the lead that occupied a double column down page 1 with a jump head inside—all under an 8 column banner line.[123]

O. O. McIntyre

It was as though even the weather was against them that evening on Thursday, April 18, 1912. Odd stood, pencil and pad in hand, at the Cunard Line's pier waiting for the arrival of the *Carpathia* and the survivors of the maiden voyage of the *Titanic*. Surprisingly, he had been assigned the job of field editor. He was grateful they hadn't stuck him in their makeshift headquarters in a cheap, rundown diner on West Street, opposite the pier.

Lightening lit up the sky, periodically giving the water a ghostly look through the fog that had rolled in earlier.

Four days after the ship had sunk, there was still great confusion about what had happened and who had survived. Everyone was desperate for news about the survivors and the sinking of the "unsinkable" ship. Newspapers were the primary source for getting that information into the hands of the public.

At just twenty-eight years old, Odd was in the middle of the story of a lifetime, and the pressure to deliver was great. Just weeks earlier, he had been certain his days at the copy desk of the *Evening Mail* were numbered, so in many ways, what had been the end for so many seemed like a second chance for him.

Hampton's Magazine had folded just a few months earlier and their savings were running out, so Odd and Maybelle decided it was a good time for Maybelle to visit her mother back in Gallipolis for awhile. Odd moved into a cheap boarding house on West Fifty-Seventh Street and was willing to take just about any job he could find. After several months of searching, he was hired by the *Evening Mail* as a copy editor, and Maybelle was able to return to New York.

The thought of being fired again and disappointing his wife was almost more than he could stand. His fear of failure was likely making the already anxious young reporter commit more mistakes than he normally would have. Although later he described the *Evening Mail* as "a rather weak sister in the field, but showing flashes of form at intervals,"[124] it was one of the oldest newspapers in the country, and he was happy to be working anywhere. Originally named the *New York Express*, the *Evening Mail* was founded as a Whig paper in 1836 by James Brooks and Erastus, his younger brother. By the time Odd was hired as a copy editor in 1911, the paper had gone through many mergers, owners, and name changes. In 1888, publisher, lawyer, and banker Elliott Shepard, husband of heiress Margaret Louise Vanderbilt, purchased what was at that time called the *Main and Express* from Cyrus Field. Field was a prominent businessman responsible for laying the first transatlantic cable. In addition to its important role in the history of New York publishing, under Shepard's ownership, the newspaper became known for the building in which it was produced. Located at Broadway and Fulton Street, and completed in 1892, the newspaper's headquarters was one of New York's early ornate skyscrapers. The powerful presses could produce nearly one hundred thousand newspapers per hour and were located in the basement, while the editorial offices were located on the tenth and eleventh floors.[125]

Although Odd reluctantly went to work each day in that ornate building, he made few friends. Many of the editors and reporters he had worked with at the *Cincinnati Post* had become as close to him as brothers, and they played as hard as they worked. At the *Evening Mail*, the staff was older and less likely to want to go out for a drink after work. These were newspaper men from an earlier era who were now no longer able to handle the difficult job of hitting the streets looking for stories, which was what Odd really wanted to do. He hated being stuck in an office. Odd wrote:

> *The copy desk was composed mostly of old newspapermen who had outlived their usefulness—pathetic and trembling creatures, who lived in perpetual dread of the blue envelope. It was one of the most unhappy and depressing of my newspaper experiences, and I cannot today pass the spot where the old Evening Mail stood without a sinking feeling.*[126]

The biggest problem with the position of copy editor was that it left no room for error in the areas where Odd was weakest: spelling, punctuation, and grammar. Everyone, including Odd, knew he was in a job in which he would never succeed. To make matters worse, the thirty-five dollars he was making each week was nearly half what he'd been making when he left Ohio less than a year earlier, and he and Maybelle were barely hanging on financially.

He was desperate enough to work up the nerve to give his boss, Theophilus E. Niles, an ultimatum: Either increase his salary, or he would be forced to find another job. That idea backfired when Niles suggested a new job elsewhere was a good idea, as it appeared to him Odd had "slumped in his work."[127]

A break from the misery of the copy desk finally came with the arrival of a new city editor who was Odd's complete opposite. Confident and outgoing, Robert Emmet MacAlarney was a graduate of Dickinson College in Pennsylvania and had gone on to study at Harvard. Spelling and grammar were not a problem for MacAlarney. Despite their differences, he spotted potential in the nervous, frightened copy editor and, after giving him better stories on which to work, he was instrumental in getting Odd promoted to assistant city editor.

MacAlarney would not have to wait long to see if his faith in the young writer was misplaced. On Sunday, April 14, 1912, a bulletin from the Associated Press office in Cape Race, Newfoundland arrived in the newsroom of *The New York Times*. It read, "At 10:25 o'clock tonight the White Star Line steamship Titanic called 'CQD' to the Marconi station here, and

Friends and family of *Titanic* passengers wait at the offices of the White Star Line hoping for news that their loved ones are among the survivors. *George Grantham Bain Collection, Library of Congress Prints and Photographs Division*

reported having struck an iceberg. The steamer said that immediate assistance was required."

In the first days after the crew of the *Carpathia*, a Cunard Line ship, pulled the *Titanic's* survivors from the lifeboats, very little was known back on shore about the fate of the ship or its passengers. Confusion and desperation for news led to false stories being printed by many newspapers around the world. Radio communication was still new and wireless messages were misinterpreted, resulting in initial reports that no passengers had died in the accident. The White Star Line, the British shipping company that owned and operated the *Titanic*, first announced that the ship was merely damaged. Executives at the White Star Line were so certain the ship was being towed to Halifax for repairs, they sent many of the wealthy passengers' family members that direction on a train. Once the truth was discovered, they had to return the anxious family members to New York to wait for information on the fate of their loved ones. On April 15, the *Evening Mail* headline announced, "Titanic's Passengers Saved; Liner Being Towed to Halifax."[128] Other newspapers included headlines like "Everyone Safe. Morning of Suspense Ends in Message of Relief," and "All Titanic Passengers are Safe; Transferred in Lifeboats at Sea."[129]

Relief was soon replaced with fear and dread when the crew from the *Carpathia* finally radioed that they had pulled 706 of *Titanic's* 2,208 passengers out of the ocean, and the Titanic was gone. The unthinkable had happened; the unsinkable ship had sunk, and many lives had been lost. To make matters worse, there was now confusion and miscommunication about which passengers had been rescued and which had perished.

While some names of survivors were telegraphed to the home office and then shared with waiting friends and family members, in the final hours leading up to *Carpathia's* arrival at port in New York City, the young men working in its telegraph office stopped communicating altogether, which frustrated many who were eager for information. One story that appeared in the *Evening Mail* on Thursday, April 18, reported the growing anger among those waiting for news:

Watchers Angered by Carpathia's Silence
Anger displaced grief today among the watchers at the White Star line offices when they learned that the defiant silence maintained by the Carpathia concerning the details of the terrible tragedy that cost so many lives cannot even be broken by the demands of the federal authorities in Washington. The dispatch concerning this information was issued at 9 o'clock this morning by the Navy department. It stated that the scout cruiser Salem has tried repeatedly, but in vain, to get some details from the Carpathia.[130]

The Associated Press sent a notice to all their clients apprising them of the status:

Carpathia Ignores Associated Press
We have no assurance that we will get any wireless news from the Carpathia, as this vessel studiously refuses to answer all queries. Even President Taft's requests for information, addressed to the Carpathia have been ignored.

A man he described as "grey faced and swollen eyed" yelled at one reporter who was working for the *Evening Mail*, interviewing those waiting outside the White Star Line offices. The exchange between him and the reporter summed up the anguish of those who did not yet know the fate of their loved ones:

What are you people if you can't get us the real story of what happened?"
he demanded. It was explained to him that the newspapers can get nothing
yet except what is snatched in meager bulletins from the Cunard air. He was
also told that the Cunard people have refused to permit reporters to board the
'Carpathia,' and that only a limited number of them would be permitted
on the pier when the rescue ship docks. 'And are you going to stand for that?'
he cried incredulously. 'Why, what do these ship people think anyway? Do
they imagine that they can hold back forever the truth about what happened
when...' And then his voice choked back and he turned away.[131]

It was later alleged that a senior official from Marconi, the company
that managed the telegraph operators, had instructed them to cease
communicating to increase the value of the news when the ship reached
port. An official with Marconi was accused of making a deal with *The
New York Times* for exclusive interviews with the operators as soon as the
Carpathia docked.

The frenzy of the public was unlike anything Odd and his peers had
ever experienced. It was in this high-pressured environment that Robert
MacAlarney would show just how much faith he had in Odd, when he
put the young assistant editor in charge of the reporters who would be
attempting to get stories from the survivors as they exited the rescue ship.

On the evening of Thursday, April 18, the *Carpathia* finally sailed into
New York Harbor. The fog that had rolled in earlier made it difficult
to see, and perhaps overcome by the sadness and a great sense of loss,
the crowd of more than 2,000 crowded on the pier was eerily silent. All
that could be heard was the distant tolling of church bells, an occasional
roll of thunder, and the steady sound of the rain that continued to fall
through the evening.

Some photographers and reporters were not fortunate enough to be
on the pier, so they hired boats of all shapes and sizes to get as close to
the ship as possible. As the magnesium flashes of the cameras went off,
glimpses of the survivors could be seen crowded on the deck of the ship,
waiting anxiously to be reunited with loved ones. The tension hung in
the air as the ship slowly passed her own berth, Pier 54, then stopped at
White Star Line's Pier 59. This was where the *Titanic* would have returned
had it not sunk. Somberly, the crew lowered *Titanic's* empty lifeboats into

Reporters interview *Titanic* survivors as they exit the *Carpathia*. *The American Press Association*

the water, returning them to the White Star Line. The *Carpathia* then made her way back to Pier 54 where she docked.

The gangways finally began to lower, and the crew prepared for the passengers to disembark. At eleven o' clock that evening, the first survivors began departing the ship as the crowd surged forward and strained against barricades that had been set up by police. The silence became a quiet murmur and then a roar as reporters began shouting questions and photographers pushed forward. The flashes of the cameras once again illuminated weary survivors as they struggled to exit the ship.

The interviews Odd and his team managed to get in the hours that followed gave *Evening Mail* readers a glimpse into a night of horrible deaths, the honor of sacrifice, and the shame of cowardly deeds done by those desperate for survival.

One reporter, possibly even Odd himself, stood in the pouring rain interviewing Dr. Washington Dodge and his wife, Ruth, who witnessed the bravery of Isidor Straus, co-owner of Macy's department store, and his wife, Ida. "Mrs. Straus showed the most admirable heroism," Dodge said. "Each time those who were helping load the lifeboats tried to get

The front page of *The New York Times* on April 17, 1912. *The New York Times*

the elderly couple to leave the *Titanic*, they declined."[132]

Dr. Dodge heard someone in the crowd plead with Straus to get in one of the boats, pointing out Straus' advanced age, to which he replied, "I am not too old to sacrifice myself for a woman." Another of the survivors, Harry "Kid" Homer, a gambler who had booked passage on the *Titanic* to take advantage of all the wealthy guests, interrupted and shared that he had seen an officer trying to physically tear Ida Straus from her husband to force her into a boat, but she had her arms wrapped so tightly around his neck, it proved impossible. Homer heard her say, "If you stay, I will stay." The last time he saw them, they were still standing on the deck of the sinking ship. At the time, Homer neglected to mention that he had escaped the *Titanic* disguised as a woman.

As Dr. Dodge began to tell the reporter about the bravery of wealthy businessman John Jacob Astor IV and U.S. Army Major Archibald Butt, he was interrupted by his wife, who wanted to share her version of what happened that night:

Yes, I saw Major Archibald Butt. I knew him because he was the handsomest man on the ship. I saw him standing by Captain Smith, alongside Colonel John Jacob Astor, and it seemed to me like those three men were in command of everything. I looked into Colonel Astor's face and into that of Major Butt, and I could see no fear. The last recollection I have of getting away in a boat was that Major Butt and Colonel Astor were standing by the side of the gangway assisting the second cabin passengers into the remaining boats. [133]

Ruth Washington also shared with the reporter that the final words she heard from Ida Straus were, "We are old people, Isidor, and we will die together."

Odd and the reporters assigned to him received high praise for the work they did in those difficult days. His talent was not in spelling or grammar, but in observing and writing about people in a way that allowed others to easily relate. This style of writing was very different from traditional reporting, and was only just beginning to be embraced by newspapers and magazines.

Odd had done better than expected on his first assignment as assistant editor, and was hopeful that this was a sign of better days ahead. After working more than forty-eight hours with no sleep, he finally returned home. Three hours after he drifted off, Maybelle couldn't resist waking him up to show him the early edition of the *Evening Mail*. In twelve-point type was the byline, "by O. O. McIntyre." As sleepy as he was, he read the story at least a dozen times.

Unfortunately, despite the good work he had done, his days at the *Evening Mail* were numbered. Robert MacAlarney soon departed the paper to accept a position as the first journalism instructor at Columbia University's School of Journalism. Odd's new boss was much more interested in traditional spelling and grammar skills than observational humor and Odd's ability to write in a style to which Middle America could relate. Odd found a note on his desk that read, "I shall have to dispense with your services Saturday."

He was once again without a job, and as he later wrote, "The real lean days had set in." [134]

10

The Letter

I am still pretty much the yokel and what success I have had in writing of New York for the out country has been due to my enthusiasm for it. I cannot walk on Fifth Avenue, Broadway or any other part of town today without experiencing a certain thrill.[135]

O. O. McIntyre

As the competition for readers grew during the early years of the twentieth century, publishers continued to look for affordable content that would appeal to the masses. Cartoons and comic strips filled that need, and could be enjoyed by readers of every age and reading level. In addition to providing entertainment for readers in a time before radio and television, some of the strips also provided satirical commentary on social issues of the day. Many of the early twentieth-century comic strip artists considered themselves to be more journalists than illustrators, and they attracted devoted fans of all ages, who followed their favorite cartoons religiously.

In 1913, while Odd was still working at the *Evening Mail*, he and Maybelle moved in with three talented friends, also in New York by way of Cincinnati, who were renting a small studio apartment on West

(left to right, seated) Odd McIntyre, Bob Brinkerhoff, Maybelle McIntyre, Harold
Webster, and Steven Tilton. (left to right, standing) Edna Brinkerhoff, Ethel Webster, and
an unidentified woman, *Courtesy the Esther Allen Greer Museum at the University of Rio Grande*

148th Street, in the Washington Heights neighborhood of Manhattan.
Bob Brinkerhoff, Harold T. Webster and Ray Rohn had worked with
Odd back at *The Cincinnati Post*, and now they were all determined to
make it in the big city.

As the son of the founder of the *Toledo Post*, cartoonist Brinkerhoff had
grown up around the newspaper business. Everyone knew of "Brinks"
as a talented artist, but he was also a gifted singer who won a scholarship
to the Cincinnati Conservatory. His musical ability came in handy in his
early years in New York, and he occasionally picked up a few dollars
singing for weddings and in church choirs. Eventually, his career as a
cartoonist took off and he became most famous as the artist of a comic strip

Cartoon by Harold T. Webster featuring Odd McIntyre.

called "Little Mary Mixup." Distributed by United Features Syndicate from 1917 to 1957, it was considered unusual at the time because it was the first comic strip to feature a young girl as the lead character.

Brinks wasn't the only roommate with a nickname. Harold T. Webster always signed his work "Webster." However, his many friends, including Odd and Maybelle, called him "Webby." He grew up in Tomahawk, Wisconsin, where his father ran the local drug store. As a young boy he

LITTLE MARY MIXUP

"Little Mary Mixup" cartoon strip by Bob Brinkerhoff. *United Features Syndicate*

began drawing cartoons and, although he had very little formal training, his natural ability led him to jobs as a cartoonist for *The Chicago Daily News* and Chicago's *Inter Ocean*, and ultimately to *The Cincinnati Post.*

Sometimes referred to as "the Mark Twain of cartoonists," Webster became famous penning strips like "The Timid Soul," "The Thrill That Comes Once in a Lifetime," and "How to Torture Your Husband." His most successful strip, "The Timid Soul," followed the adventures of Caspar Milquetoast, a timid man who, as Webster explained, "speaks softly and gets hit with a big stick."

Webster's contribution to the world of cartooning was celebrated in a feature story in *Time* magazine in November 1945, in which his portrait appeared on the cover. The article stated one of the reasons for Webster's success was his ability to present a positive image of Americans during some very troubling times:

Cover of the March 28, 1925 issue of *The New Yorker* designed by Ray Rohn, *Condé Nast*

Caspar Milquetoast is the only character Cartoonist Webster has ever given a name to—and Caspar, with appropriate shyness, sneaked into the strip as a space filler. The rest of Webster's bald-headed bores, thin, puzzled wives, and freckle-faced kids need no name; they are, when they hit the mark—as they often do—Everyman. H. T. Webster has learned to slice and serve his generous chunks of U.S. life methodically…Webster is one of the few journalists of his troubled time who has managed consistently to remind people of the news that they are human beings, and that that news is not as bad as it is generally made out.[136]

Ray Rohn rounded out the creative family on West 148th Street. Rohn was a talented cartoonist and illustrator who freelanced for *The New Yorker, The Saturday Evening Post, Collier's, Green Book,* and many other magazines. Born in Defiance, Ohio, Rohn had worked in Cleveland and Cincinnati before heading to New York with Brinkerhoff and Webster. In addition to working in the art department of the *Public Ledger* and creating a comic strip called "Bedelia's Beaus," Rohn worked in advertising, creating print ads, and designing corporate icons.

The young group of friends pooled their money and paid a cook to come in each day and prepare their meals. After they settled in, Maybelle's mother moved from Ohio and became their housekeeper, den mother, and cheerleader.

Despite the fact that money was tight for everyone, they were living in the most exciting city in the world and they had each other for support as they sought jobs in the growing newspaper and magazine industries. They couldn't afford to go out for their entertainment, so many evenings Maybelle would read out loud to the group. She read history, the classics, biographies, and popular novels of the day. The friends became very close in those early days of struggle and supported each other through their successes and failures. Odd wrote:

> *Bob Brinkerhoff is a friend of long standing. Along with H. T. Webster and Ray Rohn, we came to New York together, pitching camp in a walk-up apartment far uptown in the 140s. All of us slaved side by side for several years in the editorial rooms of the Cincinnati Post. In those first days in the metropolis we were gay, young buccaneers on the journalistic high seas. Money was so coy and reluctant, we often cut each other's hair and there were bleak days when we pussy-footed from our flat via the fire escape to avoid a rather unsentimental landlord.*[137]

As much as Odd and Maybelle enjoyed living with the group, once Odd lost his job at the *Evening Mail,* money became even tighter. To make matters worse, as Odd was dealing with failure and trying to figure out what to do next, the careers of the others were taking off. The May 1915 issue of *Cartoons* magazine featured the trio:

H. T. Webster, cartoonist of the New York Globe; R. M. Brinkerhoff, cartoonist and illustrator, and Ray Rohn, who is making a reputation for himself in Judge, make up a trio that has invaded New York successfully from the west...Webster's cartoons today are syndicated throughout the United States by the Globe Publishing Company, and have brought him merited rewards...Brinkerhoff it will be noticed has resumed cartooning, his recent work appearing in the New York Evening Post...Scarcely a week passes but that Mr. Rohn adds to the joy of life by one of his humorous drawings in Judge.[138]

Odd assumed, rightly so, that his friends wanted to move out of the studio apartment, but were staying for the sake of him and Maybelle. The last thing they wanted to do was hold their friends back, so the couple moved to room 121 of the Hotel Hargrave on Seventy-Second Street, while Maybelle's mother returned to Gallipolis.

With its heavily ornamented classical design, the Hotel Hargrave, designed in a Beaux-Arts style by architect Frederick C. Browne, is as impressive today as it was when it was built more than a century ago.

The hotel was completed in two sections—the first in 1902 and the second in 1907. It was advertised as having "comfort, refinement, and luxury at very moderate prices." Ads for the hotel touted its 300 rooms, 200 bathrooms, and the fact that it was fireproof. The hotel was also near the subway and the El, and Central Park was just a block away.

Although it was not a bad place to live, Odd sank into such a depression, he could barely leave their room. Many years later, he wrote, "The four walls of room 121 witnessed, I hope, the greatest defeats I shall ever know. Only the man or woman who has failed utterly time after time understands such a

HOTEL HARGRAVE - 112 W. 72nd St. NEW YORK

sickness of the soul."[139]

Odd and Maybelle had some very interesting neighbors while living at the Hotel Hargrave. New York Giant's infielder Eddie Grant lived in one of the brownstones across the street. Actress Alice Joyce lived in another, while comedian W. C. Fields lived around the corner. One neighbor who would eventually create a national media sensation was living right next door. Although Odd remembered Edward Browning as a quiet and unassuming neighbor, he would become one of the most successful real estate developers in Manhattan in the 1920s, and a frequent target of gossip and scandal. In 1926, he was a fifty-one-year-old divorcee when he married sixteen-year-old "Peaches" Heenan. Although "Daddy" Browning, as he came to be called in the tabloids, showered his young bride with hundreds of thousands of dollars' worth of furs, jewelry. and clothing, in ten months they were in divorce court. The trial resulted in unprecedented news coverage, much of it from the tabloids, due in large part to Peaches' dramatic testimony of her life with Browning:

> *My innocent sensibilities were astonished when he came lumbering into our bedroom dressed as a sheik and growling "woof woof" at me like a bear. Naturally, I went into a swoon. Besides, I feel that if he got to bring his pet duck along on our honeymoon, I should have been able to take my mother. The nasty thing has free reign of the house, just honk, honk, honking all day long.[140]*

As they nodded hello and shared small talk about the weather, Odd saw nothing in the quiet Browning that would indicate his neighbor would someday be the subject of one of the most salacious stories of the decade.

During this period, Odd and Maybelle also got to know another of the hotel's residents, novelist and short story writer Edna Ferber. This was long before her Pulitzer Prize for the novel *So Big* and before her novels were made into the films *Show Boat*, *Cimarron*, and *Giant*.

Although no cooking was allowed, Maybelle would sneak groceries into the hotel inside a fur muff. Odd would then sit outside the bathroom "smoking furiously" to disguise the smell of Maybelle preparing their evening meal on a hot plate. It was the only time in their years together that Maybelle cooked. Years later, J. Wade McGrath, the hotel manager, ran into Odd and, as they discussed the old days, McGrath laughingly mentioned that he knew they had been cooking, but had chosen to look the other way because he liked them.

It seemed that Odd was the only one in their circle of friends struggling to find success. He tried to sell poems, jokes, cartoons, and stories, but was finding very few willing to buy his work. *Life* bought a thing or two, and he did a story in the *Sun* for which he made twenty dollars. One has to wonder if there were any coincidence that the things he sold around this time were purchased by the publications where Webster and Brinkerhoff were working. Odd joked that his submissions to *The Saturday Evening Post* were rejected so fast, he wondered if they sent someone from Philadelphia to New Jersey to intercept and return them before they were opened.

Fortunately, the couple had inherited a little money from Odd's grandfather. Although the plan was to save it for their retirement, Maybelle insisted they use it to live on until Odd could catch a break. Although Maybelle never told Odd exactly how bad their financial situation got, before things got better, their savings dwindled to less than five hundred dollars.

Humorist Irvin Cobb was a close friend of the couple, and he wrote about Maybelle's strength during those lean years, "A thousand times, along about then, he would have quit. She kept him at the damnable deadly useless grind of it."[141]

The stress of being without a job, the feeling of failure, and not knowing what the future would bring, aggravated Odd's already fragile mental health. For the first time, his close friends observed his name was indicative of his behavior. Later, when he was better, Odd dismissed it as "chronic melancholia" and "professional gloom,"[142] but there was clearly something else going on. During this period, Odd was most likely struggling with the early symptoms of pernicious anemia, that could have greatly impacted his mental and emotional state.

If he were out with friends, Odd would suddenly, without warning, leave and run back to the hotel to find Maybelle. If friends tried to hold him or make him stay, he would react almost violently. Former roommates Brinkerhoff and Webster would spend hours trying to coax him out of his hotel room. Friends also noticed that he refused to walk near Central Park because of a sudden fear of open spaces. He shared with his closest friends that he was afraid he would die in the street if he left the awnings under which he felt protected. Occasionally, Odd's fear of open spaces got so bad, he ran from awning to awning until he reached his destination. Eventually, it was just easier to stay home.

Odd found sleep nearly unattainable; some nights were so bad he would lie awake and sob. Insomnia is another of pernicious anemia's cruel symptoms. Although Odd was used to dealing with more anxiety than most, this time it came on full force. At night, he and Maybelle took long walks through Central Park. Odd felt safe because the open spaces were hidden by the darkness. Some evenings they sat on a bench and listened to the sounds of the city while Maybelle napped with her head on his shoulder. Odd, unable to sleep, would stare into the dark and fight his demons. He became so ill his skin actually turned grey, his hair turned white, and he lost a great deal of weight. Already thin and lanky, he began to appear emaciated. With their money nearly gone and Odd trying to survive a mental state that had become unbearable, Maybelle once again pushed an idea they had discussed from time to time—what if Odd wrote a daily column about his life in New York for newspapers in small towns like Gallipolis? He could do that and never even have to leave their room. So one morning, as an act of pure survival, Odd set his typewriter up on a small, wooden table and began writing his first column from New York. He wrote it as though he were writing a letter home to his friends and family. What would interest them about the people, places, sights, sounds, and smells of New York?

There is some splendid philosophy in the story of Isidore Greenberg, known to all Lower Broadway as 'Newsie Izzy' the newsboy. 'Izzy' has been on the streets for thirteen years selling newspapers and now he is going to become a 'rah, 'rah, 'rah boy. He is going to enter Cornell and what do you suppose he is going to study? Scientific agriculture!...[143] Joe Jackson, the heavy-hitting outfielder of the Cleveland Naps, cannot read or write. Jackson comes from the mountain districts of Tennessee and began playing ball before he donned long trousers. He has been playing ball ever since and he had never had a chance to study...[144] Dixie Hines, the theatrical agent, tells of two vaudeville artists who succumbed, as Dixie put it, to matrimony...the actor husband was the first to reach the breakfast table in the morning...soon the bride arrived. 'What are you doing?' she said rather poutily. 'I'm lookin' at Mutt and Jeff,' he replied. 'It's just my luck,' she flared back, 'to marry some book-worm...'[145]

Odd's early attempts at a column were nothing like what it eventually became. His earlier writing, while entertaining, had only glimpses of the unique style that would one day make his column different from any others that had come before, or any that would come after. He was not yet comfortable enough to be himself. But, while the work he produced left more to be desired, it did provide the thing Odd needed most—hope. It gave him a reason to get out of bed in the morning and do something with his mind other than worry about the future. The column literally saved his life.

The syndication business was continuing to grow, and Odd and Maybelle thought that perhaps one of the syndicates might be interested in Odd's "letter from New York." They wrote to all the major companies and attached samples of the letter, but it was rejected by each and every one. He later compared dropping the letters down the mail chute to counting beads on a rosary. With each one he closed his eyes and repeated, "Please like these columns, please like these columns, please like these columns..."[146]

Now, as he roamed the streets trying to find work, everything he saw seemed to provide inspiration. There was even more to celebrate—and write about—when he got a part-time job with song publisher Leo Feist.

The same post-Civil War improvements in printing and transportation that allowed newspapers and magazines to reach a mass audience had

Some of the early composers, songwriters, and publishers Odd got to know on Tin Pan Alley. (left to right) Gene Buck, Victor Herbert, John Philip Sousa, Harry B. Smith, Jerome Kern, Irving Berlin, George W. Meyer, Irving Bibo, and Otto Harbach in 1920, *Al Aumuller, Library of Congress Prints and Photographs Division*

a similar impact on popular music of the day. Suddenly, sheet music was affordable and provided a way for everyone to share and perform the same popular songs. To offer publishers protection of rights and encourage the distribution of sheet music, the 1891 copyright law was passed. As vaudeville stars, mostly based in New York, toured the country, publishers began to see the benefit of having their songs performed on stage. Around the turn of the century, popular sheet music was the gold record of the day, and from 1900 to 1910, over one hundred songs sold a million or more copies of sheet music.[147] While sheet music was also produced in cities like Chicago, Detroit, and Atlanta, New York quickly became the publishing capital of the world. Around ninety percent of most song publishers' revenue came from the sales of sheet music.

As vaudeville and other forms of public entertainment continued to grow and the sales of sheet music became a significant source of revenue, a community of writers, composers, and publishers in New York came together in a strip of row houses running between Fifth and Sixth Avenues on Twenty-Eighth Street. In one story, Journalist Monroe H. Rosenfeld supposedly coined the name "Tin Pan Alley" in 1903 after he wandered around the neighborhood trying to come up with a headline for an article he had written. According to his story, he was inspired by musician Harry Von Tilzer, who produced a unique sound from his piano by weaving strips of newspaper inside it. To Rosenfeld, it sounded like tin pans—hence the name "Tin Pan Alley." However, this is just one of many tales of how the name came to be.

One of the undisputed kings of Tin Pan Alley was Leo Feist. Although Feist had begun his career in the late 1800s as a corset salesman, he had a passion for music and was, in his spare time, a composer. Frustrated that the publishers of the day rejected all his submissions, he decided to publish his music himself. Odd likely found much to which he could relate in Feist's story of success. At night, the composer would come up with new music, and during the day take it around to orchestra leaders and singers performing in New York clubs. Once he convinced the performers to use his songs, he would take copies of the sheet music around to stores that sold them to the public. Once Feist had made his first two hundred dollars, he quit selling corsets and began his own music publishing business. He is credited with introducing modern business principles to music publishing and distribution. In 1897, Feist was one of the first to open a studio and office in Tin Pan Alley. Every piece of sheet music he produced in those early years included the slogan "You can't go wrong with a Feist song." And apparently, you couldn't. Feist's company became one of the largest sheet music publishing firms in the United States.

Feist was also quick to recognize the return on the investment of promoting his music in newspapers and magazines. When he offered a job to Odd, Odd was attracted to the possibility of working in the two areas he knew the most—newspapers and live entertainment. He had fond memories of his years spent ushering at the Ariel Opera House back in Gallipolis and the hundreds of shows he saw while working as a reporter in Cincinnati. Odd also loved the energy of a group of passionate young people coming together to create something new and exciting. About Tin Pan Alley, Odd wrote:

> *Here the decaying brownstone fronts of an older New York are honeycombed with box-like stalls, and in these stuffy stalls ebullient, perspiring and coatless young men fashion the nation's popular tunes. Tin Pan Alley has the feverish energy of the 'hell-roaring' gold camp. It races along like a mill stream. The strident jangle of a hundred pianos rises above the street din. Like its raggy-gay creations, life in Tin Pan Alley is pitched in a high and furious tempo. In the 'Alley,' Youth is king![148]*

Through his freelance job with Feist, Odd was able to spend time with many of the most popular performers of the day, not as a fan, but as an insider. It was his job to get them and the music they performed into newspapers and magazines as frequently as possible. Of course, he included many of them in his column, on which he spent the majority of his spare time. Odd borrowed a copy of *Ayer's Newspaper Directory* and, starting with newspapers in Ohio, Maybelle began mailing out copies of his letters to ten newspapers each day. Included was a simple note that offered the letter for free.

Occasionally, there were other opportunities to make money. Odd was hired to help launch Dr. Friedmann's Turtle Serum in the United States.

Dr. Friedrich Franz Friedmann had arrived in New York from Germany in February 1913 claiming he had a cure for tuberculosis, the disease that had killed Odd's mother, sister, and aunt. It was still a major cause of death in the United States, especially among the poor and working class. The doctor claimed his vaccine was created by passing the tubercule bacilli "through a turtle" in a laboratory. Odd did his job well and Dr. Friedmann received a great deal of news coverage in New York in the spring of 1913. By May, however, the New York Board of Health declared the vaccine was worthless, Friedmann's institute was closed, and Odd lost a client.

Odd also did publicity for ballet master Louis Chalif of the Metropolitan Opera Ballet when he opened a dance school in an Italian Renaissance building he had constructed. Located at 163 West Fifty-Seventh Street, opposite Carnegie Hall, the building design included a number of terra cotta ornaments that reflected classical iconography of the theater, including masks, lyres, and faces.

For a while, Odd also represented Al Shean, a German comedian who, along with Edward Gallagher, was part of the vaudeville act, *Gallagher and Shean*. Although popular, the two didn't enjoy working together and Shean was ready for a solo career when he turned to Odd. He went on to perform in a variety of roles in Broadway productions.

Odd even tried his hand at sales. For four weeks he attempted to sell ads in *The Key to New York*, a magazine made available at hotels and attractions around the city. At the end of his brief sales career, he had sold no ads. He had spent a significant amount in subway fare with no compensation, but the experience exposed him to different parts of the city and gave him a chance to meet people working in hotels, restaurants, and attractions around the city. Many would later appear, at one time or another, in his letter.

As it turned out, Odd was good at this business of publicity. His fascination with popular culture and his experience working in the newspaper business had

Advertisement for the Hotel Majestic.

126

The Hotel Majestic. *The New-York Historical Society*

given him a good understanding of the content newspaper editors were seeking. Thankfully, his health was also improving, allowing him and Maybelle to once again begin socializing with their many friends.

By the summer of 1914, Odd wanted to stop doing publicity work and focus full-time on improving the letter. However, that would be impossible until it provided a real income. The couple finally gave up hope that a syndicate was going to be interested, so they decided it was time to skip the syndicate and charge newspapers for the letter themselves. They first began by including a simple note with the letter that encouraged editors to pay what they thought the column was worth. A surprising number of newspapers responded by sending checks.

Eventually, the revenue they were generating from the letter combined with Odd's publicity work enabled them to purchase an early version of a mimeograph machine. This allowed Maybelle to make even more copies of the letter to send out each week.

As a young reporter in Gallipolis, Odd had seen how pleased it made residents to see their names in print. In New York, he discovered this fascination was more universal than he had ever imagined. Occasionally, he would include someone in the letter, then mail a copy of it to that person. He was quickly making friends and signing on new publicity clients who were thrilled to see their name or the name of their business in print.

The December 1915 issue of his column included a reference to Copeland Townsend, the new manager of the Hotel Majestic Odd met at a noon service at a Park Avenue church. Odd later mailed copies of the column to Townsend with a note asking for payment of whatever he felt the publicity for the hotel was worth. Townsend replied with a check for fifty dollars and a unique proposition. Odd and Maybelle could live at the hotel, all expenses paid, if Odd could get the hotel mentioned in the press as frequently as possible.

The opulent Hotel Majestic was home to many of New York's wealthy Jewish families because of its "less restrictive social policies" for that time. It extended from Seventy-First Street to Seventy-Second Street and faced Central Park. Designed by Alfred Zucker, the luxurious twelve-story hotel opened in 1894 and offered its visitors and residents many of the most extravagant amenities money could buy at the time. The hotel featured a grand lobby, rooftop garden, and even a bowling alley. In addition to its opulence, it was noted for a design that allowed more air and light into the building than other residences of similar size. It was a place to see and be seen, and for Odd and Maybelle, it was now home.

They began hosting dinner parties, dances, card games, and other events, and invited many of their friends in the publishing and entertainment businesses. Sometimes they would have up to thirty guests for dinner, and around the table sat writers, politicians, businessmen, and actors. Odd wrote:

> *It was more of a family hotel but week after week I had the hotel on the front pages with all sorts of freak stories—some of them harmless fakes. I never fibbed to the newspapermen. In most cases I made my "plants" so obvious that they wrote kidding stories but the hotel was being talked about and its patronage boomed. Mr. Townsend was delighted. I made innumerable newspaper friends and held Friday night penny limit poker games in the Louis XVI suite serving a tip top lunch and anything in the way of drinks that the thirsts demanded.*[149]

One great example of the "kidding stories" of which he wrote involved a woman in a black mask. The article, that appeared in Judge, was clearly tongue-in-cheek:

> *Woman in Black Mask in the Papers at Last*
> *She Is Arrested, Then Set Free, and the Press Agent of a Hotel is Made*
> *Happy.*
> *The press agent of the Hotel Majestic went to bed happy last night. Madame*
> *U. S. had been arrested at last. Two or three weeks ago he informed anxious*
> *city editors that a woman wearing a black mask which she never removed,*
> *and giving the name of Madame U. S., had arrived in the hotel. He added*
> *that she was likely to get into trouble because of the mask. Last evening*
> *he won his heart's desire. Madame U. S., handsomely gowned in black,*
> *her chestnut hair carefully evident, was arrested at Sixty-sixth Street and*
> *Central Park West...*[150]

In another incident, Odd made certain the newspapers were well informed when Miss Ethel Stewart-Forster arrived at the Hotel Majestic with her pet leopard. The guest, her leopard and, most importantly for Odd, the hotel stayed in the newspapers for days. However, the stunt took an unfortunate turn when Odd invited a group of newspaper photographers to photograph the leopard in the hotel suite in which Stewart-Forster was staying. The leopard was cautiously eyeing the group but behaving well—until the flash and the popping sound of the flashbulbs went off. According to one reporter who was there, the leopard "went out of the room like a streak. He overturned one camera and broke it. He escaped into the corridor, fled downstairs to the basement and took refuge in the storehouse where the glassware for the bar is kept. Clink, clink crash!"[151] Before he was finally caught, the leopard damaged thousands of dollars in glassware.

Odd could always be counted on to provide an entertaining story—or to create one when there was nothing to write about. He once hired a dozen young women to skip rope simultaneously on the hotel's roof garden, and on George Washington's birthday, he sent out a story about a young hotel guest using a toy hatchet to chop down one of the hotel's signature lobby palm trees.

Having been a reporter, Odd had great respect for those "working the beat" and knew that little acts of kindness could sometimes make a big difference. In February 1916, opera singer Geraldine Farrar married silent screen actor Lou Tellegen at her home on West Seventy-Fourth

Street. It was the superstar wedding of the decade, but reporters were not welcome. Odd let it be known that reporters who were waiting in the street hoping to get a glimpse of the famous couple's celebrity guests could find free food and warm beverages at the Hotel Majestic. There's no doubt, the next time he needed to get a story published, many of them remembered that day.

Thanks to Odd, the Hotel Majestic was becoming known as the place where the rich and famous stayed and visited while in New York, and a rendezvous spot for local journalists, artists, and writers. Celebrities of the day who also called the hotel home included mystery writer Arthur Somers Roche, Italian sculptor and painter Prince Paul Troubetzkoy, French cabaret singer Yvette Guilbert, opera star Anna Fitzui, actress Lillian Russell, and actor Francis X. Bushman.

Suddenly, Odd and Maybelle went from cooking on a hot plate in their bathroom, to a lifestyle only afforded by the wealthiest and most successful New Yorkers. Odd wasn't just writing about the rich and the famous, he was now living in their world. He wrote, "Often we have stepped into the elevator to find a fellow passenger was none other than Geraldine Farrar, Charles M. Schwab, Harold Lloyd, or Mayor Jimmy Walker."[152]

The letter was not forgotten during this time and the mimeograph machine was kept busy each day as Maybelle continued sending out copies, soliciting new newspapers, and then depositing the checks as they came in from around the country. Just a year after Odd sat down and typed out his first letter from New York, it became clear the couple had hit upon an idea for which there was an audience. At the many dinners the couple hosted at the Majestic, Odd met or heard about subjects that he knew would interest those reading his letters. He began receiving mail back from readers around the country and was learning from them what generated the greatest response.

Odd was never one to forget his friends. When his former roommate, Harold T. Webster, married Ethel Wortz in March 1917 after a two-week courtship, Odd arranged for them to have their wedding breakfast at the Majestic. When Bob Brinkerhoff married singer Edna Patterson, the Majestic was the venue for their wedding. And according to an account of Brinkerhoff's nuptials, he almost missed his honeymoon:

Taxicab 'Bandits' Steal Bridegroom

Robert Brinkerhoff Released. Just in Time to Catch Steamship and Join Anxious Bride. Passengers on board the United Fruit steamship Calamares stood at the rail yesterday afternoon and watched a white faced young man make a wild leap for the gangplank and just make it before the vessel pulled away from her pier in the Hudson river. The pale-faced young man was Robert M. Brinkerhoff, cartoonist who was married at noon yesterday at the Majestic Hotel. After the wedding breakfast H. T. Webster and Ray Rohn, fellow artists, lured Mr. Brinkerhoff to the lobby of the hotel, where a crowd of masked persons was in waiting. They seized the bridegroom and carried him out to a taxicab, which disappeared in the west drive of Central Park. The bride, who was Miss Edna Patterson, singer, of No. 600 Riverside Drive, was waiting with friends for the return of the bridegroom. When it came time for the start to the steamship she became alarmed, and decided to go at once to the pier. In the meantime the bridegroom was pleading wildly in the taxicab to be permitted to go to the pier. His watch surreptitiously had been turned forward an hour and he was in a panic. All might have gone well, but the kidnappers had arranged to arrive just five minutes before the time for the vessel to steam. But then in front of No. 90 West Street, the taxicab broke down. The jokers, who were getting panicky by this time, commandeered another taxicab, which reached the pier just in time. The bride was relieved, but she did not wave any farewells at the kidnappers, who slunk away sheepishly.[153]

Early example of Odd's letter in the September 9, 1918 issue of the East Liverpool, Ohio *Evening Review.*

ODD JUNIOR MAYBELLE
MᶜINTYRE
WISH YOU A
MERRY CHRISTMAS

(above) One of Odd and
Maybelle's annual holiday cards
featuring their Boston bulldog
Junior.
(left) Odd and Junior. *The Esther
Allen Greer Museum at the University
of Rio Grande*

The letter was generating enough revenue by 1920 that Odd decided
he could afford to quit his publicity work. Of course, he planned to
continue promoting the hotel in his arrangement with Townsend,
as the free room and board at one of the best addresses in the city
was too good to give up. Odd and Maybelle's lives had become a whirlwind
of theater openings, fine dining, fashion, and friendships with some
of the most well-known people in the world. Odd described their life
in the hotel as "a whirl of push buttons, rushing page boys, flunkies
caparisoned in gold braid, panjandrums in frock coats, white-capped
maids with Swedish and cockney accents, arriving patrons with bright
blonde baggage who often departed through coalholes, great actresses,
merchant princes, international flyers, and derbied house detectives."[154]

By this time, they were in their mid-thirties and every spare minute was
spent producing the letter or soliciting new newspapers. They had little
time to even think about adding a child to their world, and Maybelle
later said she often thought of the letter as their baby. Any feelings of
missing out that Odd and Maybelle may have felt because they had no

children ended the day Odd walked into their suite at the Majestic with Junior in the pocket of his overcoat.

He had noticed the little Boston bulldog in the window of a Fifth Avenue pet store. Junior would become a loyal sidekick for the couple and a frequent subject in the letter. Eventually, Junior, along with other dogs Odd and Maybelle would adopt through the years, would become almost as famous as Odd himself. Junior was also responsible for a significant change in Odd and Maybelle's lives after they had been living at the Hotel Majestic for five years. In September of 1920, Copeland Townsend, not a dog lover, casually let Odd know that a room damaged by a dog belonging to one of the hotel guests was causing a change to the policy. From then on, no dogs allowed, no exceptions. He suggested Odd just get rid of Junior or take him to a kennel.

Odd had begun to tire of life at the hotel and the publicity work he was forced to do to keep it going. Naturally shy and not much of a drinker, he preferred small groups of close friends to the parties they were having to host at the hotel. By 1920, thanks to their hard work and Maybelle's management skills, they now had about fifty thousand dollars in the bank, and they were no longer dependent on their arrangement with Townsend to live the lifestyle to which they had grown accustomed. That amount of money would be equivalent to more than six hundred thousand dollars today.

When Townsend suggested Odd get rid of Junior, Odd stared at him silently for a minute. Townsend had never seen Odd angry, and was surprised at the tone he heard in his voice as Odd replied, "Junior will be gone today." A few hours later, Odd, Maybelle, and Junior were packed, a polite farewell letter was left behind, and the little family departed the Hotel Majestic for their new home at the Ritz-Carlton Hotel at Forty-Sixth Street and Madison Avenue.

Odd and Maybelle McIntyre were beginning a new chapter in their lives, while New York was about to experience an unprecedented shift in culture, economics, and politics that would come to be known as the Roaring Twenties.

11

Ziegfeld

To my notion the most auspicious of all metropolitan
first nights was that marking the opening of the
Ziegfeld Theater with a typical Ziegfeld exploitation
of girls melting into beautiful scenes and vice versa.
Everybody was there.[155]

O. O. McIntyre

Odd and Maybelle's new home, the first Ritz-Carlton Hotel in
New York, was so opulent and grand, it made "ritzy" an
adjective. In 1927, composer Irving Berlin wrote "Puttin' on the
Ritz" about the fashionable people who came and went from the tony
address. He had Odd and Maybelle's new neighbors in mind when he
wrote about "the well-to-do, up and down Park Avenue."

Millionaire real estate developer Robert Goelet built the hotel and
licensed the name "Ritz-Carlton" from legendary hotelier Cesar Ritz.
The "hotelier to kings," as Ritz was nicknamed, opened and ran many
prestigious hotels, including the famous Hôtel Ritz in the Place Vendôme,
Paris and the Ritz Hotels in London and Madrid. Ritz was celebrated for
his dedication to providing the highest levels of quality and service, which

The first Ritz-Carlton, New York at Forty-Sixth Street and Madison Avenue. *The Library of Congress Prints and Photographs Division*

The Ritz-Carlton's Palm Room which featured "Flora," a large statue by Giovanni da Bologna sculpted around 1550. *Museum of the City of New York*

135

made his hotels the best in the world. Goelet wanted that same experience in New York, and spared no expense in the design and construction of his massive showpiece at the corner of Forty-Sixth Street and Madison Avenue. The hotel had been open just ten years when Odd and Maybelle arrived in 1920, and it was still shining like new that first day they walked through the grand entrance and into the lobby called the Palm Room. The focal point of the lobby, which was filled with live plants and flowers and green wicker furniture, was "Flora," a large statue by Giovanni da Bologna sculpted around 1550. The feeling of extravagance continued in the hotel's oval dining room where bass-relief figures on the white ceiling were so "fascinating," one writer observed "with chins up, the fashionable people at the tables look like birds in a nest waiting for dainty morsels to be dropped in their mouths."[156] On each table of the dining room often sat a tall vase overflowing with pink roses.

From gilded mirrors and plush rugs, to glittering chandeliers and oversized bathtubs, those who visited or lived at the Ritz-Carlton received meticulous service from servants who catered to their every whim. No detail was left to chance. To block out the smells that could be generated by the mechanics of the elevators, vials of perfume were kept under the seats, and even the lighting was carefully designed so the jewels of the hotels guests looked their best. Many of the top chefs were recruited from Europe, and only the highest-quality of food and drink

The Dining Room at the Ritz-Carlton Hotel. *Museum of the City of New York*

was served.

After descending the curved staircase down to the ballroom one evening, a very impressed Queen Marie of Romania was said to have whispered to a friend, "Why, this is as beautiful as my palace."

There was a garden for outdoor eating in the space between the Ritz Hotel and the Carlton House, the connected building of upscale apartments served by the Ritz. The garden restaurant featured Japanese décor, with tables placed strategically under awnings designed to look like pagodas. As they enjoyed their dinner, guests could hear the sounds of a winding, man-made stream meandering between the tables and birds singing in cages hanging from cherry trees. With the Ritz signature attention to detail, the stream was filled with fish.

Although any rent at all was an increase over what they had been paying at the Hotel Majestic, reluctance on Odd's part to spend so much on a luxury hotel vanished when he saw the reaction others had to his famous address. Maybelle knew that Odd needed to project a certain image of himself to gain access to celebrities, publishers, and other leaders of New York business and industry, and the Ritz-Carlton Hotel address on his stationery went a long way toward validating his position in the world.

Shortly after they moved in, Odd got a call from his friend Gene Buck who worked for the famous showman Florenz Ziegfeld, Jr. The multi-talented Buck had found success as both an early illustrator of sheet music and a songwriter, and was one of the few collaborators with Ziegfeld on Broadway. Buck was part talent scout, part producer, and part assistant, and was one of the few who could handle working so closely with Ziegfeld. As Will Rogers wrote, "Ziegfeld can't go out in the morning and buy Billie Burke a new Royce without consulting Gene."[157]

Arriving in New York as a young illustrator with around fourteen dollars in his pocket, Buck eventually secured a studio where he created the art for more than five thousand sheet music covers, and contributed to the popularization of the art deco style of the 1920s. Ruggedly handsome, Buck was a friend and neighbor of F. Scott Fitzgerald in Great Neck, Long Island, and it's been suggested that he was, in part, inspiration for *The Great Gatsby*. Buck and his beautiful chorus-girl wife, Helen, frequently socialized with Scott and Zelda Fitzgerald, and Helen and Zelda were close friends.[158] When Ziegfeld found out Buck knew Odd, he asked him to arrange a meeting. Odd was certain he knew exactly what Ziegfeld wanted. He wrote, "I was in a flutter of excitement about it for I had a firm

Florenz Ziegfeld Jr. *Billy Rose Theater Division,*
The New York Public Library

conviction Ziegfeld wanted me to write some sketches for his forthcoming show. I was always blowing bubbles."[159]

The next day at the appointed hour, Odd arrived at Ziegfeld's office at the New Amsterdam Theater at 214 West Forty-Second Street. After being made to wait for two hours, Odd concluded that the famous showman was no respecter of other people's time. As Odd later explained, "He was the most fascinating personality I ever met. Fascinating with the irrationality that so often authenticates genius."[160]

Buck finally led Odd into the main office and left them alone. Ziegfeld, in his early fifties, was tall, elegant, and parted his iron-grey hair in the middle. As soon as Odd entered the room, it dawned on him that Ziegfeld's face had "the predatory brood of an eagle."[161] Odd also noticed the smell of expensive perfume in the air, and later learned that Ziegfeld liberally sprayed his office with expensive scents he brought back from Paris.

Ziegfeld got right to the point, and Odd's heart sank as soon as he understood he was not going to be asked to write sketches. Ziegfeld had noticed all the attention that Odd had gotten for the Hotel Majestic and other clients, and he wanted to hire Odd to do his publicity. Of course, Odd was well acquainted with Ziegfeld's shows and was flattered by the offer. Every year, the opening night of the latest *Ziegfeld Follies* production fetched crowds of spectators trying to get a glimpse of celebrities as they arrived for the show. Odd was a fan of Ziegfeld's, but he was unwavering in his plans to give up all his publicity clients so he could focus on writing the letter. One thing Odd didn't yet know about Ziegfeld was that he almost always got what he wanted, and he wasn't about to take no for an answer from Odd.

Florenz Ziegfeld, Jr., was twenty-three years old when he entered the world of show business by volunteering to help his father, a music director, book acts for the Trocadero, an entertainment venue that was created as part of the 1893 World's Columbian Exposition held in Chicago.

His father was expecting classical music and opera, but many of the performers who appeared on stage were considerably more "popular" than what his father had in mind. Ziegfeld had booked vaudeville acts like comics, singers, jugglers, and even a brass band. Much to his father's relief, the Trocadero was the hit of the exposition.

Afterward, Ziegfeld took one of the most popular performers from the show, German bodybuilder Eugen Sandow, out on tour with some other acts including singers, jugglers, and acrobats. While Sandow's performance included demonstrations of his awesome strength (like bending iron bars), Ziegfeld noticed that the biggest applause came when Sandow posed nearly nude, flexing his muscles. The act was described in *Time*:

> *Ladies would prod his dorsal, deltoid and pectoral development with carefully gloved fingers and ask if he were real. Sporting gentlemen with Damn-my-eyes and By-God-Sirs would lay their wagers on him when he matched strength with Samson, Cyclops, Atlas, Ajax or Hercules (rival strongmen). He was renowned for many years as the 'strongest man in the world.'*[162]

In 1905, Ziegfeld fell in love both personally and professionally when he discovered Polish-French singer Anna Held while touring Europe looking for new acts. Held, who became famous for her 18-inch waist and hourglass figure, is also credited

Anna Held. *Library of Congress Prints and Photographs Division* with suggesting to Ziegfeld that he produce an American version of the *Folies Bergère* cabaret music hall that was such a hit in Paris.

When the first *Follies* curtain opened in 1907, Ziegfeld forever changed American theater. He discovered talented performers like Fanny Brice, Eddie Cantor, W. C. Fields, Will Rogers, Fred and Adela Astaire, and Bert Williams, and then provided a unique venue in which that talent could be showcased. Ziegfeld also perfected the art of early entertainment publicity and was always eager to get stories about himself, his performers, and his shows into newspapers and magazines. Once, he created a national sensation when newspapers began printing the story—placed by Ziegfeld—that Held maintained her creamy complexion by bathing each day in gallons of milk.

Ziegfeld had an eye for the ladies both professionally and personally. His productions included showgirls performing in provocative costumes designed to accentuate and flatter the female form, showing as much nudity as he could get away with and still have his shows be considered "sophisticated." Many of the young women in his shows were featured in magazines and newspapers, and were among the most popular celebrities of the day. Famous showgirls through the years included Marion Davies, Barbara Stanwyck, Louise Brooks, Olive Thomas, and Joan Blondell.

Although Ziegfeld and his first discovery, Anna Held, were never officially married, their common-law marriage ended in divorce in 1912 after she tired of his public affair with performer Lillian Lorraine and his continuing problems with gambling. In 1914 he married actress Billie Burke, with whom he had his only child, a daughter named Patricia. The family lived a lavish lifestyle in Hastings-on-the-Hudson, New York City, and Palm Beach, Florida.

With each New York show and U.S. tour, the *Follies* evolved, improved, and grew in both popularity and influence. Although Ziegfeld couldn't sing, write, or dance, and had no real sense of humor, what he did have was the ability to create beauty out of chaos by keeping his eyes and ears on the reactions of the audience. In many ways, he did on stage what Odd would do in print.

When Odd met with Ziegfeld that day, he had no intention of doing publicity work for him, or anyone else, for that matter. He was looking forward to finally having more time to spend on his letter. When Ziegfeld said, "Name your price, young man," Odd threw one out so ridiculously

Sheet music for "Garden of my Dreams" from the *Ziegfeld Follies* of 1918.

high, he was shocked when Ziegfeld accepted it without even pausing. Odd then demanded that he be able to work from home, and he made it clear that this was only going to be a part-time job. Little did Odd know, nothing with Ziegfeld was ever part time, but it was certainly never boring. He wrote:

> *From that moment on, a new world opened—a world as unreal and fantastic as the illusion it sought to create. It was a vista, too, that proved invaluable as a column source in years that were to come. I learned about the magical stratum, the Rialto, from the inside—the most completely inside vantage point that could be imagined. I saw and heard the buzz of the wheels inside the wheels!*[163]

Odd's first assignment was managing the publicity for Ziegfeld's *Midnight Frolic* that had premiered in 1915 on the roof of the New Amsterdam Theater. With a start time of midnight, it was an entertainment venue for New Yorkers who didn't want to go home after the other shows had ended. *The Follies* took place in the theater below, and many of Ziegfeld's superstars appeared in the midnight shows from time to time. It was while promoting *Midnight Frolic* that Odd met cowboy humorist

Will Rogers with whom he eventually became close friends. They often traveled together, and Odd and Maybelle frequently stayed at Will and Betty Rogers' ranch when in California.

Reviews of *Midnight Frolic* were usually overwhelmingly positive, especially in the early years. A good example is this review of a 1916 *Midnight Frolic* that included a female juggler, a tightrope walker, acrobatic stunts by the Arnaut Brothers, stand-up comedy by Eddie Cantor, and a collie dog that skipped rope:

> *It is certainly the best ever and as an entertainment for those to whom sleep is no object, it would be hard to beat. One might possibly wish that the frolic could be started an hour earlier, which would be late enough to accommodate playgoers, but that is the nearest thing to adverse criticism that the writer—not being a night owl—can think of. Gene Buck, Dave Stamper, Ned Wayburn and Joseph Urban have collaborated in the production of the new series and it is enough to say that it does full justice to the superlative reputation of its creators. Whoever selected the beauties can be freely quoted as an authority on the feminine pulchritude. In addition to the snap, brilliancy, originality and gaiety of the ensemble dances, the costumes, music and scenery, the program comprises many remarkably*

(left to right) Eddie Cantor, Florenz Ziegfeld, Jr., Sammy Lee and Irving Berlin (at piano) with the Ziegfeld Follies during rehearsals for the 1927 production. *Billy Rose Theater Division, The New York Public Library Digital Collections*

clever and entertaining specialties.[164]

Working for Ziegfeld wasn't easy, especially for Odd. "I do not see how anybody could work for him long," he wrote. "As a conversationalist he is delightful and stimulating. But when he becomes an employer, he is a tyrant."[165]

One major problem was that Odd stayed up very late—sometimes not even going to bed until dawn—and then slept until noon. If Ziegfeld had a thought or idea, he thought nothing of calling Odd at six in the morning. According to all accounts, Ziegfeld loved to communicate, and he used

Ziegfeld Follies performer and star of *Sally*, Marilyn Miller. *Billy Rose Theater Division, The New York Public Library Digital Collections*

every tool available to him at the time. He sent hundreds of long telegrams each week, made calls on his phone constantly, and had long letters and notes typed and mailed or sent by messenger. Many times Odd witnessed Ziegfeld dictating cables about mundane topics that would cost hundreds of dollars to send.

By this time, Odd had become a master at getting items placed in the newspapers and magazines, and had developed a network of contacts who were well placed in New York media. Ziegfeld was hard to impress, but he was very impressed with Odd. So much so that he gave him a large raise and the job of promoting *Sally*, a new musical comedy that featured singer and dancer Marilyn Miller. Already an established entertainer when Ziegfeld put her in the *Follies* of 1918, she became an icon in his production of *Sally*.

This gave Odd the opportunity to experience the genius that was Florenz Ziegfeld Jr. up close, as he was part of the show's development from the beginning. On one hand, Ziegfeld micro-managed every aspect of the show. On the other, he would miss appointments and have twelve people waiting in his office while he was picking out robes in a high-end men's clothing store on Fifth Avenue. He also frequently fixated on a single idea and made sure everything relating to the execution of that idea was done exactly the way he wanted it. For example, Odd was there when Ziegfeld decided one of Miller's costumes needed refurbishing. Ziegfeld first wired Miller, suggesting that the costume should be sent to the cleaners. Then he called the company manager on one of his many telephones and repeated the request. In succession, he called the wardrobe mistress, the stage manager and Miller. He still wasn't done. Odd added, "And as an afterthought he sent a telegram to the cleaning establishment and called their manager."[166]

The production costs of *Sally* hit a record-setting two hundred and fifty thousand dollars. Odd noted that, although the rehearsals were chaotic and no one seemed to know what was going on, when the curtain rose on opening night, everything went smoothly.

Sally introduced the song "Look for the Silver Lining" and was a huge hit in New York, running for more than five hundred performances and touring for over a year, winning nationwide acclaim. Odd himself sat through more than one hundred and fifty performances and claimed to have never been bored or distracted once. Marilyn Miller became one of the biggest performers of that era, and some consider her Ziegfeld's biggest star. Even Ziegfeld himself fell hard for Miller, although the feeling was not mutual. After the death of her husband, Miller infuriated Ziegfeld when she married Mary Pickford's brother, Jack.

Several times Odd infuriated Ziegfeld and he was either fired or he quit, but a few days would pass and they would both carry on as though nothing had happened.

Although Ziegfeld didn't have much of a sense of humor, Odd told a story of a time when Ziegfeld exhibited a rare moment of wit, even if it was of the sarcastic variety. The showman and his family were sailing for Europe in late February 1922. Odd had photographers and reporters at the pier who took photos and interviewed him with the intention of writing a story for the next day's issue. Meanwhile, in Norfolk, Virginia, the *Roma*, a huge dirigible, crashed to the ground, killing thirty-four men. After Ziegfeld arrived in London, he looked over the New York newspapers and saw nothing but news of the disaster. He wired Odd, "Sorry you sneaked me out of town."

Odd was in a unique position to observe both the good and the bad parts of Ziegfeld. He wrote, "A queer impresario—this Ziegfeld. He can sulk over a nickel and smile over a burst of extravagance that plunges his confreres into despair. Daily he nurses a new and imaginary grievance…

he swims up from sleep every morning at 6 o'clock to grab a telephone and whine his woe."[167]

Odd was growing weary of being the one on the other end of the phone listening to Ziegfeld's woes. He wanted to spend more time working on the letter, but Ziegfeld's demands were growing and taking up too much of Odd's time. One morning they argued and a few hours later Odd received a very wordy letter firing him. When Ziegfeld called the next day acting as though nothing had happened, Odd resigned, once again. This time, as Odd put it, "he stayed resigned." He told Ziegfeld, "I like you Flo as a friend, but you haven't got enough money to hire me for another day."[168]

Odd remained in Ziegfeld's trusted inner circle and they continued to speak frequently. The *Midnight Frolic* ended, as Prohibition made it too difficult to make a profit on a nightclub, and the *Follies* formula began to tire toward the end of the 1920s. However, Ziegfeld's real masterpiece was yet to come.

Now considered a watershed moment in the history of American musical theater, the curtain rose on Ziegfeld's *Show Boat* in 1927. Based on a book by Odd's friend Edna Ferber with music by Jerome Kern and lyrics by Oscar Hammerstein, it was something that had never before been seen on stage. Combining serious storytelling with musical performances and dance routines, it was also the first time black and white performers shared a stage as equals. Although Odd had not worked for his friend for several years, included in the program was an article he had written as a tribute to Ziegfeld.

Like many others, Ziegfeld lost everything when the stock market crashed in 1929. He staged a revival of *Show Boat* in 1932 and produced some radio programs, but the mood of the country had changed. He struggled with his health for a few years and died in Hollywood on July 22, 1932.

Odd remembered his friend in an article in *Cosmopolitan*:

> *He was symbolic of a fabulous era—an era the like of which this generation will never see again. He knew beauty in human flesh from A to Z…for three years I was as close to him as anybody in the world of theater glamour. I was his press agent, and in priming the pumps to feed his insatiable vanity, I was in the whirl of a mind that seemed in constant chaos, yet paradoxically was as straight and sure as an arrow.*[169]

12

Syndication

Only those who have done it know the agonizing strain of preparing a daily article year in and year out. It becomes a horrible ordeal. My system of writing varies from most men doing the same sort of daily chore. I do not take notes and I never know exactly what I am going to write until I sit down at my typewriter in the corner of my bedroom in pajamas—a system that has become a fixed habit.[170]

O. O. McIntyre

In the early morning hours of November 11, 1918, sleepy reporters camping out at Woodrow Wilson's White House finally received the news they had been waiting for—the armistice had been signed and the World War was officially over. As New Yorkers filled Fifth Avenue early that morning, newsboys could be heard up and down the street shouting the headlines from the various newspapers. Blazoned across the front page of the *New York Times* that morning was the headline, "ARMISTICE SIGNED, END OF THE WAR! BERLIN SEIZED BY REVOLUTIONISTS; NEW CHANCELLOR BEGS FOR ORDER;

OUSTED KAISER FLEES TO HOLLAND." The *New-York Tribune* led with the headline, "GERMANY HAS SURRENDERED; WORLD WAR ENDED AT 6 A.M," while the *New York Journal's* headline, "VICTORY HERE; KAISER FLEES," filled the entire top half of the front page. Horns were blowing and ticker tape streamed from the windows of the buildings above.

Odd and Maybelle heard the church bells and car horns. Odd quickly dressed and ran down to Broadway and Forty-Second Street, where he captured for his readers the excitement of that day. He wrote, "At Columbus Circle a girl in expensive furs jumped from a taxicab and rushed to the curb where a French officer was standing. She kissed him on the mouth before the amazed officer knew what was happening...all motor traffic on Fifth Avenue was diverted to Madison Avenue and the sidewalks and streets were playgrounds."[171] It was a new day in America, both literally and metaphorically, as the sun rose over the East River at the end of Wall Street.

The newspaper business was again undergoing a time of radical change. While the actual number of newspapers was decreasing steadily, circulation was increasing. In his account of that era, *Only Yesterday*, historian Frederick Lew Allen noted that between 1914 and 1926, the number of daily newspapers in the country dropped from 2,580 to 2,001. Sunday editions dropped from 571 to 541 but, during that same period, total circulation rose by 8,000,000.[172]

Many of the newspapers in the larger cities were combined into chains like Scripps-Howard or Hearst. Independent newspapers were either absorbed into the chains or were closed because they couldn't compete. With all these new readers came an even greater need for a steady supply of fresh material, and much of it was provided by syndicated content, including cartoons, puzzles, editorials, and columns written by personalities—like Odd McIntyre. Illustrators, photographers, journalists, and columnists no longer had to work in the city where their newspapers were based. Much of the syndicated work was being done in New York, and those who were doing the work were influencing an entire nation by contributing to a mass popular culture. New York had become one of the most influential and creative places on earth, and nowhere was that creative energy more evident than in Odd's letter. By 1922, he had found the voice and the professional persona he would use for the next two decades. He made sure his readers knew that, although he

One of Odd McIntyre's column headers in the early 1920s.

lived among popular entertainers, giants of publishing, and captains of industry, he was really just like the folks reading his column in small towns and communities around the country. "Come along and let me show you all the fun we're having here in New York," he seemed to exclaim. However, it was usually followed by "But really, I would rather be there with you at the breakfast table in Smalltown, U.S.A."

His columns melded small-town newspaper reporting, the energy of Tin Pan Alley, the spectacle of Ziegfeld's *Follies*, and the sophistication of the Ritz-Carlton. Unnecessary words were eliminated and the style he used made errors in grammar and spelling seem intentional or, at the very least, forgivable. Occasionally, Odd even created his own words to communicate thoughts or feelings and, with headings like "Thingumbobs" and "Thoughts While Strolling," sections of his letter were written in a seemingly disconnected stream-of-consciousness style. It could easily have come across as nonsensical, but Odd was somehow able to make it come together and create a clear picture for readers of what it must be like to live in New York. While critics rolled their eyes at columns like this one, many interpreted Odd's letter as factual:

Thoughts while strolling around New York: A turbaned Hindoo. With giggly girls at his heels. One of Manhattan's great criminal lawyers. A lion's head on a dwarfish body. A silver cocktail set in plush window settings. Walter Lippmann. He's going to join the World staff, too. The cry of a catbird. Um-m-m! Pumpkin pies in bakeshop windows. Now the cops are wearing steel jackets to stop bootleggers' bullets. There goes Elsie Ferguson! Dan, the Telescope Man. Points out Old Sirius the Dog Star to timid yokels. He's been at the same corner for twenty-two years. A pursed up scarlet mouth. Hungry eyes. Plying the oldest profession...Strangers emerging from the Grand Central runways with the look of a startled faun. I've spent my last cent on those weight machines. There's no thrill like seeing your own photographs in a strange photographer's window…that looks like Tom Mix. I like his description of the swell New York dinner. He said the only thing he recognized was a radish. Laughing, bright-eyed commuters going home from matinees. New York's gayety is almost too unflagging. It savors strain. Dusk begins to fall. Night brightens into an electrical fantasy. The metropolis tingles with a new sort of happiness. Shadows unreal and remote, appear. So do dinner flasks. Enough thoughts for one day.[173]

Odd gossiped about entertainers of the day, but usually left out anything too unflattering. If he did say something negative about a public figure, he usually countered with something negative about himself to somehow make up for it. While his publicity days were over, he was still attracted to celebrities and the glamour associated with entertainment.

When it came to movies, Odd was an early adopter and was a champion of the new medium of silent film, just like he was of theater, books, and music. In this September 1921 column, he wrote about early movie stars Mary Pickford and Douglas Fairbanks:

Mary and Doug were quartered at the inn where I also reside before sailing for Europe. Josef, my waiter, who has a Weberfieldian accent, also attended to their wants. Life ran high on our floor. Guests were constantly peeping

Actors Douglas Fairbanks, Mary Pickford, and Charlie Chaplin with film director D. W. Griffith, 1919.

through the slits in doors to see the movie stars go and come. And Josef would drop a plate of hot soup any time to reach the hall when the news flashed of their going and coming by that mysterious magic of hotel telepathy. Josef had confided to me that he had histrionic ambitions and prefers the screen as a means of exploiting his talents. I don't know movie requirements, but Josef moves his lips when he reads and can wiggle his ears, so he may have a great future. Incidentally, Mr. Fairbanks and Miss Pickford were the despair of theatrical companies along Broadway. They attended several 'first nights,' and the people turned out to watch them more than they did the performance.[174]

Odd knew the celebrities of the day, but more importantly, many of them knew him. Occasionally, he both celebrated and criticized this new kind of fame that was being created by silent films:

Little Jackie Coogan honored me with a personal call the other morning. If you are a patron of the silver sheet you know Jackie, for at the tender age of 6 he has had fame that comes to few in a lifetime. His salary is staggering. In a very short time he became as famous as Charlie Chaplin and Mary Pickford... The little chap had just recovered from an illness due to the heavy demands upon his time by his first visit to Manhattan. He was followed about the streets trailed by an army of reporters and photographers and generally lionized wherever he went. He appeared more interested in my dog than any other member of the household, and the dog, who has not the slightest sense of proportions, immediately secured a towel and engaged Jackie in a romp that left them both panting... One can not help but have a feeling of sympathy for the lad, despite the success he has achieved. There is something about his wistful expression that gives one the idea that he is rather tired of it. He is guarded like a princeling, cut off from the companionship so essential to boyhood and basks in a reflected glory that he little understands.[175]

When it came to celebrities, Odd could be counted on to know what was going on behind the scenes:

Charlie Chaplin has a great love for fine music and he always admired Enrico Caruso. He told a friend he would like to meet the great singer. The friend arranged the meeting and they went to the dressing room in the Metropolitan opera house. Caruso was having a bad evening and was not his usual genial self. They were presented: 'Well' said Caruso to Chaplin

"I understand you are the Caruso of the moving picture business.' Quick as a flash Chaplin replied: 'Yes and I understand you are the Chaplin of the grand opera business.' It was chilly after that.[176]

Although he was surrounded with the biggest and the brightest celebrities of the day, Odd rarely missed an opportunity to "take himself down a peg or two," as in this story where he implied that, next to his friend, movie star Rudolf Valentino, he looked like Pipe Ben Turpin, a cross-eyed comedian from the silent film era who used exaggerated facial expressions for laughs:

In a distant city the other day I shared the distinction of being guest of honor at a dinner with Rudolf Valentino, the movie star. As we were leaving the dinner a group of girls clotted about the entrance to see Valentino. I followed at his heels and a voice shrilled: 'Pipe Ben Turpin!' Incidentally, Valentino strikes me as being a very earnest young man who is really bewildered by his success. He appears to have a genuine sense of gratitude for his sudden elevation. He made a convincing and cleverly worded talk and is taking advantage of every opportunity to improve himself.[177]

Back at *The Cincinnati Post*, Odd had worked alongside some of the leading muckrakers of the day and, although he had witnessed the change that could come from powerful writing about social issues, that was never really his intention with his column. One *New York Times* critic wrote, "Mr. McIntyre is plainly a man who is himself and with no decoration is what the public wants. Many thousands who read next to nothing else read what he has to say. He does not need to strain for their attention and he has the good sense not to try."[178] Most of Odd's observations on social issues were just that—observations, and the intention was usually to entertain more than to inform. On the problem of drug addiction, he wrote:

A shiver of fear has reached those who live in the phantom world of drug addiction in New York. Dr. Simon, head of the narcotic squad, has written to wealthy drug addicts that they must take a cure or face arrest and exposure…Drug addicts have a partnership in that silent understanding that links them into something closer than casual acquaintanceship. Several meetings have been held at which the rich rubbed elbows with the dregs of the underworld. They were facing the tragedy of their supply being cut off...at the narcotic clinic on the Bowery below Canal Street, where the bilge waters of the city tide and flow and eddy, curtained limousines arrive every hour and empty their heavily veiled patients. Sometimes they are screaming in delirium. One broke away from her captors and rushed up to a laborer in crumpled corduroys. She kneeled at his feet, extracted a chamois bag of jewels from her bodice and baring her arm shouted: 'Quick, for God's sake, the needle!' It developed that he was a peddler and in her agony she had recognized him.[179]

Like a friend casually chatting over dinner, Odd sometimes reminded readers of people, places and things in the past, and the way things were in the good old days:

Many of us who remember the 65-cent dinners of fifteen years ago with a bottle of free red or white wine—but why revive all that? There are some still living who can remember when druggists were druggists. Indeed I can remember back before the pocket lighter when it was natty to strike a match on the heel without losing a step, but I don't want to play this anymore. I'm going back too far.[180]

Occasionally, his tone was that of an old, opinionated uncle. He eagerly shared his thoughts on everything from food, fashion, and the social ins and outs of the day. He especially disliked show offs:

That studied nonchalance that is peculiarly Manhattanese does not always indicate the real New Yorker. It is a veneer, and when cracked probably reveals a man whose chief claim to fame is winning the standing broad-spit on the courthouse steps back home. This careless indifference is affected in various ways. Arriving for the premiere of a play after the second act is now the vogue. Sending oneself a telegram while at a dinner party and then not opening them is another. Wearing a polo hat and carrying a mallet down the avenue is still another.[181]

Above all, Odd's column included a great deal of humor in the form of stories, jokes, or witty observations:

There is a poetic beat to the name of a floral shop in the tunneled depths of one of the railroad terminals. Odink, Florette and Trickle…the nomenclature. Another rather poetic name is that of a lunchroom on Sullivan Street. It is run by Wow, Dow and Gow. They should advertise 'Good Chow.'[182]

Everything Odd had done—his successes and his failures—came together in his letter, and among many newspaper readers around the country it was becoming the first thing they turned to each day. However, few knew the real secret to his financial success was actually Maybelle.

On August 18, 1920, the 19th Amendment to the Constitution was finally ratified, declaring that American women, like men, deserved all the rights and responsibilities of citizenship, including the right to vote in elections. No one had to explain to Odd the power of womanhood. He knew that without Maybelle, he would very likely still be back in Gallipolis working at the *Journal*. It was Maybelle who kept the couple going when times were lean. She was the one who pushed Odd to keep producing the letter, and when Odd was in one of his "states of melancholia," it was she who made sure the letter was completed and sent to newspapers around the country. When the two of them had made the letter so successful that several syndicates were interested, they both knew who was going to be the best negotiator. Years earlier, they had experienced rejection after rejection as they tried to convince the syndicates that the letter would be a popular syndicated column.

One was particularly painful. Odd left several copies of the letter with Harvard-educated Clinton Tyler Brainard, president of McClure Newspaper Syndicate, the first syndicate in the nation and one of the largest. Brainard was unimpressed, and when Odd called to gauge his interest, Brainard, full of condescension, gave him a lecture on the difference between news and publicity. He concluded with, "No way would I ever put anything like this in my newspapers." As Brainard hung up the phone, he looked over at his secretary, Charles Vincent McAdam, and shook his head. McAdam had also read the columns Odd sent and didn't agree. He could see the public appeal in what Odd was writing. But he was just a secretary, so he continued working, although he always remembered Odd's column and the way Brainard had rejected it so coldly.

Through the years, McAdam worked his way up in the syndicate business in several New York companies, including International Features and King Features. While out on the road he would see Odd's letter from New

Odd and Maybelle aboard the *Mauritania*, 1922. *The Esther Allen Greer Museum at the University of Rio Grande*

York appearing in local papers, and he would remember that day back in the McClure office. McAdam's dream was to start his own syndicate, and he even had a brief meeting with Odd and Maybelle, but they were hesitant to turn the letter over to someone just starting out.

By the summer of 1922, McAdam, along with Virgil Venice McNitt, had founded the McNaught Syndicate. One evening, McAdam was leaving a performance of the *Ziegfeld Follies* when he ran into Odd in the lobby. The two began discussing the letter and the sudden interest from syndicators. McAdam asked Odd to consider syndicating the letter with McNaught.

Maybelle set up a meeting with McAdam and McNitt, and on a cool spring afternoon in May 1922, she nervously slid into a chair in a conference room at the McNaught Syndicate offices in the New York Times building, across the street from the New Amsterdam Theater. She later laughed about how, because she and Odd were headed to a party immediately afterwards, she was overdressed for the meeting in a black satin coat trimmed in ermine with a matching muff. In the conference room, Maybelle sat on one side of the table while a row of McNaught publishing executives and their legal counsel sat on the other. She looked down and noticed her hands were shaking, so she thrust them deep inside her muff so they wouldn't be able to tell just how nervous she really felt. Maybelle knew exactly what she wanted and what she felt was fair to compensate the couple for their years of hard work, and she had no intention of accepting any less.

This was her moment. At times, she had been the only person alive who believed in Odd. She supported his career when he experienced failure after failure, and she had waited patiently in Gallipolis while he got his newspaper career started. She had encouraged him to accept the position in New York, and it was she who had worked hard to make sure they survived until he could catch a break. She took care of him physically, mentally, emotionally, and now, financially. Friend and humorist Irvin Cobb wrote, "Through all those earlier years of discouragement and heartbreak, and all through these latter fat ones, Odd had the same boss the firm started out with—general manager, private secretary, social buffer, budget director, financial advisor, almoner, trained nurse, hand holder, brow rubber, mentor and guide, all rolled into one."[183]

When the negotiations were over, Maybelle walked away with one of the most lucrative syndication contracts in history. Odd would receive five hundred dollars per week and sixty percent of the profits for three years. They would renew the agreement every three years until Odd's death. In a true testament to Maybelle's important role, in later years, the syndicate paid her a thousand dollars per month to manage Odd.

Charles McAdam, who had that chance encounter with Odd at the *Follies* and then won the contract to syndicate the letter, became a close friend of President Dwight D. Eisenhower and presidential candidates Thomas E. Dewey and Al Smith. Later in life, Joseph Kennedy offered McAdam one million dollars to run John F. Kennedy's presidential campaign, but he declined. McAdam made an additional connection to the world of newspaper chains in 1948 when his son, Charles Jr., married Sally Gannett, the daughter of publishing giant Frank E. Gannett.

The McNaught Syndicate soon signed agreements with many others, including columnists Will Rogers, Irvin Cobb, Dale Carnegie, Walter Winchell, and Abigail Van Buren, and comic strips like *Joe Palooka* and *Heathcliff.*

For nine years, Odd had not had a single day of vacation. He worked an average of fourteen hours per day, and in nine years, he had not left Manhattan. He was exhausted, underweight, and still not sleeping well. It was time for a vacation.

Odd and Maybelle had dinner at Louis Sherry's new restaurant at 300 Park Avenue and, in Odd's words, "ordered everything on the menu except the date of the month."[184]

When Odd and Maybelle first began sending out the letter, they called it "McIntyre's New York Letter." Some newspapers printed it using different titles like "Day by Day," "Once Overs," "Manhattan Minutes," or "The Great White Way." Later, several newspapers began using "New York Day by Day" and eventually that name stuck and was used by most newspapers.

After dinner at Louis Sherry's, they grabbed a taxi and headed to the Cunard Pier to board the *Mauretania* bound for Europe. Then, at least for a few weeks, "New York Day by Day" became "Europe Day by Day," and the couple was finally able to enjoy some much-deserved rest.

13

Cosmopolitan

I have been contributing to Cosmopolitan without a break for more than fourteen years. Longer, the editor tells me, than any other writer. Thus I am privileged to ruminate and remember when. One cannot perform such a chore so steadily without a tinge of sentimentality.[185]

O. O. McIntyre

In 1922, it had been a little over a decade since Ray Long had recruited Odd to New York to work for *Hampton's Magazine*. While Odd was finally experiencing a measure of success, Long's rise in the world of magazine publishing had been nothing short of meteoric.

His achievement in Chicago as the managing editor of *The Red Book Magazine* had proven his ability to determine the content that would sell magazines. Part of Consolidated Magazines, Inc., *Red Book* was founded in 1903 by Lewis M. Stumer, Abraham R. Stumer, Benjamin J. Rosenthal, and Louis Eckstein. The foursome had first found success in the 1890s with the Chicago Mail Order Company, a business that sold a variety of women's hats and accessories. As the role of women in American

The cover of *The Red Book Magazine.*
November 1922.

society evolved, so did the products they sold in their catalogs. By 1909, their main catalog had grown to nearly one thousand pages filled with clothing, toiletries, furniture, and appliances. The money the company made in the mail-order business had been invested well, and the partners eventually owned real estate, clothing stores, drug stores, and restaurants.

A sister magazine to *The Blue Book Magazine* and *The Green Book Magazine*, *The Red Book Magazine* name was chosen by Trumbull White, the magazine's first editor in 1903, because, in his words, "Red is the color of cheerfulness, of brightness, of gayety." Much to the surprise of the publishing world, within two years, their little magazine had gained an impressive circulation of over 225,000. Although it included articles intended to appeal to every member of the family, regardless of age or sex, it had already been established that women were more likely to buy both magazines and the products advertised inside. The cover of each issue featured an illustration of a modern, young woman against a bright red background. Inside was a combination of short stories and non-fiction articles on topics like mystery, travel, and romance.

Significant increases in literacy and population growth, and improvements in the transportation, printing, and advertising industries created a boom in the magazine business in the early decades of the twentieth century. Around the time Ray Long first pulled his chair up to his desk at *Red Book* in 1922, there were more than 3,500 magazines published in the United States. Many American families subscribed to multiple magazines, and newsstands were plentiful in cities and towns around the country.

Most American consumers had more leisure time and expendable income than those in previous generations, and those who produced consumer goods saw magazines as a way to make potential customers aware

Ray Long and Odd McIntyre were friends, colleagues, and eventually, relatives. *The Esther Allen Greer Museum at the University of Rio Grande*

of the latest and greatest products. As revenue from advertising increased, the price of magazines was lowered, which caused the number of subscribers to increase—generating even more advertising revenue. Now that so many more Americans were living in cities, they were turning to stores and mail-order catalogs for things they had previously grown or built on their farms.

Several "breakthrough" products were now fighting for ad space in magazines. In 1906, industrialist Will Keith Kellogg purchased his first ads selling Corn Flakes and, by 1915, the company was spending more than a million dollars each year on advertising. In 1911, Proctor and Gamble hired advertising agency J. Walter Thompson Co. to launch Crisco, its new vegetable shortening. Ads touted Crisco as, "An absolutely new product. A scientific discovery, which will affect every kitchen in America."[186] That same year, Woodbury Soap Company became the first company to use sex appeal to sell a product when they began running magazine ads that promised women who used their soap would have "skin you would love to touch." In 1936, Woodbury would become the first company to use nudity in American magazine advertising.

Early Woodbury Soap Company ad.

With more customers shopping and more products from which to choose, it was time for a drastic improvement in stores where food and toiletries were purchased. In 1916, Clarence Saunders opened Piggly Wiggly, the first self-service grocery store, in Memphis, Tennessee. For the first time, shoppers no longer had to depend on a clerk to hand them the goods they wanted, as was the case in a traditional general store. Ads for Piggly Wiggly touted a "new way to shop that has quickly become a nation-wide vogue." The power to choose among products was now in the hands of the consumers, and thanks to the growth of transportation, many of the same products were on grocery store shelves around the nation. Manufacturers of consumer goods could now view the whole nation as a potential marketplace, and magazines provided a way for them to get their products quickly in front of potential customers.

Early Piggly Wiggly ad.

The more readers a magazine could get, the more potential customers for advertisers. Ray Long had a knack for getting readers because he quickly comprehended the public's fickle tastes. This allowed him to produce the kind of magazine he knew the public would buy. Long also appreciated the importance of good design, photography, and illustration. It was no longer enough to have interesting articles—more and more, magazines readers wanted to be visually entertained as well.

As Long applied those principles to *Red Book*, circulation grew, as did advertising revenue. Under his direction, the magazine's subscriber base grew from 225,000 to more than 400,000.

Publisher William Randolph Hearst noticed the results Long was getting and was eager to get the talented editor working for him, instead of the competition.

In 1905, Hearst had expanded his empire to include magazine publishing with the launch of *Motor* magazine. He later purchased *Cosmopolitan*, then quickly added *Good Housekeeping*, *Harper's Bazaar*, and others to his growing stable of periodicals.

While *Cosmopolitan* was selling an impressive one million copies each month, Hearst, frustrated because the circulation had not grown for two years, was determined to get Long at the helm of his flagship magazine. However, Long would agree to the terms, then suddenly back out. Months would pass and Hearst would offer more. Long would accept the terms, then back out again. The salary negotiation took more than two years, but on January 1, 1919 Long officially became editor of Hearst's *Cosmopolitan*.

The *Cosmopolitan* that Long took over was, as one writer of the day described it, "full of Robert W. Chambers and Gouverneur Morris, and consisted largely of sex against a background of either high adventure or of high society."[187]

Long felt the public was tiring of the type of articles that filled the pages of *Cosmopolitan*, and began looking for young writers who produced work that he himself wanted to read. A 1931 feature on Long in *Fortune* magazine referred to him as "a literary barometer knowing when the rain is coming before the drops have begun to fall. He must be able to predict in advance the point of popular acceptance and the point of popular saturation."[188]

Long improved the quality of the writing, increased the stable of writers from ten to twenty, added more illustrations and photographs, and changed the way they were used within the magazine. Other magazines primarily used photos and illustration in boxes, but Long's designers began incorporating them into the stories and headlines. *Cosmopolitan* began looking unlike anything readers had seen before. Long also began recruiting popular writers from other magazines, including Irvin Cobb, Fannie Hurst, Rupert Hughes, Arthur Summers Roche, and W. Somerset Maugham. A big believer in taking care of his writers and paying them premium salaries, he was able to get some of the best poets, novelists, and short story writers of the day to write exclusively for *Cosmopolitan*.

Especially important for the advertising revenue, after improving the quality of the publication, *Cosmopolitan* saw significant growth of subscribers who were high-earning city dwellers and an especially important target for advertisers.

While the other magazines were usually associated with Hearst, *Cosmopolitan* was, without a doubt, Long's baby. He read manuscripts six hours each day during his four-day workweek and twelve hours during his weekend, and he approved each and every word that appeared in the magazine. Unlike other editors, Long frequently made editorial changes and suggestions to even his most respected writers' work, and they usually listened. Always on the hunt for new talent and trends, he let his assistants know that, although he never wanted to see routine correspondence, notes from readers, or comments mailed to the magazine, all letters from struggling young writers were to be taken to him to be read personally.[189] By doing this, he occasionally found undiscovered talent who would end up writing exclusively for *Cosmopolitan*.

Two things happened in July 1922 that would once again connect Ray Long and Odd McIntyre. Since returning to New York, Long had been trying to convince Odd to submit something to *Cosmopolitan*. In one instance, Odd and Long met for a few days in Cincinnati, where Odd's column was very popular with readers. When they arrived and word spread around town, so many calls were coming into the hotel asking for Odd that they had to bring in an additional operator. Long was astonished and told his friend, "If that many people read your stuff in Cincinnati alone, there must be millions of others elsewhere. And if they read you in newspapers, they'll read you in *Cosmopolitan!*"[190]

Odd always declined, claiming to be too busy with the letter or his publicity work, but in reality, the many rejections he had received from magazines still haunted him, and he wasn't certain he could do it. But Long persisted, and the August 1922 issue of *Cosmopolitan* included a photo of Odd with his bulldog, and an announcement that his new monthly article would begin with the next issue.

Readers who paid the thirty-five cents to purchase the September 1922 issue of *Cosmopolitan* could flip through and read "The Social Error of Being Well Fed" by George Ade, "Reminiscences" by Lillian Russell, "Old Ben Alibi" by Irvin S. Cobb, "The Metropolitan Touch" by P. G. Wodehouse, and Odd's very first Cosmopolitan article, "A Vignette of New York." From then until his death, every single issue included an article by O. O. McIntyre.

The style of his monthly magazine column was completely different from

BRIDE OF EDITOR WHOSE MARRIAGE WAS A SURPRISE

MRS. RAY LONG.

Romance Revealed When Ray Long and Wife Sail for Europe.

All but a few of his closest friends were surprised to-day to learn that Ray Long, editor of the Cosmopolitan Magazine, editor-in-chief of the International Magazine Company and Cosmopolitan Books Corporation, was married July 25. The secret was revealed by the sailing of Mr. Long and his bride yesterday on the Aquitania for Cherbourg.

His bride, who was Miss Lucy Virginia Bovie, twenty-four years old, of No. 66 West 47th Street, is well known in this city. She is a cousin of Mrs. O. O. McIntyre of the Ritz-Carlton.

The wedding took place in Westport, Conn., at the home of Judge George Hyatt. Leon Gordin, an artist, Mrs. Gordin and Percy Anderson, also an artist, were the witnesses of the marriage.

Wedding announcement of Ray Long and Lucy Virginia Bovie from the *Evening World* on August 2, 1922.

the letter, and provided an opportunity for him to expound on things he liked—or didn't like—and to showcase his very unique style of writing. In that first article he shared more about the city he had grown to love:

Gray dusk comes with a mysterious hush to Union Square. The moon hangs its slight crescent on the sky and there is a soft gravity about the trees and the walks, turning purple in the haze. The lamps, pale and ungleaming, are strung like so many beads about the shadowy lawns. It is that magic hour when New York pauses its skyrocket rush—the hiatus between the end of the workday and the beginning of evening pleasures. The shrill of the newsboy crying of murder, divorce and a world wet with tears, the clatter of giant hoofs against cobblestone, the jangle of surface cars, shriek of motor sirens and screech of the elevated spun high in the clouds are stilled.[191]

Around this time, Ray Long was in his mid-forties. Although he was a small man and not traditionally handsome, he was sophisticated, well dressed, and knew everybody who was anybody in New York. He kept his thin mustache closely trimmed, his shoes shined, and wore clothes purchased from the best shops on Fifth Avenue. Now divorced from his second wife, he was single, wealthy, and lonely. He was a frequent visitor to Odd and Maybelle's home at the Ritz-Carlton, and it was there Long met Lucy Virginia Bovie, Maybelle's cousin, also from Gallipolis. Long and the much-younger Bovie married on July 25, 1922 and quickly had a son, Ray Long Jr. Long was now not only one of Odd's biggest fans, he was family.

Throughout the 1920s, Odd's articles in *Cosmopolitan* included vivid descriptions of various New York neighborhoods, including Tin Pan Alley, Broadway, and Fifth Avenue. He shared the New York he was experiencing in the 1920s and the 1930s, but also the New York of the past, creating a colorful historical record of the city:

The Bowery is no more! The picturesque midrib of New York's East Side squalor has flung off tattered garments. Instead of shiny serge, there is now the faint rustle of silk…Gold Tooth Fannie who once lived on the Avenue and fed the poor at dawn from a banjo-torched cart. The Sullivans—Big and Little Tim! Owen Kildare, the Bowery poet. Spike O' Day who pawned his peg leg each morning and retrieved it at night with a beggar's spoils…

Through the '20s and '30s, more then 170 issues of *Cosmopolitan* magazine included an article written by Odd McIntyre. In the April 1933 issue, he shared with his readers the story of his and Maybelle's courtship.

Sophie the Scrubwoman whose life-sized painting now hangs in the Doyers Street Mission. Blind Toots the singer of Chatham Square. Stubby Toliver the Bowery hackman. Salvation Annie! All are gone![192]

Considering Odd's past experience, it's no surprise his profiles of celebrities became one of his specialties, and he frequently wrote features on the most popular personalities of the day, including jazz musician Paul Whiteman, boxer Gene Tunney, his former boss Florenz Ziegfeld, playwright Anita Loos, and opera singer Marion Talley. Sometimes his profiles were of individuals he knew well from New York's social scene.

He wrote details that pulled back the curtain on the world of entertainment, and he shared his version of what the world was like for those who worked on the stage, in radio, and in the movies. While what he wrote about the culture of the day wasn't always positive, it was always entertaining:

In the Broadwayesque section of New York termed the Roaring Forties is the lair of the Gold Digger. There, with pouting lips, baby stare and dégagé smile, she lies in wait for those who go intriguing incog. The past year has been "pay dirt" in the flaming Gulch of the Diggers. Men in high places who have strayed from peaceful hearths to seek Understanding Women have plunged spectacularly to social, financial and domestic ruin. Their bleached bones are the 'Stop, Look and Listen!' signs along the way. One was untrussed by a murder, another by blackmail and countless others by the inexorable law that has a way of dealing with the faithless.[193]

Much of American popular culture was being created in New York and then spreading throughout the nation faster than ever before, and Odd was there to provide his observations, as in this Cosmopolitan article titled, "The Men Who Dope Out Your Slang":

Café's, tea-rooms, hotel lobbies and theater foyers crackle with wise cracks. If some jester invents one in the morning it is almost certain that the same night the stage—from self-assured comedians to "wonder kiddies" of vaudeville—is wafting the wheeze. And the next day it sweeps Manhattan like a fire in the prairie brush…the popularity of American slang is easily traced back to George Ade. Though for years he was about the only originator, the field is now crowded. The most gifted and prolific fashioner of slang is T. A. Dorgan, known to millions of newspaper readers as "Tad," the cartoonist. It was Tad who had one of his cartoon figures say, 'Yes, we have no bananas.' Tad also immortalized: 'Easy on the whip, Phil, it's a hired horse,' 'Up with the napkins, here comes the soup,' 'Dead from the neck up,' and 'There's gold in them hills, boys!'[194]

Odd also wrote of his and Maybelle's occasional travels to other states like California and Texas and countries like Paris, London, and Mexico. Frequent topics also included his childhood in Gallipolis and his passionate love of his dogs.

Odd was on his way to being the most popular newspaper and magazine writer in the country, and was certainly among the highest-paid. He had everything money could buy, a beautiful wife, close friends, and he lived in the most exciting city in the world.

To a casual observer, it would appear that Odd McIntyre had finally made it and should be the happiest man on earth. But as was the case with some of Odd's writing, things were not always as they seemed.

14

Pernicious Anemia

I am 37 years old—love dogs and people. I belong to the Forty-sixth Street Pants Pressing Club. I have the general contour of the Australian anteater, am addicted to loud shirts, sleeping late of mornings and vanilla ice cream with hot chocolate sauce. I like mystery stories, dislike carrots, The New Republic, prints of the Mona Lisa and Chic Sale is my favorite actor. And I have not taken a drop of medicine in seven years. So be it![195]

O. O. McIntyre

What was really wrong with Odd McIntyre? Historian E. L. Huddleston summed it up as, "Odd had trouble just coping." He wrote:

Most of his life was a fight against fears: of dropping dead in the street, of open spaces, of the telephone, of debt, of being slapped on the back, and of someone picking lint from his coat. Besides his phobias, he endured an often debilitating inferiority complex, persistent insomnia, and a chronic hypochondria that had turned him against doctors at an early age.[196]

A few references to his symptoms appear in Odd's own writing and in that of his friends who were around at the time. Using humor, he allowed some of his fears and obsessions to figure slightly into his public persona. For example, after persuading Maybelle to go with him to watch an early silent movie starring Lillian Gish, he wrote in his daily column, "In the afternoon with my wife, poor wretch, to see the film drama, *Way Down East*, and the best thing ever I saw, and yet I can find but faint praise for the film plays. Walked among the theater hordes going home and tried to stifle my fear of crowds but could not. Dined on ham and fried apples, and read a little in the Bible. And so to bed."[197]

He wrote he was so afraid of open spaces, it was years before he could cross Central Park's south meadow. He went through a strange phase of not being able to speak to someone on their second meeting, unless the other person spoke first, and he was suddenly struck with a fear of the barbershop:

> *I was seated in a barber chair, when all of a sudden, as though struck by lightening, I was in a panic. I simply had to get out of that chair! My haircut needed only a few finishing touches but I could not wait. I made some crazy excuse and rushed off all atremble, and never since have been able to sit in a barber chair. I have tried valiantly, but I get no farther than the door before my heart begins looping the loop. The barber now comes to my home and I am perfectly composed.*[198]

Journalist Joseph Bryan III wrote a not-so-flattering article in the *Saturday Evening Post* about Odd, in which he noted his well-publicized clothing obsession. He wrote, "Sixty dressing gowns hang in the closet of O. O. McIntyre's Park Avenue apartment. Thirty pairs of day pajamas, and another thirty for sleeping are folded in his wardrobe." Bryan also wrote of the bounty Odd shipped home from Paris after a visit. Odd estimated he had shipped "200 neckties, 200 canes, 200 bathrobes, 100 pairs of socks, 100 shirts, fifty suits of Japanese-silk underwear, sixty pairs of pajamas, sixty suits, fifty pairs of shoes, three dozen hats and handkerchiefs past counting."[199] Odd himself wrote about his large collection of clothing and accessories, turning it into one of his many "quirky" personality traits.

A writer for *The New York Times* observed that "naturally shy, his illness had infected him with a genuine fear of open spaces and it was torture for him to go about seeking material for the column he was determined to write."[200] Charles Driscoll, Odd's editor at McNaught, wrote that he observed Odd's "halting step, unwillingness to rise from a chair and difficulty in turning his head."[201]

Odd and Maybelle became extremely defensive about his obvious health problems, and anyone who brought them up, especially in the later years, found they were no longer welcome in the McIntyre home or in their small inner circle of friends and associates. Driscoll remembered, "During all the years of struggle, triumph and greater struggle, the subject of illness was taboo in the McIntyre household. Those who mentioned it were not welcome guests, and were not invited to return."[202]

Friends learned any attempt to encourage Odd to seek professional help was futile. He sometimes attributed his dislike of doctors to several childhood operations he had on his sinuses that he claimed had been "unnecessary." His heels were dug in and he was not going to see a doctor under any circumstances.

Another contributing factor to Odd's stubbornness was his religion. Although he rarely mentioned religion in his writing, since 1918 he and Maybelle had been followers of Christian Science. They were introduced to Christian Science by their neighbors Mr. and Mrs. William F. Spatt. Odd was experiencing a painful growth, possibly lesions, on his lower back, which made it difficult to sit. Spatt offered to take him to a local Christian Science practitioner, who supposedly healed him. Although he never wrote about it, Maybelle told a friend that Odd frequently said he would not have had courage to continue his career had it not been for Christian Science.

Founder of Christian Science, Mary Baker Eddy.

The "Scopes Monkey Trial" of 1925, in which John Scopes' was brought to court for teaching evolution, led to a nationwide debate over religion and science. Scientific and medical discoveries were happening rapidly, and many Americans were struggling to adjust their own personal beliefs. The battle was frequently covered in newspapers with headlines like "Religion Shakes Science's Hand," "Religion Has Nothing to Fear from Truths in Biology," "Rev. E. M. L. Gould Finds Evolution Supports Religion," and "The Rev. L. H. Bell Warns of Science Displacing Religion."[203]

Some Protestants, primarily young, urban city-dwellers, adopted a more modern view of religion, accepting a flexible approach to Christianity that incorporated modern science. Others, primarily located in rural, middle America, remained dedicated to traditional and conservative Christianity. Like other areas of popular culture, religion was undergoing an era of change.

In the 1920s, many had lost fathers, sons, and brothers in the first World War, and more than 675,000 Americans had died in an influenza pandemic that ended in 1919. Those who were mourning loved ones were eager to embrace Spiritualism, in which communicating with the dead was considered a possibility. There was a surge in the sales of Ouija boards, and séances became mainstream as people gathered to listen to a medium relay messages from their deceased friends and family members.

In Los Angeles, evangelist Aimee Semple McPherson, founder of the

Evangelist Aimee Semple McPherson. *The Foursquare Church*

Angelus Temple, Church of the Foursquare Gospel, began using the new technology of radio to broadcast her dramatic Pentecostal messages around the world. Her church services featured enthusiastic vaudeville-like performances by professional actors and musicians, and spellbinding sermons in which her flowing robes were on full display. She laid hands on the sick, asking God to heal them. McPherson's church became a major tourist attraction and its five thousand seats weren't enough to hold all those who came to hear her preach. She was the first to incorporate modern entertainment elements into church services.

Odd and Maybelle's preferred religion, Christian Science, was founded in 1879 by Mary Baker Eddy. It taught that sickness was an illusion that could be stopped by prayer, which was most effective when not combined with medical treatment. Avoiding doctors, even when seriously ill, was a significant part of the church dogma.

It's hard to know how faithful Odd really was to Christian Science. When he was younger, he drank and smoked, both of which are very much discouraged in that religion. Driscoll observed that Odd always kept a dictionary and a Bible on his desk, but he also noticed Odd described his religion as being "interested in science" rather than calling himself a Christian Scientist. Inside the front cover of his dictionary was a quote from Eddy that read, "A knowledge of the science of being develops the latent abilities and possibilities of man. It extends the atmosphere of thought, giving mortals access to broader and higher realms. It raises the thinking into his native air of insight and perspicacity."[204]

Odd once wrote in his column that he was planning to attend church the following day. He had no specific denomination in mind but planned to drop by whichever neighborhood church "struck his fancy" during his morning walk. He continued, "I rarely hang enraptured on the words of the pulpiteer. Much of a sermon's portent, its ecclesiasticism, escapes me…I have never set myself to a serious deciphering of the unknowable, I only know that I believe."[205]

Unfortunately, even if Odd's past experience and his religion had not discouraged him from seeing a doctor, it would not have made much of a difference. His various mental and physical symptoms can now be attributed to one illness—pernicious anemia. When the body is unable to digest vitamin B12, it results in a lack of healthy red blood cells and an insufficient amount of oxygen getting to the body's tissues, including the brain. Although it's nearly non-existent today because treatment is so readily available, during Odd's life, little was known about the cause or effects of the disease, and it brought on a long, painful decline and eventual early death.

The symptoms of the disorder could include impaired concentration, weakness, insomnia, severe depression, panic disorders, phobias, and obsessive compulsive disorders—all issues that Odd struggled with, and which worsened with age. Another frequent symptom of pernicious anemia, lesions on the spinal cord, could explain that first medical problem that resulted in Odd's visit to a Christian Science practitioner back in Cincinnati.

Many patients struggling with the disease also experienced a change in the color of their skin, their hair turned gray or white, and they had significant weight loss—all symptoms Odd experienced in New York in the early 1920s. In many photos, Odd appears gaunt and unhealthy, and looks considerably older than he actually was.

His illness also hampered his ability to see his family, with whom he still maintained frequent contact. Odd's father, stepmother, and members of his mother's family all still lived in Plattsburg, Missouri, and his sister Kate lived nearby. It's interesting that, although he was now a highly-successful New York columnist with fame and fortune, he was still trying to impress his father. Shortly after Maybelle renegotiated Odd's contract in February 1925, Henry McIntyre opened his mailbox to find what appeared to be a business letter from New York. In fact, it was from Odd's syndication company and read:

Dear Mr. McIntyre:

I have just received a letter from your son who is now in Europe in which he suggests that I might be interested in telling you about our new contract. Just before he sailed, we signed an agreement for three years. The first year at $900.00 a week and the second and third years at $1,000 a week, with probabilities of a still larger return through a percentage division of proceeds. I am sure you must feel proud of a son who has made such a remarkable success of life. He is now one of the two or three favorites with newspaper readers all over the United States.

Very sincerely yours,

V. V. McNitt, President

The McNaught Syndicate

It's unlikely Henry McIntyre ever found a way to let Odd know if he were proud of him. If he did, Odd never wrote about it. What he did write, however, was a tribute to his father for the April 1925 issue of *Cosmopolitan*. He applauded his father, who was then 71, for being "one of the truly great Americans." In the article titled "My Dad," Odd wrote, "In my opinion he is one of the mightiest of American assets...he belongs to the brotherhood of Common Men and without them sometimes I feel that our nation would face anarchy and ruin."[206]

Odd also tried to impress his father by bragging about his connection to famous people in New York. Although they both wrote for *Cosmopolitan*, Odd had not yet met well-known humorist Irvin Cobb. After attending a dinner in which Cobb was the guest of honor, Odd wrote a letter to his father and bragged that he had "had dinner with Irvin Cobb the other night." He failed to mention he was simply a member of the audience. Of course, Odd assumed Cobb and his father would never meet, so it would do no harm to exaggerate his connection a little.

Later, Cobb was on a speaking tour and happened to stop in Plattsburg, Missouri. Henry McIntyre met Cobb at the train station and insisted his son's "close friend" should stay at his house instead of in a hotel. The temptation to eat a home-cooked meal was so great, Cobb took Henry McIntyre up on the offer, even though he didn't actually know Odd. Henry then invited all of Odd's Plattsburg friends and family over. Although he had never even been formally introduced, Cobb played along and acted as though he and Odd were best friends.

When Cobb returned to New York, he contacted Odd and the two met for the first time. Cobb and his wife, Laura, became Odd and Maybelle's close friends and traveling companions, and the story of how he met Odd's father was one of Cobb's favorites.

Odd's stepmother, Henry McIntyre's second wife Sultana Duncan, died on April 3, 1925 at their home on Broadway Street in Plattsburg. She had been active in the Plattsburg Baptist Church, and the minister who had officiated their marriage eighteen years earlier conducted her funeral. Odd was unable to attend because he was so ill, and the family received a wire that Odd had muscular rheumatism of his neck and shoulders, was run-down, and it would be too dangerous for him to travel. In June, it was reported in the *Plattsburg Leader* that Odd was in such bad shape, he had been unable to leave his suite at the Ritz-Carlton for nearly two months.

Although Odd had agreed to speak at the twentieth annual Plattsburg

Henry McIntyre near the end of his life. *The Esther Allen Greer Museum at the University of Rio Grande*

Chautauqua in August 1925—an event Henry McIntyre helped arrange—Odd was again too sick to travel and had to cancel. In September, he wrote to his father that for the first time in many weeks, he was able to bathe, shave, and dress himself. One family friend reported, "Odd looks badly. He is in bad shape physically—otherwise he would have been in Plattsburg to see his father long before now."[207]

Henry McIntyre's health was also failing. At his seventy-second birthday party on July 29, 1925, it was reported that, "although he is unable to eat very much of anything, he likes for his friends to eat and enjoyed the friends and family members who came to wish him a happy birthday."

Odd was in Paris on May 31, 1926 when he received a telegram that his father had died of heart disease at his home in Plattsburg. His obituary mentioned his work to get the Kansas City and North Railroad into Plattsburg, his role in securing the town's first telephone company, the fact that he was chairman of the Red Cross, and that during World War I, he spent much of his time supporting local soldiers.

Although Odd was unable to attend his father's funeral, he no doubt took notice of the sentence in Henry's obituary, "Henry's chief pride was in his own children, Oscar Odd McIntyre and Mrs. Katie Tabb of Kansas City." In the end, Odd finally received a small bit of public acknowledgment that his father had been proud of him, even if someone else had written it.

The pernicious anemia that kept Odd away from events like family funerals was not likely to get better on its own. The definition of pernicious is "having a harmful effect, especially in a gradual or subtle way," and until 1926, it was indeed very harmful, resulting in the early death of nearly one hundred percent of its victims. The disease struck men more than women, and was found to be more prevalent among those, like Odd, who had Scottish heritage.

Pernicious anemia also caused an "exaggeration of native traits," meaning Odd's natural tendencies would have been dramatically intensified. This would explain his obsession with buying and saving clothes that he never wore, his fears of poverty and death, and his paralyzing shyness. In one instance, a young Joan Crawford requested that Odd sit next to her at a dinner. He was unable to speak more than a word or two and never even glanced at the actress sitting next to him. In another, he was asked to address a group gathered for a dinner. He took the podium for a brief moment, said hello, looked at the audience, then sat back down. Lucrative offers to be on the radio were customarily rejected without any consideration, and he used his column as an excuse. However, it's more likely his painful shyness and fear of failure were the real reasons he preferred to stay hidden behind his typewriter.

While some aspects of the disease were somewhat understood by the late 1920s, the cure remained elusive. One physician, Philip M. Lovell, wrote in a 1929 article in the *Los Angeles Times*, "Pernicious anemia is a condition in which the blood either lacks the red hemoglobin substance or far more likely, is deficient in blood cells themselves…but what causes the blood 'factories' to break down?" He then pointed to the typical American diet as a reason for the disease's prevalence. He wrote, "Our modern civilized diet, with its one hundred and twenty pounds of white sugar per capita, with its one hundred and twenty pounds of meatstuffs and its average cup-and-a-half of coffee or other similar drinks per day, furnishes a background of why pernicious anemia is a very common condition."[208]

Of course, Maybelle's concern about Odd's health was greater than anyone else's. As someone who read many newspapers and magazines each week, she was obviously looking for suggestions on how to treat her husband's various maladies. If she suspected that he had pernicious anemia, she may have taken the advice given by Royal S. Copeland, a physician, newspaper columnist, and senator from New York, in an article he wrote in 1928:

In the treatment of pernicious anemia, everything which would be fatiguing must be avoided. Long hours of work, long rail trips, sightseeing, worry and anything else which uses up energy must be forbidden. Frequent rest periods should be insisted upon. The diet should be nourishing and, above all, made appetizing. If any special foods are not to be taken the doctor will tell the patient. He will also prescribe medication. Greatest good in such a case may be accomplished by helping the sufferer to be cheerful and enjoy life as he finds it.[209]

Unfortunately, none of Dr. Copeland's tips would cure someone suffering from pernicious anemia. However, a cure—or at least a first step toward finding one—did come in 1926 when physicians George Whipple, George Minot and William Murphy saw significant improvement in their pernicious anemia patients who ate a half-pound of raw liver every day. For their groundbreaking work, the three physicians won the Nobel Prize in 1934. When Dr. Minot received word that he had been awarded the Nobel Prize, he was standing at the bedside of a pernicious anemia patient. He said, "Only nine days ago, this man was dying. By means of a needle we have injected liver extract into his system. Now he is sitting up, shouting for food, reading a newspaper."[210]

Sadly, there would be no such quick recovery for Odd, even though with the right medical care, his quality of life could have been vastly improved. By the middle of the 1920s, he was forced to struggle with long periods of serious illness, while simultaneously enjoying greater fame and fortune than he had ever dreamed possible.

15

Pop Culture

Not a week passes that I do not visit one of the great railroad terminals to see the crack fliers thunder in. There is always drama at the gates. I see movie stars, flowering with orchids, on their first lap of a journey to Hollywood. Shackled prisoners off for many long, gray years at Sing Sing. Sometimes a president...all manner of people interest me. I have found that the gunman, the thief, the prostitute, the confidence man and all the odd human flotsam spewed up from a great city's depths are searching for happiness—and missing it—just as many of us do.[211]

O. O. McIntyre

Even though Odd still wrote fondly of Gallipolis, and occasionally he and Maybelle discussed returning to visit, New York was now home. He wrote, "I love New York devotedly. There is no other city in which I would care to live." And if New York was home, his readers around the world were his family. He was receiving hundreds of letters from fans each week, and if he mentioned liking or needing something in his column, days later his mail would explode as that item would arrive at his address from all over the nation. After he mentioned his robe was getting shabby, he received hundreds of robes in the mail—that he donated to charity. In the next column, he jokingly mentioned that his car was looking pretty bad, too.

It's likely part of Odd's mass appeal was based on his writing about many different subjects. The comments, critiques, and observations in his columns and articles were about every aspect of popular culture, including newspapers, magazines, movies, fashion, fine art, books, restaurants, history, sports, and even his thoughts on the social norms of the day. He then threw in a bit of gossip about celebrities, businessmen, and politicians for good measure.

Sometimes many of those subjects were covered in one paragraph. For example, in January 1925, he wrote, "People who bore me: 'America's sweetheart' movie stars, doctors who announce schemes to prolong life 25 years and cannot cure whooping cough, wonder kiddies of vaudeville, women who smoke cigarettes in hotel lobbies and artists who wear Elbert Hubbard ties."[212]

Of course, as a writer himself, he was especially fond of his fellow wordsmiths both personally and professionally. With the money to travel, he and Maybelle were frequent visitors to Paris, where Odd became friends with many of the writers referred to as the "Lost Generation." The group was supposedly nicknamed when Gertrude Stein commented to Ernest Hemingway, "All of you young people who served in the war. You are a lost generation. You have no respect for anything. You drink yourselves to death."

This group of creative American expatriates, who had come of age during World War I, was disillusioned by what America was becoming in the 1920s. As a whole, they felt that morality, patriotism, and faith were no longer important, and it was impossible to live the way others had just a generation before. Living a bohemian lifestyle, frequently in Europe, they tried to make sense of the world through their writing. In addition to Stein and Hemingway, writers associated with the Lost Generation included F. Scott Fitzgerald, T. S. Eliot, E. E. Cummings, and Hart Crane.

Although he was not publicly identified with the group, Odd was right

Harry's New York Bar in Paris, France was a frequent hangout of Odd McIntyre and the writers who came to be known as "The Lost Generation."

there with them as they wrote, danced, sang, and drank. Ironically, for a group who wanted to escape American culture, much of their socializing took place at Harry's New York Bar in Paris. Much of the bar's interior was literally from New York. When Clancey's Bar in Manhattan closed because of Prohibition, American jockey Tod Sloan had it dismantled piece by piece and shipped to 5 Rue Daunou, where it was named The New York Bar. Later purchased by Harry MacElhone, a former bartender, and renamed Harry's New York Bar, it became a popular hangout for Americans looking for a taste of home while living in or visiting Paris. In the words of one customer, "It had the smell and flavor of where you had come from."[213] To make it easier to find for those who didn't speak French, the bar's advertising featured the tagline, "Just tell the taxi driver: Sank Roo Doe Noo."

George Gershwin was said to have composed "An American in Paris" at the bar's piano, and other writers like F. Scott Fitzgerald used the bar as a favorite place to work. Harry's was also included in fiction. In Ian Fleming's *From a View to a Kill,* James Bond recalls visiting the bar during his first time in Paris at age sixteen. Fleming wrote, "That had started one of the memorable evenings of his life, culminating in the loss, almost simultaneously, of his virginity and his notecase."

Odd was a frequent patron when in Paris, even helping MacElhone

(left) Official membership pin of the Brotherhood of the International Barflies. (right) The official membership book of the IBF that lists Odd as "Big Blue Bottlefly."

come up with a club for the most dedicated customers—the Brotherhood of the International Bar Flies. The IBF, as they called it, was a "secret and fraternal organization devoted to the uplift and downfall of serious drinkers." Members could identify each other by their IBF lapel pin that featured a dead fly on a sugar cube. They each received a bright red book, with the club logo on the front that listed Odd as "big blue bottle fly" and president, and McElhone as "exalted blue bottle fly" and vice president.

Underneath the member's name, and authorized by MacElhone's signature, it noted that the bearer was a "member in good standing of this trap and is entitled to buy and drink in all other traps of the I.B.F. and in the U.S.A." It added that the member was "entitled to confidence and respect of all Bootleggers, Rum-hounds, Ticket-speculators, Night-Club Doorkeepers, Headwaiters and Bartenders in all parts of the globe." Members had to agree "as they flew through life in the great swarm, they would never sting a fellow member."

No club is complete without an official song and the IBF had one— with words and music by O. O. McIntyre. "Buzz Buzz Buzz" included the lyrics, "There are bar flies east and there are bar flies west; Bar flies near and bar flies far."

There were, in fact, members near and far. Gatherings continued in New York when Odd returned home. Periodically, there was even an IBF newsletter that listed the best bars, or "fly traps" as they called them, around the world. While Odd's fellow members included writers F. Scott Fitzgerald, Thorton Wilder, and Ernest Hemingway, non-writers were certainly not excluded from the club. Boxer Jack Dempsey, coach Knute Rockne, and fashion designer Coco Chanel were among those who could be spotted wearing the IBF pin and ordering cocktails at bars around the world.

Although Odd still considered himself more of a reporter than anything else, he was an avid reader and loved spending time with talented writers of all genres. In April 1925, Odd's friend and fellow IBF member F. Scott Fitzgerald published *The Great Gatsby*. The novel, critical of the consumer culture and materialism of the time, followed Midwesterner Nick Carraway as he moved to New York and became friends with a group of spoiled, young people living the "American dream." Odd and his friends read it closely to see if Fitzgerald had included any characters inspired by them in his tale of riches gone wrong.

Fitzgerald's personal scrapbook includes a clipping from Odd's April 18, 1923 column in which he noted Fitzgerald was a neighbor of sports columnist and short story writer Ring Lardner, and humorously played off the egos of both writers:

> *F. Scott Fitzgerald and Ring Lardner are neighbors at Great Neck, L.I. In the morning when the young author who glorified the flapper springs out of bed he sings through an open window: 'Oh the great Fitzgerald is just out of bed. Just out of bed. O, the great Fitzgerald!' And soon across the space booms the voice of Lardner: 'The mighty Lardner prepareth to shave. Soap suds and lather! O, the beautiful sylph-like Lardner.' Neighbors have been trying to mitigate the annoyance but to no avail. For Fitzgerald and Lardner continue their rhyming fooleries at intervals all during the day.*[214]

Journalist Harold Ross, another of Odd's friends, published the first

(left) Ernest Hemingway and (right) George Gershwin in the early 1920s.

issue of the *New Yorker* in February 1925, while his friend and former neighbor, Edna Ferber, won a Pulitzer Prize that year for her novel, *So Big*. Odd also spent long evenings chatting over dinners with Theodore Dreiser, whose *American Tragedy* was also published in 1925. Dreiser and Odd were so close, he would be among the last visitors to the McIntyre home before Odd's death. Odd and Maybelle were frequently in attendance at the dinner parties of Nobel Prize-winning author Sinclair Lewis. His novel, *Babbit*, a satire of American culture, was an immediate bestseller in 1922 and was followed in 1926 by the Pulitzer Prize-winning *Arrowsmith*. Lewis declined the award and wrote, "All prizes, like all titles, are dangerous. The seekers for prizes tend to labor not for inherent excellence but for alien rewards; they tend to write this, or timorously to avoid writing that, in order to tickle the prejudices of a haphazard committee."

In addition to literature, the music of the 1920s and the technology that made it more accessible helped define the decade; and Odd was there to write about it.

After the *Titanic* disaster and then through the First World War, radios were primarily for military use. The first real broadcast directed at non-military personnel took place in 1920, and covered the results of the election that ushered Warren G. Harding into the White House. After that, Americans became obsessed with the radio, and soon manufacturers added speakers that allowed people to listen together, rather than having to use headphones. Almost overnight, gathering together around the radio became a ritual among families of all income levels in large cities, small towns, and rural areas alike. By 1925, there were more than four million radios in homes across the country, with more than six hundred stations broadcasting news, music, sports, entertainment programs and, of course, lots of advertising.

Odd listened to one of the earliest New York stations, WMCA, that broadcast from a circular, glass-enclosed studio on the twenty-fourth floor of the McAlpin Hotel at Broadway and Thirty-Fourth Street. Using the slogan "Where the Searchlight Flashes and the White Way Begins," the station aired a variety of content, from New York Giants baseball games and lectures on Christian Science, to music by bandleader Rudy Vallee and one of Odd's favorites, singer and comedian Eddie Cantor. The Radio Corporation of America, known as RCA, broadcast across the street from the New York Public Library from a tower on the roof

Freeman Gosden playing Amos Jones and Charles Correll playing Andy Brown on the radio program *Amos & Andy. Courtesy Library of Congress Prints and Photographs Division*

of Aeolian Hall, twenty-one stories above West Forty-Second Street. At the top of the radio antenna was a metal ornamental globe that cast a shadow across Fifth Avenue.

The jazz revolution that was taking place in cities from New Orleans to Chicago to New York could also be heard live on the radio. Each week, WHN broadcast programs from the Cotton Club, a "whites-only" nightclub run by gangster Owney Madden in New York's Harlem neighborhood. It catered to an upper-class clientele thirsty for illegal booze, beautiful girls, and great music. While the audiences were all white, the entertainers were mostly black. Jazz musicians like Fletcher Henderson, Duke Ellington, Louie Armstrong, Ethel Waters, Billie Holiday, and many others appeared at the club and contributed to the popularity and growth of the genre.

The music from Tin Pan Alley that Odd had promoted just a few years earlier could now be heard far beyond its original New York neighborhood. In 1925, favorites among radio listeners included Cole Porter's "I'm in Love Again," Irving Berlin's "Remember," and brothers Ira and George Gershwin's "That Certain Feeling."

While New York was certainly a hotbed of broadcasting, the beauty of radio was that it could originate from anywhere. On the other side of the country, the Warner brothers had no intention of being left behind. In March 1925, their new radio station began broadcasting from its studio lot on Sunset Boulevard in Hollywood. It was used to spotlight the various entertainers Warner Bros. was featuring in its movies. In an effort to put their existing movie production facilities to use, they experimented with placing a microphone on movie sets so audiences could listen in as the movies were made.

As they discovered, people loved hearing the stories as much as they enjoyed seeing them on the big screen. Very quickly, dramas like *Amos 'n' Andy* kept audiences entertained with serial programming for which they would return day after day. *Amos 'n' Andy* featured white actors Freeman Gosden and Charles Correll as two black men, Amos Jones and Andy H. Brown. It's hard to comprehend just how popular it was at the time.

Today, it may seem like a show filled with racist overtones and clichés of African-American life during that period, but at the time, it was a big hit with both black and white audiences. Movie theaters began turning the show on in the lobby when it aired, to keep people from going home to listen to the radio. Just four months after the show first aired, it had more than forty million listeners every single evening. A *New York Times* review of *The Adventures of Amos 'n' Andy, a Social History of the American Phenomenon* summed up the universal appeal of the show:

> *Unlike most blackface characters, those in 'Amos 'n' Andy' reflected many values common to lower middle-class Americans. White audiences could empathize with the universal aspects of the experiences of the black people depicted on the program—financial problems, personal relationships, even reactions to contemporary events—while laughing at their supposed ethnic traits. As Mr. Ely points out, Gosden and Correll walked a tightrope, plying white audiences with traditional racial stereotypes but cleverly muting their harsher overtones.*[215]

Odd himself had little time to listen to the radio, and knew little about the actors other than the fact that they had created a national phenomenon. He wrote a feature on *Amos 'n' Andy* for *Cosmopolitan*, in which he noted, "In less than a year, they have become the outstanding marvels of the radio world—supreme minstrels of the air whose homely philosophy of the commonplace has made them beloved in almost every household in the land."[216] To write the feature, he sat down with the two performers in his living room for an interview that lasted about an hour. He began the interview in hopes they could explain to him what they were doing to create this radio program that had everyone hooked, but Gosden and Correll were just as confused over their success as Odd. He wrote, "In all my years of interviewing successes, accidental and deserved, I never saw more conspicuous examples of complete bewilderment. They act as if they were holding something that would at any moment explode in their hands."[217]

A big question among those working in the news and entertainment industries was whether people would really spend money at the movie theaters if they could listen to entertainment like *Amos 'n' Andy* for free in their homes. Others worried about whether the public would stop reading newspapers and magazines if they were spending all their time going to the movies and listening to the radio. There was no question these new sources of entertainment were killing vaudeville. Mass media was undergoing rapid change, whether people in the business liked it or not. Some were able to adapt and take advantage of the new transformative technologies, while others were not, and their businesses and careers eventually failed.

As Odd's former boss Benjamin B. Hampton wrote in the first sentence of his book, *A History of the Movies*, "Many men, through many years, searched for ways to make pictures appear to move."[218] By the mid-1920s, they had and there were more than 20,000 movie theaters in the United States alone. For a nickel, the audience could watch a short showing of a silent reel of film, frequently accompanied by a piano. At first, nickelodeons appealed to a working-class audience, but after effective storytelling became part of the moving picture production process, they became popular with every sex, age, and income and in every part of the country. Rich and poor, young and old, men and women, everyone loved the moving picture show.

Small storefronts were no longer suitable for growing audiences, so large, ornate movie palaces were built and huge organs were installed, along with room for orchestras to provide the soundtrack for the stories taking place on the large screens. In 1914, Odd watched the Strand Theater being built in Manhattan at 1579 Broadway. Costing a million dollars to build, it was unlike anything New Yorkers had seen before. *The Brooklyn Daily Eagle* reported:

The Strand, the new $1,000,000 theater at Broadway and 47th, said to be the largest and most luxurious photo drama theater in the world, and the first of its kind erected in New York City, will open its doors to the general public on Saturday night at 7 o'clock, and the performance will commence at 8:30 p.m. The premier will be devoted to an invited audience representing the celebrities of every walk of life in the metropolis as well as the general public. A revelation in constructive and decorative beauty is promised when the Strand is opened. Every modern device for public comfort and safety has been incorporated. The building is fireproof in every respect and the auditorium will seat almost 3,500 people...In addition to the two organs built in the theater, there will be an orchestra of twenty-five players and a quartet of grand opera singers...The picture story chosen to open the theater is the Selig photo drama of Rex Beach's novel, 'The Spoilers.'[219]

In a post-war patriotic flourish, the article added, "It is an American story by an American author, produced in America for the premier of the biggest American photo drama theater, which was also built by Americans with American capital."[220]

The Warner brothers embraced radio, even though at first they saw it as a promotional tool for their movies rather than as an independent medium. With the slogan "Movieland—Lights, Camera, Action," they

The audience preparing to enter Warners' Theatre before the premiere of *Don Juan* starring John Barrymore. *National Archives and Records Administration*

capitalized on the country's new love of the silver screen and used radio to create a demand for their moving pictures.

While the movies were a huge success, it was frustrating that the technology did not allow audiences to hear what was happening on screen. Of all the Warner brothers—Harry, Al, Sam, and Jack—it was Sam Warner who had most championed the radio station, and who had been the most involved in its development. Although it was impossible at the time to sync audio and video, recorded sound at least allowed the audience to have some sound along with the moving pictures. But when Western Electric demonstrated a new technology for syncing audio with film, Sam Warner knew he had found what he had been looking for. Initially called "Vitaphone movies" and dismissed as a fad, the technology allowed audiences to finally hear what was happening on screen.

The first Warner Bros. Vitaphone movie, *Don Juan*, was released in 1926 and starred John Barrymore. The audio for the film, recorded by the New York Philharmonic, was an instant success. After its premiere at Warner's Theater in New York, a reviewer for *The New York Times* wrote, "A marvelous devise known as the vitaphone, which synchronizes sounds with motion pictures, stirred a distinguished audience in Warner's Theater to unusual enthusiasm at its initial presentation Thursday evening."[221]

Before the movie, the audience enjoyed a variety of acts including a Vitaphone recording of Odd's close friend Will Hayes, who was president of the Motion Picture Producers and Distributors of America. The recording featured Hayes delivering a speech congratulating the developers and the Warner brothers on the technological achievement of sound combined with moving pictures. *The New York Times* reviewer noted, "There was no muffled utterance or lisping in the course of the talk; it was the voice of Hays, and had any of his friends closed their eyes to his picture on the screen they would have immediately recognized the voice. Every syllable was audible and clear."[222]

That same year, Warner Bros. released other Vitaphone movies, including *Broken Hearts of Hollywood* featuring Douglas Fairbanks Jr. and Louise Dresser, *While London Sleeps* starring Rin Tin Tin, and several others that featured a musical score and sound effects.

Just like other areas of popular culture, fashion trends of the 1920s changed almost overnight, especially for those living in metropolitan areas.

More expendable income and access to shopping, along with an increase in the availability of newspapers, magazines, radio, and movies—and a thriving advertising industry—meant that men and women could see how they should look, and where they could buy the clothing and accessories to look that way.

A dramatic increase in exposure to celebrities and the clothes they wore also greatly contributed to the fashion trends of that day. From Coco Chanel's little black dress and Clara Bow's flapper ensembles, to Louise Brooks' bobbed hair and Pola Negri's fur boots, female celebrities were setting fashion trends that women around the country were following. And men were no different; Rudolph Valentino inspired them to slick their hair back, while Charles Lindberg's popularity resulted in the sale of hundreds of thousands of leather jackets. Hats were important and men wore top hats, newsboy caps, or the black bowler hat popularized by Charlie Chaplin.

For someone who often referred to himself as a "hick," Odd had a very unique sense of personal style, and he lived in the most fashionable city in the United States. He wrote, "Today I'll still follow a snappy dresser along New York streets in the manner of a dog following a covered wagon."[223] He frequently wrote of his tendency to wear bright colors and patterns, and claimed his friends said his taste in clothes was atrocious. He described his wardrobe as "a cross between a Harlem sheik and a circus parade gone wrong."[224]

Friend Irvin Cobb wrote that Odd's style of dress caught the blinking eye the way P. T. Barnum's funeral must have. He wrote, "He's the kind who will go into a tailor shop and pick out something suitable for a fancy vest and then have a whole suit made of it." However, he added, "People say he is a striking figure and most distinguished-looking and all such drivel, and, doggone me, much as I hate to confess it, the skinny, gray-headed scoundrel somehow or another is just that."[225]

Novelist Rupert Hughes remembered running into Odd one day as he was stepping out of Delmonico's restaurant at Fifth Avenue and Forty-Fourth Street. He was so startled by Odd's gray-checked suit, white spats and "audacious" hat, he gasped. "Good Lord, Mr. McIntyre, you look like a professional gambler!" Ray Long later told him he couldn't have paid Odd a higher compliment.[226]

Odd could write about the fancy clothes he was wearing in such a humble way, it appealed even to those who would never wear a cravat or carry a walking stick. In one instance, he wrote of having lunch in that oval-shaped dining room of the Ritz-Carlton. When he heard the sounds of a "fire wagon" outside, he ran to the window. Although he carried a walking stick and wore spats, a rather "modish" suit, a cravat that blended with his brightly-colored shirt, and a pearl-white hat, the excitement of a potential fire still held a thrill for him, because it had only been twenty years since he had been "yanked from the south end of a north-bound plow."[227] He may have looked like a "city slicker" on the outside, but he was telling his readers, "Beneath it all, I'm just like you."

Comments about what he saw both men and women wearing in New York were frequently woven into his column

Odd McIntyre's personal sense of style combined urban sophistication with a unique flair that usually caused him to stand out in a crowd. Spats, a top hat, and a cane became part of his public identity. *The Gallia County Historical Society*

and magazine articles, and he could be counted on to share his opinions. For example, although he wore white spats, he wrote, "The white spats of the New Yorker are more than a bit of gaudy fashion clap-trap. They are a symbol, and the transplanted yokel is in reality trying to live up to that symbol. About him are fellows trying to live up to the monocle, the valet, and the silk hat."[228]

From color and fabrics to accessories, Odd was somehow able to write about the topic in a way that did not alienate his primary audience of middle Americans. Even something as simple as the sudden prevalence of the color brown, became more interesting when covered by Odd:

This winter the prevailing note in men's clothes was brown. And to what length it was carried! Brown the shade of an autumn leaf, brown of deep mahogany, rust-brown, walnut-stain brown, tobacco-brown and chocolate. Brown scarves, walking sticks, hats with tiny brown feathers in the side, brown shoes, brown shirts and collars—'kerchiefs. Spats, cuff buttons and even the wrist watch straps were toned in with the general ensemble. By spring the prevailing color may be a Mediterranean-blue and should it be, the veteran chameleons will be doing their stuff.[229]

Although he always wore the latest trends himself, he often wrote as though he were as puzzled by fashion as those who were reading his column. "You can't keep up with the fashion makers who keep the style in the hollow of their head," he wrote. "The seasonal styles started off atrociously. Every hat had a feathered gadget in the band. Then the feather pickers went on strike or something and now the classy dressers are wearing little tufts of color ribbon where feathers once sprouted." And as though all his readers were, like him, struggling to keep up with the latest fashion trends, he added, "Be brave men!"[230]

He also frequently mentioned the fashions he observed his friends and associates wearing. Flo Ziegfeld wore "riotous shirts and screaming cravats," Charles Schwab appeared at the Ritz for lunch "with a carnation in his coat lapel, a wing collar with flaring polka-dot bow tie," while Irvin Cobb was "regally enthroned in a house gown of deep silken purple with gray cord and lapels and two-toned chevalier house boots to match." Odd wrote that for several nights in a row he stood at the stage entrance of the old Century Theater at Sixty-Second Street and Central Park West just to watch Vernon Castle "saunter out in a milk white suit and lavender sport shirt."

Odd also pointed out when the shirt-waist evening frock for women was the "hoop-de-doo" of the moment, as he called it, or when canes for women came into fashion, but went out again almost immediately. He wrote, "A lady's cane shop opened as a tribute to the new fashion. It was not the fad of the flapper who flits lightly from one fashion foible to another…no one seems to know why the craze was so short lived."[231]

Odd also covered sports. In the 1920s, no sport provided more spectacle and drama than boxing. The popularity of the sport grew quickly and some boxers became household names. The biggest matches were built up in the media for weeks and drew thousands of fans, while hundreds of thousands more listened on the radio. Boxing's appeal was lost on Odd, however—he felt it was symbolic of a "thin veneer of civilization allowing something ugly to peep through."

What Odd could relate to was an underdog's struggle for success. He loved a David and Goliath story, and he found a little bit of David in boxer Gene Tunney. They met in the winter of 1925, when they were both staying at the same luxury resort. It was the opening of racing season, and Odd and Maybelle were on the clubhouse veranda socializing with Biltmore Hotel founder and avid horseman John M. Bowman, Florence Ziegfeld's wife Billie Burke, politician and activist Dudley Malone, dancer Irene Castle, and others. Odd decided to step outside for a moment and ran into Tunney. Born in Greenwich Village, Tunney had been small as a boy, but turned to boxing as a way to defend himself against neighborhood bullies. While in France with the Marine Corps during World War I, he won the American Expeditionary Forces heavyweight championship. After returning to the United States after the war, he won several major fights, including the light heavyweight championship. He was known to spend hours studying and learning about the strengths and weaknesses of each opponent and, in addition to preparing physically and mentally, he focused on the technical aspects of boxing.

That day at the resort, Odd admired Tunney's white golf outfit and cap, while the well-read Tunney was excited to meet someone whose column he read in the newspaper. As the two talked, they noticed a flurry of activity taking place at the entrance to the veranda. They walked closer and realized boxer Jack Dempsey and his entourage had arrived. Dempsey had been the world heavyweight champion since 1919 and was one of the most popular athletes in the world at the time. When he wasn't winning boxing matches, "Kid Blackie" as he was nicknamed, made public appearances, staged boxing exhibitions, and even appeared in a movie. Tunney had met Dempsey shortly after Dempsey won the heavyweight championship, when the two happened to be on the same ferryboat. Tunney began to study the champion's moves and was ringside at his matches every chance he got.

As Odd and Tunney stood watching Dempsey's dramatic entrance at the club veranda, Tunney whispered to Odd, "There's the champion."

He then explained to Odd that they knew each other, and stepped back a little as though Dempsey needed even more room to pass by. Odd watched as Dempsey came closer and Tunney prepared to greet the champion, but Dempsey only glared at Tunney as he passed by without stopping, and gave not even a flicker of recognition. Odd was embarrassed for the young boxer, but Tunney just said, "Perhaps he didn't recognize me."

Odd and Tunney saw each other frequently that winter. At one dinner party, Tunney was in the corner playing checkers with another guest while several others tried to remember a quotation from English poet Samuel Taylor Coleridge. One of the guests whom Odd referred to as a "rather boorish Englishman," sarcastically said, "Perhaps Mr. Tunney will enlighten us." Tunney surprised the others and thrilled Odd when he recited the quotation in full, and then shared the meaning.

On September 23, 1926, Gene Tunney's preparation and determination paid off when he defeated Jack Dempsey at the Sesquicentennial Stadium in Philadelphia and won the world heavyweight title. In December, Odd wrote a column about the young boxer titled "My Friend Gene Tunney."

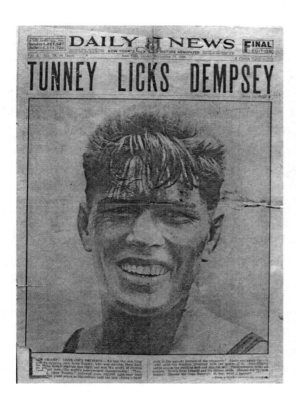

Portrait of Gene Tunney, *The Harris & Ewing Collection, Library of Congress*

The September 24, 1926 issue of the New York *Daily News* that featured challenger Gene Tunney's defeat of Heavyweight Champion Jack Dempsey at Sesquicentennial Stadium in Philadelphia.

In the article, Odd focused on Tunney's humility, hard work, and dedication to his family. He wrote, "He convinced me of something I have not always believed. That is that a man can be a prize-fighter and also a scholar and a gentleman."[232]

Odd's readers also knew he could write about both the best New York restaurants of the day, and the ones that were long gone. Of one such restaurant, he remembered, "Many sturdy eating havens now are shuttered. Among them is Daly's, so long on West 59th Street. It employed peroxided waitresses who, after several visits, might call a patron 'Dearie.' The proprietor drifted from table to table and inquired about things."[233]

Readers also counted on Odd to let them know where they could spot a celebrity in New York. A mention in his column usually resulted in a bustle of tourists at the restaurant looking for a celebrity. He wrote, "Dinty Moore's Café has suddenly become one of the celebrity luncheon places, along with the Algonquin and Sardi's. Among those I saw lunching there recently were Anita Loos, John Gilbert, Gilbert Miller, Edgar Selwyn, Major Bowes, Arthur Hornblow, Marjorie Oelrichs and Joe Schenck."[234]

Odd made sure his readers from out of town who visited the city never left New York hungry. He put his stamp of approval on the minestrone soup at Moneta's on Mulberry Street, the beef à la mode at Fraunces Tavern at Pearl and Broad, the frog legs at Ben Riley's Arrowhead Inn on Depot Lane, the pig knuckles and sauerkraut at Luchows' over near Union Square, the filet of sole at the Pierre Hotel off Fifth Avenue, the Coney Island hot dog at Feltman's, the fried pork chops at Manny's on Fourth Street, and the spaghetti at Sardi's over in the basement at 246 West Forty-Fourth Street.

Odd McIntyre's New York was crackling with excitement and the energy of change. The bands were loud, the women beautiful, and the food delicious. And it was even better because—as Odd saw it—every restaurant was full of celebrities. He loved knowing the rich and the famous and loved writing about them even more. He admitted, "If I see Charlie Chaplin on the street, I turn and follow him until he is swallowed up by his hotel or wherever he's going."[235]

On some occasions, his admiration would turn into real friendship. Such was the case with the silent film actor who came to be known as "the Latin lover," Rudolph Valentino.

16

Rudolph Valentino

Valentino said to me, 'It sometimes worries me that you might think that, because I invite you to the first showings of my films with me, I am seeking a little publicity through the things you write. It would please me if you would never mention me in any of your articles. I would like to think our friendship transcends that.' He was tremendously sincere and, until he died, I never mentioned him after that until his passing.[236]

O. O. McIntyre

As he had befriended the stars of Broadway, the *Follies*, and Tin Pan Alley, Odd was also quick to support those who captured the nation's attention on the big screen. Among his closest friends in the early 1920s was Rudolph Valentino, one of the most popular actors of the early twentieth century, and the first male actor to rise to the status of icon.

He emigrated from Southern Italy to New York in 1913 at the age of eighteen. First living on the streets and in Central Park, he worked as a

194

Rudolph Valentino and his wife, silent film costume and set designer Natacha Rambova in a 1922 photo by photojournalist and early celebrity photographer James Abbe. *The Billy Rose Theater Division, The New York Public Library*

tango dancer, and later performed on the vaudeville circuit. After a move to Hollywood and a series of roles in silent films, Valentino experienced his first major success in 1921 in *The Four Horsemen of the Apocalypse*. Directed by Rex Ingram, the silent movie was a huge success and became the top-grossing movie of 1921, beating out Charlie Chaplin's *The Kid*. It became the sixth best-grossing silent film of all time. Valentino's role of Julio, a young heir to an Argentinean cattle baron, included a smoldering tango scene which, when combined with the performance in his next role, *The Sheik*, turned Valentino into a superstar. He was forever typecast as the brooding, irresistible lover. His performance inspired a tango craze in the United States, launched fashion trends like gaucho pants, and was responsible for a sudden increase of Latin influences in American art and interior design.

After a rocky first marriage, Valentino fell in love with costume and set designer Natacha Rambova while working on his movie, Camille. Although still not divorced from his first wife, Valentino and Rambova had a quick wedding in Mexico in 1922, after which Valentino was arrested and charged with bigamy. He then publicly battled his studio for better compensation, as he was making the studio a great deal of money while being paid very little. He was sued by the studio and was

(top) Promotional photo of Valentino and Agnes Ayres for the 1921 silent film, *The Sheik*. (bottom) Promotional photo of Valentino for the 1922 silent film *Blood and Sand*.

unable to continue making films until his contract ended. The celebrity lifestyle was expensive even then, and Valentino had spent everything he had made.

It was during this period in the mid-1920s that Odd met Valentino in Chicago and, as Odd noticed, Valentino may have been down but he wasn't out. He and his wife took time off from making movies to go on a United States tango tour sponsored by Mineralava Beauty Clay. Odd later admitted that until he met Valentino in person, he had assumed the worst about the actor. What he discovered was that Valentino was extremely humble and quite insecure about his fame. Complete awareness of his success never quite sank in for the man who came across as so confident and sure of himself on film.

Odd joined Valentino at a screening of one of his movies that had provided a rare opportunity for the actor to try his hand at comedy. While the audience was laughing, up in the curtained box where the stars of the movie and VIPs were sitting, Odd glanced over and noticed the actor looked terrified as he waited motionless for the reaction of the audience after each of his lines.

While Odd and Valentino seemed to have very little in common, somehow they became great friends. It's possible that Odd's struggle for success appealed in some way to Valentino who shared many of his own problems with the columnist. After Valentino's death, Odd wrote that his friend came to him many times "perplexed, harassed, and soul-spent— but never defeated." He added, "His courage was boundless."[237]

Valentino often made fun of Odd's flashy clothes. Occasionally, Odd would open his mail to find a cheap

July 1922 cover of *Photoplay* magazine featuring an illustration of Valentino as Julio in *Four Horsemen of the Apocalypse* by artist Tempest Inman.

197

clip-on tie that Valentino had mailed from some exotic port of call that was, in Odd's words, "the color of poisonous wallpaper." Valentino had a great sense of humor. He was once invited to the McIntyre's house for a gathering on a warm summer evening and, anticipating the loudness of Odd's outfit, he arrived wearing fur earmuffs.

Odd appreciated Valentino's sense of humor, but what most impressed him about his friend was his humility. One evening, Odd and Maybelle arrived at the Ritz-Carlton with Valentino and Natacha Rambova. As they stood talking in front of their car, a crowd began gathering to get a glimpse of the superstar. As the crowd grew larger and noisier, Valentino leaned in and whispered to Odd, "I think something must have happened at your hotel." He had no idea that the "something at the hotel" was his arrival.

After the release and huge success of *The Eagle* in 1925 and *The Son of the Sheik* in 1926, Valentino was at the height of his stardom, and many reviewers claimed his performance in *The Son of the Sheik* was the best acting of his career.

A few months after the opening of *The Son of the Sheik*, Valentino collapsed in his suite at the Ambassador Hotel in New York and was rushed to the hospital. After an operation to remove his appendix and treat gastric ulcers, his prognosis was good. Sadly, eight days later, on August 23, 1926, an infection would take his young life. At 3:30 a.m., Valentino looked up at his doctor and asked, "Doctor, do you know the greatest thing I am looking forward to?" He smiled and continued, "I am looking forward to going fishing with you next month. I hope you have plenty of fishing rods. Mine are all in California."

Odd always felt Valentino was greatly misunderstood, so it was ironic that his actual last words were in Italian so no one present knew what he had said. Valentino slipped into a coma and died a few hours later. He was only thirty-one years old.

Celebrity news coverage, especially of the death of someone as well-known as Valentino, was still very new. The spectacle in the days following his death took everyone involved by surprise, and is one of the earliest examples of the ugly side of fame.

As his body lay in state at the Frank Campbell Funeral Parlor at Broadway and Sixty-sixth Street in Manhattan, more than 100,000 fans crowded the streets around the building. Women were said to have torn at their clothes and collapsed because of their grief. Rumors

A crowd gathered at the Frank Campbell Funeral Home to view the body of Rudolph Valentino.

that several young women around the country had committed suicide began to spread.

Valentino and Natacha Rambova had divorced in 1925 and Valentino had been dating both *Ziegfeld Follies* showgirl Marion Wilson Benda and Polish actress Pola Negri. With her well-deserved reputation as a diva, Negri added to the theatrics around Valentino's funeral. Wearing layers of flowing, black silk, with much of her face dramatically covered by veils, she fainted multiple times in the days surrounding his death and funeral, usually when there were cameras around. At one point she threw herself on his coffin, hysterically sobbing. For Valentino's funeral, Negri spent a small fortune on a huge blanket of 4,000 blood-red roses with white roses in the middle that spelled out "Pola."

Valentino's open casket was on display for the public to pass by and pay their respects. Throughout the day, more than ninety thousand people came with the hopes of seeing Valentino's body. When his manager, George Ullman, walked outside among the fans waiting in the drizzle, he noticed many of them were joking and laughing, not at all mourning his friend's death. After he observed what he called a "sordid, disgusting, irreverent...sorry spectacle, a sort of vulgar circus affair to which the public showing had been reduced,"[238] he had the doors to the funeral home shut and ended the viewing permanently. A few hours later, the hundreds who still waited became angry and the crowd slowly grew to thousands as others began gathering to observe the spectacle created by a combination of angry fans and trouble-makers. Just before midnight, the police began trying to drive away the crowds to avoid a riot, but a small group of about a hundred broke through the police barricades and made it into the building. However, Valentino's coffin had already been removed. A public funeral procession that had been planned in New York was canceled, and the body was sent to California for the funeral. Held at St. Malachi's Catholic Church, that was also known as the Actor's Church, the services were open to only a small group of Valentino's friends including Mary Pickford, Douglas Fairbanks, and Gloria Swanson. No press was invited, but Gloria Swanson's husband, Henry de La Falaise, found a photographer for the *Daily Mirror* hiding in the church choir loft. He grabbed the photographer and forcibly threw him down the stairs of the church, shattering his camera.

Rudolph Valentino was the first movie star to achieve a level of iconic celebrity that only increased after his early death. In the years to come, that list would grow to include others like James Dean, Marilyn Monroe, Elvis Presley, and Bob Marley.

The last conversation Odd had with Valentino before his died took place in Paris just a few months earlier. Odd, Maybelle, and Maybelle's mother were staying in an apartment at 22 Avenue Henri Martin for a few months. As the sun set, Odd sat on a bench with Valentino, who was also in Paris at the time, watching the Eiffel Tower in the distance while discussing their latest projects and exchanging gossip about their mutual friends. Eventually, it was time to say good-bye. Odd's last memory of Valentino was watching him "swing down the Avenue des Champs-Elysées with his head held high."

When George Ullman wrote a book about Valentino in 1926, he asked Odd to write the foreword. In remembering his friend who made such a lasting impression on the world in such short time, Odd wrote:

> *As I write these lines to my friend, I think of those far worthier lines of*
> *Edna St. Vincent Millay:*
> *My candle burns at both ends;*
>   *It will not last the night;*
> *But ah, my foes, and oh, my friends—*
>   *It gives a lovely light!* [239]

17

Friends

A truism about friendship is this: Firmness and age, as with trees, only flourish in good soil. That's why crooks never remain pals long. Thinnest friendships are gushiest. And bustling geniality is always unstable... enduring friendships are bulwarked in the Ruth and Naomi saga: 'Wither thou goest, etc.' I haven't a surplus of such loyalty. But it does exist."[240]

O. O. McIntyre

Although he always had a special appreciation for those in the publishing industry, Odd McIntyre met a lot of successful people who worked in a variety of fields, and many of them considered him a friend. People like iconic businessmen Messmore Kendall and Charles Schwab, movie czar Will Hayes, radio announcer and war correspondent Frazier Hunt, bandleader Paul Whiteman, editor Robert H. Davis, and restaurateurs like James "Dinty" Moore all had warm relationships with Odd.

Everyone knew he could be counted on to be there in times of need. He and Maybelle's apartment was the first place theatrical producer and

Odd and Maybelle and friends at one of the many parties they attended in the 1920s. At this New Year's Eve party, Maybelle (bottom row, center) is sitting between George Gershwin and Rube Goldberg (reclining), while Odd is on the back row (third from right) along with Roy Howard and Ray Long (fifth and seventh from right). Groucho Marx is on the bottom row in the far right of the photo. *The Esther Allen Greer Museum at the University of Rio Grande*

composer Earl Carroll went for breakfast after completing a six-month sentence in an Atlanta prison. Carroll was one of the early celebrities to learn the hard way, it isn't the crime, it's lying about it that will send you to jail. He was convicted of perjury after lying about a party he had given in which the centerpiece was a nude woman bathing in a tub filled with illegal booze.

Odd frequently loaned friends money, even when he knew he most likely wouldn't be repaid. He also loved to connect people in one business with those in another, in an effort to help them both.

The autographed photos on the wall of Odd's home included one from Charlie Chaplin, who wrote "To O. O. McIntyre, a man who sees and feels the passing show." The inscription on a photo from William Randolph Hearst read, "To O. O. McIntyre who has an amazing ability to delight everyone and offend no one. From his admiring associate and friend." On her photo to Odd, comedienne Sophie Tucker wrote, "Dear O. O. McIntyre, Please may I be one of the many to grace the walls of your memory room. Love and Regards." Bandleader Paul Whiteman signed his, "To my best press agent from the world's worst fiddler."

Odd knew everybody who was anybody in New York, and during the years when things were going well, he and Maybelle spent nearly every night eating in the best restaurants, seeing the best plays, and attending parties of the rich and famous. But there were only a few individuals with whom he became truly close. At the top of that list were humorists and actors Irvin S. Cobb and Will Rogers, and philanthropist William Clifford Hogg.

After a number of years on the forefront of the business of celebrity, Odd was no longer as impressed by fame as he was on that first bus ride down Fifth Avenue. He was now more likely to be drawn to quiet displays of humility and the confidence that came from those who had talent to back up their celebrity. Odd recounted a story in which he was at a Hollywood party where Charlie Chaplin was the "fair-haired boy" of the evening. Odd was not a fan of Chaplin at the time and considered him "overrated." As he observed the guests crowding around the celebrated actor, he also noticed a solitary, shy stranger sitting in the corner. He wrote, "Chaplin turned from his clowning and settled himself in a chair beside the abashed guest…soon they had their heads together and were indulging in mutual laughter." He added, "It was a big evening for the visitor, as well as a heartening gesture from a reigning celebrity."[241]

An early publicity photo of Charlie Chaplin.

Afterward, he became one of Chaplin's biggest fans.

Odd was usually inclined to become closest to those who, like he and Cobb, proudly proclaimed their rural heritage. Odd loved the fact that, although he was a literary legend, Cobb still called a window a "winder" and put the accent on "po" in policemen.[242]

Cobb was born in Paducah, Kentucky in 1876, and by age nineteen was managing editor of the Paducah Daily News. In 1904, he moved to New York, where he became a staff writer for Joseph Pulitzer's New York *World*. Cobb achieved success through his syndicated newspaper articles, the stories he wrote for magazines like *Cosmopolitan* and the *Saturday Evening Post*, and his more than sixty books. He honed his skills working as a reporter, but found his greatest success when he shifted to storytelling through other mediums. In 1916, his stories about a fictional, mint julep-loving judge in West Kentucky named William Pitman Bishop were compiled in a book, *Old Judge Priest*, that became a bestseller and was later turned into a film starring Will Rogers.

Many of Cobb's books, articles, and short stories were turned into silent films, and he even made the move to the other side of

the camera, appearing in ten movies. Cobb was at the right place, at the right time, with a unique look that allowed him to perform certain character roles for which there was no equal in Hollywood. With a rotund shape, large fleshy jowls, bushy eyebrows, and fish-like mouth, that often held one of his ever-present cigars, Cobb was instantly recognizable, and unlike anyone else working on early Hollywood movie sets. His years of experience as a journalist and writer, and a deep intelligence that was somewhat unexpected given his physical appearance, made him one of the most entertaining

A portrait of Irvin Cobb taken by photographer Clifford Lutter. *Jody Lutter*

Irvin Cobb
presenting Shirley
Temple with a
miniaturized
version of the
Oscar at the
seventh annual
Academy Awards
in 1935.
*Academy of
Motion Picture Arts
and Sciences*

celebrities of the day. Odd once noted that Cobb was the only writer
he knew who could face an audience in a theater and "run away with
the show." That ability came in handy when Cobb hosted the seventh
annual Academy Awards in 1935 at the Biltmore Hotel in Los Angeles.
Frank Capra's romantic comedy, *It Happened One Night*, won the top five
awards, including best actor and actress for Clark Gable and Claudette
Colbert. Also that year, Shirley Temple became the youngest actress to
receive an Oscar when Cobb presented her with a miniaturized version
of the statue.

For Odd, Cobb's success in Hollywood was less impressive than his
connection to the journalism of days gone by. In the foreword for a book
about Cobb written in 1938, Odd wrote:

Early vaudeville promotional photo of Will Rogers. *The Library of Congress Prints and Photographs Division*

To me he is one of the last links with an honorable writing era, representative of a day when there were no gutter tabloidism, keyhole peeping and reputation-wrecking journalism. He belonged to the illustrious period when clean-minded newspapermen drank their rye neat at the Martinique and Doc Perry's, got drunk like gentlemen and took over the line of the cab driver for a spin up Broadway as a red sun bleared an eye over Manhattan…what we newspapermen like about Cobb is that he prefers to remain a newspaper reporter.[243]

The admiration was mutual. Cobb was possibly one of the biggest fans of Odd's writing. About Odd, he observed, "He rarely says anything clever out loud, but when he sits down at his typewriter, along with the rest of the grist, out comes cleverness by the ream—and it's not always surface smartness, either, which so abundantly clatters forth; but frequently is the aptly-phrased expressions of a sound philosophy and a very shrewd, very canny gift of observation, plus a gorgeous sense of human sympathy and human charity."[244]

While both Odd McIntyre and Irvin Cobb merely reminded their fans

Will Rogers and Irvin Cobb from Odd's personal collection of photographs. *The Esther Allen Greer Museum at the University of Rio Grande*

that their feet were firmly planted in their rural upbringing, their mutual friend, Will Rogers, used his western roots to catapult himself into fame.

William Penn Adair Rogers was born in 1879 to a prominent Cherokee Nation family in what is now Oklahoma. Rogers performed his cowboy act on stages around the world, wrote books, newspaper columns and magazine articles, performed on the radio, and made more than seventy movies. By the early 1930s, he was the highest-paid movie star and, without a doubt, one of the most famous men in the world.

Odd first became friends with Will Rogers when they were both working for Ziegfeld and Rogers was one of the acts performing in the *Midnight Frolic*. They continued to cross paths professionally, and eventually became close friends.

Odd was privileged to experience a side of Rogers that only a few got to see; he referred to it as a "divine comedy that cannot be transplanted to the stage, screen, radio, or printed word."[245] Odd felt Rogers was at his best "with a napkin tucked in his badly fitting collar and squared off before a bowl of chili in some hole-in-the-wall beanery."

In October 1931, Odd wrote a column about Rogers for *Cosmopolitan*, that celebrated his friend's humility in the face of his great fame. He began, "Living as I do in the perfumed purlieus of a city where a fevered army of climbers, social, political and financial, indulge in a constant and heartbreaking struggle to scale the heights, I am always perked up by the thought of a Will Rogers."[246]

Odd recounted numerous examples of his first-hand observations of Rogers being just like "regular folks." Odd spent time with Rogers and his family at their home in California, gossiped with him in Hollywood dressing rooms, walked with him along London's Strand, and bunked with him at a political convention. Odd and Rogers attended the 1928 Democratic convention in Houston, Texas, at which New Yorker Alfred E. Smith was nominated to run against Republican Herbert Hoover, who won the election.

That night, Rogers, who was always fidgety, began to get on Odd's nerves. During the proceedings, Odd wrote, Rogers "snaps his jaw 100 times a minute and when he is not wiggling his feet, he is shifting from one hip to another or rolling a lead pencil between his palms." Finally Odd could take no more and leaned over and whispered, "If you can't sit still, go home."[247]

(top, left to right) Will Rogers, Irvin Cobb, Emma Kerns, Odd McIntyre, and Will Hayes spending the day at Rogers' California ranch. *The Esther Allen Greer Museum at the University of Rio Grande* (bottom) The group prepares for a ride on Roger' new buggy. *The Will Rogers Memorial Museums*

In the spring of 1933, Odd and Maybelle decided to take Maybelle's eighty-one-year-old aunt, Emma Kerns, to Hollywood. They spent part of their trip at the Rogers' Santa Monica ranch with an interesting group of friends. In addition to Will and Betty Rogers, the guest list included

Will Hayes and his wife, Irvin Cobb and his daughter Elizabeth, and Florenz Ziegfeld's widow, actress Billie Burke. Rogers was excited to take some of the group out for a ride in his new wagon. As they headed down a road that had been recently cut into the hills on the ranch, the mule pulling the wagon began to gallop. Things really got out of control when the brake on the wagon stopped working and the mule continued to pick up speed. Fortunately, the ranch foreman was riding alongside and was able to regain control of the runaway mule. Betty Rogers, Billie Burke and Irvin Cobb had had enough of mules and wagons for the day and opted to walk back down to the ranch house.

Odd and Maybelle had great respect for Betty Rogers. Will and Betty had three children and a solid marriage, and she was a strong supporter of her husband's work. Odd wrote that if Betty Rogers shook her head after her husband tested out a performance on her, Will Rogers would return to his study to work on it until she approved.

Rogers was also an advocate for aviation and often used his own newspaper column to champion commercial air travel, still in its infancy in the early 1920s. In an article Odd wrote about Rogers for *Cosmopolitan*, he noted that, next to a bucking horse, Rogers most loved the air—much to the worry of his wife, who was trying to keep her husband on the ground. In a horrible foreshadowing of a sad day to come, Odd added, "And Mrs. Rogers is right. To lose Will Rogers not only would be a personal loss to her and many others, it would take on the proportions of a national calamity."[248]

After Rogers read a proof of the article, Odd received a telegram from him:

Thanks Odd for that piece about me in 'Cosmopolitan.' Ray Long sent me an advance proof. You sure had to tell some whoppers to make me out to be a regular fellow. It may offset the terrible opinions of some of the intellectuals. Those birds have never been able to figure out why you and I haven't starved to death long ago. If it wasn't for our own country folk we would, too. Betty joins me in best to you all. Come on out to Hollywood. It was never funnier than right now. Give Irvin my regards.[249]

Another mutual friend of Cobb, Rogers, and Odd was William C. Hogg. Odd made the acquaintance of Hogg, called Bill by his friends, around 1918 through Ray Long. One of the richest men in Texas, and a son of the state's twentieth governor, Hogg was very interested when he heard that Odd was the go-to man for theatrical publicity, and one of the few publicists the great Ziegfeld himself trusted. A few weeks after they first met, Hogg contacted Odd and asked if they could meet to discuss a sensitive topic. They met in the lobby of the Ritz-Carlton, and Odd noticed Hogg seemed nervous and more intent on tearing up a matchbox than getting around to what he wanted to ask.

William C. Hogg. *The Will Hogg Foundation*

Finally, after looking around to make sure no one was listening, he began. Hogg was a friend of Earl Carroll, who had lost a lot of money in the theater. Carroll had a new play coming out that Hogg thought could be a hit, and Carroll definitely needed one, as he was broke. Hogg knew Carroll had no money for publicity so he wanted to hire someone to promote the play, but under the condition that it never be revealed who was paying the bill. As Odd would later discover, Hogg frequently used his money to help those in need, but always anonymously. Although Odd was much too busy to take on another client, he subcontracted the work and the play was a hit. In 1922, Carroll used his significant earnings to build the Earl Carroll Theater at 753 Seventh Avenue, and remained unaware for many years the part Hogg had played in helping him survive a tough time.

In Hogg, Odd found a down-to-earth friend with whom he and Maybelle would enjoy first-class travels around the world. He could have been talking about himself when Odd described Hogg as "a human anomaly, at once cosmopolitan and the backwoods jasper."[250] Irvin Cobb described Hogg as an iceberg, because "only the craggy tip was revealed to the stranger's casual eye...he was a bundle of contradictions that clashed like cymbals."[251]

Hogg traveled to exotic locales, and owned luxurious homes and ranches in California, Houston, New York, and Mexico. He had a love of architecture, fine art, and gourmet food, as well as hunting, fishing, and cattle farming, while living the lifestyle of a gentleman rancher.

In addition to his secret philanthropy, giving away millions of dollars to education and fine arts charities, he fought for those who were less fortunate, and it was said "the soil of Texas is littered with the broken political bodies of men who had opposed him in his battles for civic righteousness."[252]

Hogg's temper and profanity were nearly as legendary among his friends as his generosity. Odd remembered a story that illustrated both sides of his friend. Hogg once became so angry at a waiter who brought cold bread to the table, he flew into a rage and, as a result, the man was fired. Feeling guilty, he then bought the waiter his own restaurant, and "tossed in a cottage for his family to boot."[253]

Hogg, Odd, and Maybelle were frequently joined on their travels by Hogg's sister, with the impossible-to-forget name, Ima Hogg. With a home and office in New York, Hogg often visited the Ritz-Carlton to spend time with Odd and Maybelle. When in town, Irvin Cobb also began joining them for a late brunch. The more time Hogg spent with them at the hotel, the more he was convinced purchasing their own apartment would provide both a better investment and a nicer quality of life for the couple. Although this wasn't the first time Odd and Maybelle had thought about moving, Charles Driscoll remembered Odd once said that if it hadn't been for Hogg, they would have spent the rest of their lives at the Ritz-Carlton.

It wasn't like Odd was afraid to spend money. In 1929, his mother-in-law, or "Mud" as he affectionately called her, suggested they buy a car rather than pay a taxi to shuttle them around the city every night. Odd thought it seemed like a good idea, so he sent Maybelle and her mother off to purchase a Rolls-Royce. Odd wrote a check for twenty thousand dollars and from then on, the McIntyres were chauffeured around the city in luxury.

One day Hogg took them to see an apartment he had picked out for them near his own on Park Avenue. At their first sign of hesitancy, he practically forced them to buy it. He knew if he waited, Odd would come up with a reason to stay put. Their new apartment building, located at 290 Park Avenue, extended from Forty-Eighth to Forty-Ninth Street. Odd and Maybelle purchased the entire sixth floor which

Maybelle holding Billy while sitting in their first Rolls-Royce limousine. *The Esther Allen Greer Museum at the University of Rio Grande*

included nine rooms and an Italian stone fireplace that extended from floor to ceiling. Odd's office, where he wrote each day, was located off the dining room in a small alcove.

This wasn't the first time Hogg used his skill of forceful persuasion on Odd. One winter, Odd's illness was hitting him even harder than usual, and Maybelle was discouraging visitors. Odd refused to leave the apartment, and had lost a considerable amount of weight. Hogg decided it was time to take matters into his own hands and get Odd to a warmer climate to recuperate. Of course, he refused to go, but Hogg wouldn't take no for an answer. He set the date and told Maybelle to be ready. He would take care of everything. The day arrived, and Hogg showed up at the Ritz-Carlton with a whole crew of movers to pack Odd and Maybelle's clothing and accessories into trunks. Odd mumbled there was no way he was going to Florida, sat down at his typewriter, and pretended not to notice the flurry of activity going on around him.

Odd and Maybelle returning home to New York after a trip to Europe. *The Esther Allen Greer Museum at the University of Rio Grande*

The movers began taking the luggage downstairs and, as the last trunk left the apartment, Maybelle picked up Billy, their deaf Boston terrier, and headed downstairs.

Finally, the room was empty except for Odd and Hogg, who said, "Come on, we're shoving off." Odd stood up, looked Hogg in the eyes and said, "You're shoving off, maybe. I'm not going anywhere." Without another word, Hogg picked Odd up like a baby and carried him to the elevator, set him down, and pushed the button to take them to the lobby. When they arrived downstairs, Odd found quite a spectacle.

Three cars were lined up and ready to go. The entourage included several servants and assistants, a cook, and two young journalists Hogg had hired to track down stories for Odd while he was in Florida. Never one to miss a detail, Hogg had even brought along a female dog as a companion for Billy.

Odd later credited that trip to Florida with saving his life.

On trips abroad, Odd was more comfortable with a routine, and preferred to stay in the same cities and hotels during most visits. However, in the summer of 1930, after spending a few weeks in Paris, Hogg convinced the couple to join him for a motor tour of Germany, Belgium, and Holland.

Vacationing with Hogg was quite an experience, and that first evening in Paris set the tone for the rest of their vacation. Hogg met them at the pier and escorted them to the brand-new, luxurious Hotel Prince de Galles on Avenue George V.

That evening, the group attended a show at the cabaret music hall Folies Bergère, and afterward, had dinner at Ciros with Hogg and the star of the show, Josephine Baker. Baker was creating a sensation with her act in which she wore little more than a skirt made from a string of bananas. A few nights later, the group, including Baker, went to a performance by Mistinguett, an iconic cabaret singer who performed at the Folies Bergère and Moulin Rouge, and was the highest-paid performer in the world at the time.

The weeks in Paris were spent visiting museums and attractions, eating in fine restaurants, and shopping. Maybelle noted in her diary several things she had purchased, including a black and pink knitted dress, a black crocodile suede bag, a silk dress for her mother, and an overcoat for Odd. Ima Hogg arrived on June 4 and, a few weeks later, they had two cars loaded down for their trip. They stopped in Liège, Belgium for the Exposition of 1930, and then explored Amsterdam, the Rhine, Frankfurt, Berlin and other cities. To commemorate the trip, Hogg gave Odd a black pearl and Maybelle a sapphire vanity case.

The McIntyres and Kate Small returned to New York, while Hogg and his sister stayed in Germany. As they parted, Odd yelled out the window, "So long Bill, you big stiff." Hogg humorously thumbed his nose at Odd and disappeared into the crowd.

Odd and Maybelle arrived home in time to spend July 4, 1930 watching fireworks with Ray and Lucy Long and their son, Ray Jr. It had been almost twenty years since Ray Long had picked up Odd and Maybelle at the train station when they first arrived in New York.

In just two decades the couple had risen to a place of prominence in the entertainment and publishing world, and had been part of an economic boom that changed the world forever. By 1930, however, the celebration of wealth and excess was coming quickly to an end.

Maybelle kept a small diary while decorating their new home, so we know that after approving samples for carpet and draperies at Macy's on July 7, 1930, she and Odd went to see Earl Carroll's *Vanities* at the New Amsterdam Theater. This was the eighth version of *Vanities* that Carroll had produced. Similar to Ziegfeld's productions in that they featured vignettes of dancers, comedians, singers, and lots of beautiful women, Carroll's productions tended to include more nudity than the *Follies*. Comedians Patsy Kelly and Jack Benny—in his Broadway debut—hosted the Vanities of 1930. While watching the show that warm July evening, Odd must have smiled as he thought back to the day more than ten years earlier when Bill Hogg asked Odd to help him make Carroll's play a hit.

On Saturday morning, August 2, 1930, Odd and Maybelle had their first breakfast in their new apartment. Maybelle's mother, who had been living at the Algonquin Hotel, moved in with her daughter and son-in-law. Of course, the family also included Billy, the Boston terrier. Not all the furnishings and decorations arrived on time, so Billy spent his first night howling in the middle of the uncarpeted living room.

O. O. McIntyre illustration by James Montgomery Flagg. *The Esther Allen Greer Museum at the University of Rio Grande*

Odd's new study included bookshelves on which he placed some of his favorite books, most autographed to Odd by a leading novelist of the day. He also displayed gifts—many of them handmade—that were sent to him from readers around the world. His portrait, inked by illustrator James Montgomery Flagg, also sat on the shelf. Flagg's best-known illustration was the iconic 1917 poster of Uncle Sam pointing to the viewer above the headline "I want you for the U.S. Army." At the height of his career, Flagg was the highest-paid magazine illustrator in the world, and Odd cherished the portrait Flagg had done of him for a magazine article.

Several months after moving into their new apartment, Odd and Maybelle received a cable from Ima Hogg that read, "Brother has undergone an emergency operation." A few anxious days went by, but they were relieved just a bit when they received a telegram from Hogg letting them know he looked forward to having breakfast with them in their new home when he returned to New York.

Hogg would never get to see Odd and Maybelle in the apartment he had helped them find. Days after the telegram arrived, they received devastating news from a cable sent by one of Hogg's brothers. Hogg had died at the age of fifty-five due to complications after an operation to remove gallstones.

Irvin Cobb was on a hunting trip at the Bob White Lodge in North Carolina when he received the news about Hogg's death. He took the next train to New York and headed straight from the station to Odd and Maybelle's apartment where they could grieve over the loss of their friend together. The McIntyres, Irvin Cobb, Ima Hogg, and a few other friends accompanied Bill Hogg's body to the Hogg's home in Houston.

Odd was grateful Cobb was there to tell jokes and funny stories about their times with Hogg. He wrote, "Six of us who loved Bill Hogg with a devotion rare among men accompanied his body to Texas. You may be shocked that we laughed much of the time. It is the mood that Bill, in the casket ahead, would have loved...we began to feel that Bill was right along with us. And who can say he wasn't?"[254]

Odd wrote about Hogg in his column, "I loved him as few love their favorite brother. For twelve years our lives have been almost constant companionship. He was my guide, my counselor, my friend."[255] Charles Driscoll remembered he had never seen anyone so devastated by grief, and he was certain Odd never really got over the loss.

While the Wall Street crash of 1929 signaled the beginning of one of the most catastrophic decades in American history, for Odd and Maybelle, the death of Bill Hogg in 1930 was the start of several years of great struggle, heartache, and death.

18

Enemies

There is in New York a band of intelligentsia known as 'A Group of Our Serious Young Thinkers.' It is their self-imposed task to think for the poor nit-wits who are known as the public...it is told that one of them tried publicly to show his disdain for Will Rogers because of his persistent use of 'ain't.' And it is recorded that Rogers took a reef in his chewing gum and replied, 'I notice that a lot of guys who ain't saying ain't, ain't eatin'.'[256]

O. O. McIntyre

Odd McIntyre was not a fan of the group that came to be known as the Algonquin Round Table, and some of those in the group were not fans of his.

Their first gathering took place at one of the round tables at the Hotel Algonquin at 59 West Forty-Fourth Street in 1919. Owner Frank Case saw opportunity in catering to those in the entertainment and publishing businesses, and celebrities could often be found either staying in the hotel or eating in the hotel's restaurant.

The famous round table lunches began when publicist Peter Toohey and Hippodrome press agent Murdock Pemberton invited *New York Times* drama critic Alexander Woollcott to lunch at the Algonquin to pitch a story about up-and-coming playwright Eugene O'Neill. Woollcott shut them down, rejecting the idea almost immediately, and choosing instead to fill the remaining time with stories of his recent exploits in Europe during the war. He spent so much time talking about himself, the two decided, as a joke, to arrange a "welcome home" luncheon for Woollcott and invite all the theater critics and

Alexander Woollcott.

newspaper editors in New York. The program included a variety of speeches, each to be given by Woollcott himself. The lunch was such a hit, they decided to gather again the next day, and again the day after that, and soon their daily luncheons became the stuff of legends. In addition to Woollcott, the high-profile writers, editors, actors, and publicists who lunched at the Algonquin included Robert Benchley, George S. Kaufman, Dorothy Parker, Heywood Broun, Harold Ross, Edna Ferber, and many others. "The Vicious Circle," as they jokingly called themselves, became famous for their witty observations and clever comments, often made at the expense of each other—or those who weren't considered worthy of being invited. As Edna Ferber recalled, if the group disapproved of you, they were "merciless."

Odd celebrated much of the modern popular culture of the era, and certainly benefitted from America's fascination with the writing, art, fashion, and entertainment that was coming out of New York at the time. However, his personal philosophy tended to be more conservative and better aligned with those from the previous generation. Even though he was only a few years older than most of those trading barbs at the Round Table, their snobby sophistication and sarcastic wit were lost on him.

The Hotel Algonquin at 59 West Forty-Fourth Street in the early 1920s.

He wrote, "The group represents adolescent genius in the loop of time. Having discarded swaddling clothes and climbed down from their high chairs, they are out to ride knowledge to a fall. They go in for things if you know what I mean."[257] Charles Driscoll wrote that Odd considered many of those in the group to be "a bit too precious, possibly a mite pretentious, and not wholly genuine."

Individually, many of them were misfits, rebels, or outcasts, but their luncheon allowed them to essentially write their own celebrity into being. Working as a group, they had extraordinary influence on the literature of the 1920s. Odd wrote, "If one of the thinkers writes a play, a short story, a bit of verse or a novel, the others slide down their brass poles, gallop to their typewriters, wrinkle their brows and swell their mighty paean of approval."[258]

Odd was occasionally a target of their disapproval. Charles Driscoll had attended a few of the lunches when he first arrived in New York and personally witnessed several "round-table hate canticles directed at McIntyre."[259]

Frank Case tried frequently to get Odd and the group together. Because his mother-in-law lived there at the time, Odd was a frequent visitor to the hotel and one of Case's close friends, but Odd never sat down with any of those he considered part of "that Algonquin crowd," as he called them.

By the early 1930s, the group began drifting apart. Some moved to Hollywood or Europe, while others got too busy for long daily lunches. Edna Ferber wrote she knew the end had come when she arrived at the Algonquin to find a family of tourists from Kansas sitting at the table waiting for a menu. Odd must have had a slight smile of sarcasm on his face when he wrote in his October 23, 1931 column, "Thoughts while strolling: What became of the Algonquin Round Table?"[260]

Even with the Algonquin Round Table dismantled, Odd's unique style of writing, combined with the image he himself had created and promoted, made him an easy target for parody.

In the fall of 1933, celebrated columnist, short story writer, and satirist Ring Lardner asked editor Harold Ross to check with Odd to see if he would mind if he parodied Odd's column for the *New Yorker*. Odd replied that he would be "flattered pink" and asked Ross to tell Lardner "not to spare the horses." Titled "Odd's Bodkins" and written in a hospital where he was being treated for tuberculosis, the article appeared in the October issue of the magazine and was the last piece of non-fiction Lardner wrote before his death.

Playing off Odd's penchant for name dropping, he wrote, "Home for a moment to slit my mail and found invitations from Mussolini, Joan Blondell, Joan Crawford, Joan of Arc, President Buchanan, Joe Walcott, and Louisa M. Walcott…breaking bread in the evening at the office of J. P. Morgan & Company and sat between Bernie Shaw, H. G. Wells, Charlie Dickens, Lizzie Barrett, Will Thackery, Lottie Brontë, Paul Whiteman, and Bill Klem." Odd's free-flowing style of stringing unrelated thoughts together, while popular with his readers, was easy for Lardner to parody: "One-word description of Franklin Delano Roosevelt—President…Mayor O'Brien is the image of Joan Crawford…Tallulah Bankhead and Jimmy Durante have profiles exactly alike…Damon Runyon's feet…Kate Smith is a small-town girl who became nationwide in a big city…Two of my favorite people—Senator Long."[261]

The piece allowed Odd to show he could laugh at himself. However, he also took the opportunity to put down other critics of his writing. He wrote, "I think my wife will testify that no reader could possibly have laughed more uproariously than I at the burlesque. I aroused the neighbors. Several have attempted biting satire since Lardner's passing, but they lack his delicious gift. They exploit only a mean-tempered pettiness…"[262]

One individual who exhibited "mean-tempered pettiness" was publisher John C. Farrar. He had begun his career as a poet and held a great deal of contempt for Odd. Speaking with Farrar one day, Charles Driscoll asked him about his dislike of Odd. Farrar said Odd had insulted him in his column but added that he didn't care to elaborate. When Driscoll asked Odd what he had written in his column about Farrar, all Odd could remember was that he had referred to Farrar at some point as a "pale young poet." In Driscoll's version of the story, Odd wrote a note to Farrar and the two reconciled. However, it seems that either Farrar's grudge remained, or Odd later committed some new offense.

Farrar had become the editor of *The Bookman*, a literary journal, in 1927. In 1928, he wrote an editorial about Odd that began, "For a long time now I have been wanting to take O. O. McIntyre seriously. Yet, somehow things have conspired against me."[263] He went on to say that he was angry at the columnist because Odd had written that the magazine he was editing "could have been edited just as well by the veriest office boy."[264]

Farrar wrote that although Odd's friends immediately began assuring him that Odd didn't mean it, he had never received a personal apology. Farrar then went in for the kill:

> *Mr. O. O. McIntyre is the little boy Cinderella who came out of Gallipolis, Ohio, lives at the Ritz, consorts with famous people, and realizes that, after all, the 'Folks Back Home' are the best. He never lets you forget it. He tells you the first time he saw an artichoke he didn't know what to do with it. Nevertheless, you know darned well that he can handle an artichoke now with the best of them…he does not hesitate to extol the waitress, as long as she is a simple waitress; but when she becomes a purse-proud waitress, he pricks her with his ready pin…he watches like a snake, until he sees them becoming aware of their station. Then he strikes with his fangs.[265]*

Hopefully, Farrar appreciated Odd's column eight years later, on September 8, 1936, in which Odd applauds Farrar's successful transition from "pale, young poet" to "ruddy and robust" businessman:

> *Johnny Farrar is a refutation of the old saw: 'You cannot make a*

businessman out of a poet.' Only a few years ago he was strumming his lyre, a delicately pale, blue-eyed dreamer who had come down from the green hills of Vermont to the big city. Today, as one of the heads of a publishing house, he is a ruddy and robust figure in one of the most highly competitive fields of merchandising. If he turns out a sonnet these days it is solely for his own amusement. His time is spent at a desk surrounded by secretaries and push buttons. [266]

Although Odd claimed he never intentionally wrote anything that harmed anyone—and for the most part, that was true—he wasn't shy about letting readers know which celebrities he didn't care for. For example, in 1933, he wrote about British comedienne Beatrice Lillie, whom Noel Coward had recently referred to as "the funniest woman of our civilization." Odd wrote in his column, "I grow increasingly churlish toward the art of Beatrice Lillie. Each season she comes back with a clashing of cymbals and an Algonquin accolade. Her faked stumbles, studied coyness and off-key 'Pulleaze' were amusing the first time but after a few years I am cloyed." [267] Odd's insults weren't lost on Lillie. After receiving a hearty round of applause at an event where she was being honored, Lillie commented, "I wish O. O. McIntyre could hear this!" When he heard that, Odd wrote, "I wish so, too. It would be different, for most of the applause which I have heard for Miss Lillie has come from a first night claque." [268] A claque was the name for members of a Broadway audience hired specifically to applaud those on stage.

As the economic depression of the 1930s continued, Odd's writing evolved and reflected the times. He was no longer a wide-eyed yokel experiencing the magic of New York for the first time every day; he was now America's wise old uncle who wanted everyone to remember the "good old days" while facing the challenges ahead with a positive attitude.

By 1932, one in every four Americans was jobless and one in every four farms had been sold because the farmers couldn't afford to pay the taxes. It was a world turned upside down. While those in urban areas were going hungry because they couldn't afford to purchase food—or couldn't find it if they had the money—on the farms that did survive, crops were destroyed and livestock slaughtered in order to create more demand. By 1934, half of all home mortgages were in default and banks were foreclosing on a thousand homes every single day.

In 1933, President Franklin D. Roosevelt introduced the New Deal, with the goal of bringing about "relief, recovery, and reform," that was desperately needed. One interesting aspect of the Great Depression was that, despite the dire situation, there was not a great deal of anger and bitterness. Americans seemed, in most cases, to take personal responsibility and embrace again some of the ideals that had been left behind during the 1920s. Lawrence W. Levine wrote in an article in "American Culture and the Great Depression" for *The Yale Review*, "The remarkable thing about the American people before reform did come was not their action but their inaction, not their demands but their passivity, not their revolutionary spirit but their traditionalism."[269]

One aspect that permeated the culture during the period was that of "pulling oneself up by one's own bootstraps" and the hope that, with the right amount of determination and hard work, it would be possible to rise above the challenges of the day and find success once again. Levine points to the advertising of the day as an example. An ad in 1932 promoting the International Correspondence School included the headline, "It's Time for Action!" In another ad, a businessman declares, "I'm one of thousands of businessmen who have been sitting tight, waiting for business to return to normal...now I'm tired of waiting for a miracle to happen. I'm going to do something about it—myself. I've determined that my salvation lies in my own hands."

Many Americans were also less likely to use material possessions to position themselves in society. As Odd noted, "The New York custom to 'put up a front' has changed to 'be yourself.'"[270]

Odd used his writing to celebrate the new spirit he

Front page of New York's *Daily News* the day after the stock market crash. *New York Daily News*

New Yorkers hoping for work as they line up outside an employment agency in the late 1930s. *Library of Congress, Arthur Rothstein Collection*

saw among his fellow New Yorkers. In a 1933 *Cosmopolitan* article, he wrote, "Everywhere I notice a new grandeur to living. Not the grandeur of the million-dollar yacht; the daily new fortune on Wall Street...and all the insane extravagances of a world drunk with dollars. But the grandeur of simplicity."[271] He contrasted that idea with what he had experienced just a few years earlier, "Anyone who lived in New York during those opulent feverish years before the crack-up couldn't throw a dinner party without being host to a millionaire or so...but now they haven't, as Irvin Cobb puts it, 'one yacht to rub against another,' but after their travail of despair, they have found a new zest to the business of living."[272]

Odd and Maybelle gave up the extravagance of travel—their last trip to Europe was in 1932—not because of a lack of money, but because Odd's health had deteriorated to the point that travel was too difficult. Also, with Will Hogg gone, it just wasn't as much fun as it had been before.

As he had during the previous decade, during the Depression Odd used his column to describe what it was like to live in New York City. About Wall Street, he wrote, "Restaurants, catering to noonday trade, are ghostly with empty white table tops. Thousands who, since the crash went to the financial district merely as a gesture until things righted, have finally abandoned daily trips. Those who have not jumped from windows are

225

in seclusion…as goes Wall Street, so goes its army of small tradesmen whose livelihood depends on the street's prosperity."[273]

By 1933, Odd and Maybelle had been in New York for twenty-two years, so his column became a place where some of the physical changes the city experienced could be recorded:

> *For those who have not seen the metropolis for 20 years the most astonishing changes are in 1, 2, 3, order—Broadway, Fifth avenue and the avenue and the borough of the Bronx. The Bronx, once a scatter of bosks, now sports an expansive Champs Elysees known as the Grand Concourse. Radio City blots out the old avenue skyline. Austere landmarks along the street—the Vanderbilt mansion, old Hotel Savoy and Delmonico's—are supplanted by spires as high as the sky and, at the moment, they are as empty as the horns of plenty. Millionaires Row, north, now is deluxe apartments. The only distinguishing marks of George M. Cohan's Broadway are his theater, the Criterion, Empire, Churchill's corner and the Hotel Astor. Broadway's present make-up is not the result of an orderly change, but represents downright decadence, sloughing off into a rotting phosphorescence of peep shows and penny-a-dance halls. Prim rows of duplicate brownstones, running off either side of Broadway and Fifth Avenue, are nearly obliterated. The few remaining are speakeasies or chopped up for recessed niches of trade and walkup flats. And you'd never believe that the once-beautiful W. 72nd could become such a jade among streets.*[274]

Odd still looked for opportunities to include humor in his column. Deborah Walker Hartwick, who wrote about his portrayal of the Great Depression in his column, noted his frequent mention of humorous signs seen around New York:

> *A frequent subject for McIntyre's column was the signs in business windows. A dramatic upper Broadway sign said, 'After 35 years of fair and faithful service—now closing our hospitable doors for evermore.' Another said, 'We cater to yachts,' and underneath was written, 'You mean, We did.' McIntyre also commented on a bank sign that read, 'Open 10:30 – 2:30,' by saying, 'Optimists.' He told of a sign in a West Twenty-Ninth Street restaurant that read, 'Don't hesitate to ask for credit, as we have the most polite way of refusing.'*[275]

Along with some of the old enemies Odd made during the 1920s, the 1930s brought a few more. Odd was just one of the many celebrities in the crosshairs of gossip columnist Walter Winchell, who sometimes referred to him as "Mcintyresome" or "The very Odd McIntyre." In one of Winchell's columns, under the headline "Oh! Oh! McIntyre," he took apart and disproved a paragraph Odd had written about Cab Calloway. He wrote, "Cab is not saddle-colored. He was not born in a small town in Missouri. He does not wear dicty clothes in zebra patterns. He does not set the pace for Harlem swells. He is not a sheik, but spends most of his time at home with his wife. Other than that, O. O. McIntyre is correct."[276]

Someone Winchell had angered began sending daily postcards with Winchell's address typed on one side and insults written in green ink and signed "the Old Copyreader" on the back. Winchell suspected Odd, and even had a bit of evidence, so he began to taunt Odd in his column. "We know the identity of the ambusher, the sniper or the hit and runner...I thought I would die from the thrill when the investigators told me that the distinguishing mark on my favorite anonymous letter writer's machine was an 'M.'"[277] He was prepared to name the offending party in his column when William Randolph Hearst sent word to Winchell that his campaign against Odd needed to stop immediately.

One insult that hurt Odd more than others came in the form of a particularly harsh and very public accusation of plagiarism. Shortly after *The Big Town*, a collection of Odd's columns, was published in 1935, writer Christopher Morley claimed some of the phrases and comments in Odd's writing came from Morley's own column. He sarcastically wrote, "When I'm low in mind, or feel any sort of spiritual ullage, I have an unfailing consolation. At any rate, I say to myself, O. O. McIntyre likes my stuff. And how." He continued, "I don't want to seem foolish. If Mr. McIntyre needs to divot the Green

Christopher Morley. *Courtesy the Library of Congress Prints and Photographs Division*

now and then for his newspaper syndicate; I've run a daily column myself and I know it's a tough job. But when he gets into the bookshops then I feel a certain sense of trade honor is involved."[278]

Morley then listed thirty examples of Odd's writing that he considered too close to his own. Included were examples like "A sweet and dangerous opiate is memory, the bliss of anxious thought," compared to Odd's "No opiate is so deadening as memory; the despair of anxious thought." Or Morely's "Her hand flying merrily over the keys like a white hen picking up corn," compared to Odd's "Watch my fingers fly over the keyboard like a hen pecking at corn."[279]

Odd had always been a fan of Morley, and occasionally featured him in his column with comments like, "Personal nomination for the most accomplished American essayist—Christopher Morley," "The most perfect verbal silversmith, to my notion, is Christopher Morley," and "Some subtle essayist—Christopher Morley is my choice—should beglamour the old-time livery stable." Odd's frequent praise of Morley made the accusation even more difficult for him to understand.

In response, Charles Driscoll publicly pointed out that many of the references were years apart, and included phrases for which there were few alternative words. He fired back, "In no instance were large gobs of similar copy quoted…and after all, why should the most successful columnist in the business take the copy of the most unsuccessful—copy that was long ago proved unsalable." He added, "I should say that Mr. Morley, whose 'Bowling Green' column is perhaps the least read in the history of journalism, is capitalizing on Mr. McIntyre's popularity."[280]

Publicly, Odd simply said, "If it did happen, it happened unintentionally." Privately, there was a settlement. According to Max Shively, who interviewed Maybelle for a thesis he wrote on Odd in 1980, Maybelle and the McIntyre's attorney met with Morley and he was willing to accept a settlement of fifteen hundred dollars.

The toll it took on Odd was not only financial, however. Driscoll remembered, "His health was in a precarious condition at the time, and it did seem for a while that this savage thrust by a man he liked and admired might kill him. Odd carried that wound to the grave."[281]

19

Loss

Note to my biographer: To the end I kidded myself
a fellow could have devoted friends no matter what
happened. Just a pushover for sentiment. So my
windswept tatters, longing for a pinch of even a dry
sad smile. Ten millions in this lunatic city and not
one who cares. Not one to bring back faith. Not one
to join me in what looks like a swell nervous
breakdown.[282]

O. O. McIntyre

While the nation endured an economic depression, Odd and
Maybelle struggled with the loss of several members of their
inner circle of friends and family. In the summer of 1933,
Maybelle's mother, Kate, then eighty, returned to New York from
her annual visit to Gallipolis. It was obvious she was seriously ill, and
her friends in Gallipolis had been shocked by how bad she looked.
She died shortly before Christmas that same year. Lucy Long and
Maybelle accompanied her body home, where she was buried in Mound
Hill Cemetery, high on a hillside overlooking the Ohio River and the

Maybelle's mother, Kate Small, was a big part of the couple's life in New York. *The Esther Allen Greer Museum at the University of Rio Grande*

town of Gallipolis. Odd was too sick himself to leave New York, but wrote in his column that not a single hard word ever passed between them. "When I stumbled and fell," he wrote, "I took my bruises to her."[283]

Other than Maybelle, no one was more responsible for Odd's success than Ray Long. It was Long who showed up at the *Herald's* offices in Dayton in 1906 and recruited Odd to join him at *The Cincinnati Post*. In 1911, it was Long who made the phone call inviting him to come to New York for the job at *Hampton's Magazine*. By convincing Odd to submit an article to *Cosmopolitan* in 1922, Long added an aspect to Odd's career that contributed greatly to his fame and made him an equal among some of the most talented writers of the early twentieth century.

In 1926, Long had been promoted to president of Hearst's International Magazine Company, essentially making him the most powerful magazine publisher in the world. Well known for paying top dollar for the writers and illustrators who appeared in *Cosmopolitan*, he was in a position to help those in whom he saw talent. As long as profits at *Cosmopolitan* stayed strong, Hearst was willing to let Long have complete control. However, when Hearst forced the merger of *Hearst's International Magazine* with *Cosmopolitan*, he set a goal for Long of two million subscribers. By 1929, not only had that goal not been met, profits were down by forty percent.

Cosmopolitan and other magazines were not alone in their decline. The depression also hit the newspaper business hard. Between 1929 and 1933, newspapers lost around forty percent of their advertising revenue. Thousands of reporters, editors, illustrators, photographers, and others working for newspapers found themselves out of a job. Some newspapers and magazines folded completely, while others merged with larger chains. Meanwhile, radio news coverage was growing. Stations were being purchased and merged to create large networks. The National

Broadcasting Company and Columbia Broadcasting System were profitable in the early 1930s, and many advertisers placed fewer print ads in favor of radio commercials or sponsorships of entire programs. On March 12, 1933, President Roosevelt took advantage of the new medium when he delivered the first "fireside chat." Americans discovered that hearing the president's words out of his own mouth was a very different experience from reading them in a newspaper or magazine.

However, there were areas where newspapers and magazines did continue to excel. As the politics and economics of the world became more complex, Americans turned to newspapers for more analysis and in-depth coverage of current events. With this expanded role of newspapers in society came an increase in syndicated columnists giving their opinions on local, national, and international news. Although Odd began having more competition—there was also an increase in the type of personal column he had been writing for more than fifteen years—he was still at the top when it came to circulation and mass popularity.

Even though much of the blame for *Cosmopolitan's* decline could be placed on the depression and increased competition from radio, Hearst's faith in Long had begun to waiver. He shifted management of the editorial budget to a finance committee, just like other publications in his publishing empire. He also brought in a general manager, Richard Berlin, to monitor and manage the business aspects of the magazine, and Berlin reported directly to Hearst and Hearst Corporation general manager Thomas White. Essentially, *Cosmopolitan* was no longer Ray Long's magazine.

As James Landers points out in, *The Improbable First Century of Cosmopolitan Magazine*, Richard Berlin was no fan of Ray Long's way of doing business. He continually pointed out to Hearst and White areas where he felt money was being wasted.

Long had been giving away small hardcover books as premiums to the magazine's subscribers. *My Story That I Like Best*, first released in 1926, included the favorite stories of *Cosmopolitan* writers Edna Ferber, Irvin Cobb, Peter B. Kyne, and others. More than half a million of these books made it into American homes during the giveaway, and contributed to the popularity of the writers. *My Favorite Story*, printed in 1928, featured the favorite stories of authors like Fannie Hurst, Ring Lardner, and W. Somerset Maugham. In 1929, a selection of Odd's stories, *Twenty-five Selected Stories of O. O. McIntyre*, was so popular, it was followed in 1932

Ray Long with Roy Howard in the mid-1930s.

with *Another Odd Book: Twenty-five Selected Stories of O. O. McIntyre.* The introduction of *My Favorite Story*, written by Long, reveals one of the secrets of his success—selecting writers who could tell stories to which readers could relate. He wrote, "Many of our writers were writing for the publication when I became its editor. Most others came into the group within a fairly short time after I became editor. They feel at home there. They feel that they know you and you know them. And in talking to you, as they do in this book, they express themselves with a frankness that could be possible only under those conditions."[284]

Hearst and the other executives felt premiums like this were a waste of money and did little to increase subscribers or advertising. Berlin was also quick to point out that there was a huge file of unused stories and illustrations, including thirty or so Harrison Fisher covers, for which Fisher had been paid three thousand dollars each. He also uncovered more than forty contracts for other highly-compensated writers and illustrators that, in many cases, could not be broken for two or three more years. Hearst was very concerned.

In a March 1931 profile in *Fortune* magazine, titled "The *Cosmopolitan* of Ray Long," the magazine was called "the book that Mr. Long makes" and "the expression of his own shrewd vigorous tastes." One has to wonder what William Randolph Hearst thought when he picked up *Fortune* and read that Long "not only edits the *Cosmopolitan* magazine, he is the *Cosmopolitan* magazine."[285] Hearst may have set the magazine down and thought, "Not for long."

Whether Hearst was angered by Long taking so much public credit for *Cosmopolitan*, or Long decided he couldn't work on a magazine over which he had no real control, four months after the article ran, Long resigned with a public statement in which he noted that he and Hearst were parting as friends, and that they had never had a serious disagreement.

The next few years were tough ones for Long. Soon after departing *Cosmopolitan* and Hearst's International Magazine Company, he left for the Pacific Ocean, telling friends he needed to get away and write. After a while, he was reported missing, and some even thought he had died. When Long finally came out of hiding, he told friends he had simply been trying to do for himself what he had done so successfully for others. During his absence, the publishing business he had started went bankrupt. He then spent some time in Hollywood writing and editing movies for Columbia, then Fox, and finally, Metro-Goldwyn-Mayer. Nothing seemed to stick. After a career that had been filled with successes, Long was struggling to find his way. For a very short time, he became editor of Bernarr Macfadden's *Photoplay* and *Shadowland* magazines and an associate editor of *Liberty*. The man who had been the highest-paid editor of all time, and who had contributed to the success of hundreds of writers and illustrators was suddenly unable to catch a break. His friend Roy Howard noticed that Long, a heavy drinker and smoker, looked horrible and was very jittery. He thought there was no way his friend was going to be around much longer if he didn't change his ways.

Pulp fiction novelist and Long's friend Jack Woodford, wrote in his autobiography:

> *I saw Ray in Hollywood. The first time in the 'Photoplay' offices there. They had given him a job. And I do mean a job. Not a position. I never before or since felt so sorry for anybody. The great Ray Long didn't even have an office in the 'Photoplay' office. He sat at an outer desk like someone was trying to humble him. Wearing a cheap cardigan sweater. Looking totally defeated and hopeless but nevertheless, his magnetic personality still glowing. If a man ever had courage, he had it. And it would be necessary with Hearst breathing hot on the back of your neck.*

On July 9, 1935, Long was living and working in Beverly Hills while his wife Lucy, from whom he was likely estranged, and their thirteen-year-old son, Ray Jr., remained in Greenwich, Connecticut. Long's maid, Helen Amdt, noticed he seemed "unusually morose," and had been in a dark mood all afternoon. Later that evening, while she was taking a telephone message for him, Amdt heard a shot. She ran into his bedroom where she found Long crumpled to the floor, unable to move. He had put a rifle in his mouth and pulled the trigger. While the bullet severed his spinal cord, it left him alive but unconscious. He was rushed to Beverly Hills Hospital where he died on the operating table. He was just fifty-seven years old.

Ray Long's small funeral was held on July 11 at a local mortuary with services performed by Rupert Hughes and a small number of friends, including Roy Howard and Irvin Cobb, in attendance. His wife stayed in Connecticut, telling reporters she was too sick to travel. During the service, Hughes said, "One does what one had to do. Ray felt that he had no more to give others, and so he took his own life…it breaks my heart when I think of those last few moments when the thought came to him that he could best serve his friends by removing himself from among them."[286]

Of his friend, Irvin Cobb wrote:

> *I treasure the memory of this dwarfish friend of mine, whose brain was as sharp as his heart was kindly; who could, with a wired message inspire a struggling writer or revive a despairing one, could with a deft hand soothe the ruffled plumage of some successful—and therefore nine times out of ten, temperamental—writer. It was Long who worked such wizardry with typefaces that he made captions tell tales and by-lines to illustrate the text.*[287]

Several months later, Long's ashes were scattered in the Catalina channel off Santa Monica by his friends Roy Howard and novelist Peter Kyne, and Long's son, Ray Jr.

Another loss for Odd and Maybelle came in 1933 with the death of their bulldog Billy. Odd's love for dogs was well documented in his writing through the years, and Billy had become somewhat of a sidekick for the columnist and his wife.

After their Boston bulldog, Junior, had been run over at the corner of Forty-Fourth Street and Fifth Avenue, Odd and Maybelle had been looking for another dog to help fill the void. Billy first captured their attention because, while the other dogs were rolling around, jumping and barking, Billy sat motionless like a "statue of despair." As Odd wrote, "It was his tragic loneliness that smote us." When they discovered much of his aloofness was because he was deaf, Odd quoted the words of Kipling, "we gave him our hearts to tear."

The little dog crossed the ocean with them sixteen times, and frequently accompanied them in the limousine. Toward the end of Billy's life, another Boston bulldog joined the family when painter and stage designer Ben Ali Haggin needed to find a home for his dog, Nimble, after he and his wife had had a baby. Unwilling to upset Billy at night, Odd and Maybelle kept Nimble in the back of the house while Billy continued sleeping in their room.

There were times when Odd's life was filled with such depression from his illness, only his dogs could comfort him. Of one of those times,

Odd wrote, "There was a day when my world seemed to collapse about me. From the utter depths of poignant despair I saw nothing but the blackness of utter futility. There seemed to me to be no way out." Billy sensed Odd's anxiety and he felt a "cold, dewy nose" nuzzling his hand. "I looked down into pleading eyes set in the quizzically cocked head of a faithful dog. Then he trotted into another room and returned with a rubber ball, which he placed at my feet and backed away expectantly as though to say, 'Come on old partner, there is a lot of fun left in this life.' It was the first glimmer of hope I had had in days and it affected me profoundly. My courage was buoyed and from that moment I carried on."[288]

There were some bright spots for Odd in the mid-1930s. Composer Meredith Willson, whom Odd met shortly after moving to New York, composed the *O. O. McIntyre Suite* as a tribute to Odd. The composition, which was performed by the Paul Whiteman Orchestra in 1934, included four parts: "Thingamabobs," "Sunday Night in Gallipolis," "Thots While Strolling," and "Local Boy Makes Good." The original composition included only three sections, but Whiteman requested a fourth, so Willson composed "Sunday Night in Gallipolis." In his April 9, 1934 column, Odd wrote that one evening in New York, he tried to listen to a broadcast of the suite being performed in San Francisco. Because of static, he was only able to hear "a few snatches," but he was very flattered by Willson's tribute.

The score of "Thots While Strolling" was later used for "Whose Dream are You," performed by Bing Crosby and the Les Paul Trio in 1945. Willson also composed the score for Charlie Chaplin's *The Great Dictator*, wrote the music and lyrics for the hit Broadway musicals *The Music Man* and *The Unsinkable Molly Brown*, and composed "It's Beginning to Look a Lot Like Christmas" and "May the Good Lord Bless and Keep You."

Despite the good moments, more grief was right around the corner. In late summer 1935, Will Rogers hired famous aviator Wiley Post to fly him through Alaska in search of new material for his column. On August 15, they left Fairbanks, Alaska. A few miles from Point Barrow they got lost, so they landed in the water to determine their location. When they took off again, an engine stall caused the airplane to crash, killing both men.

On August 22, 1935, newspapers around the country ran Odd's tribute to one of his best friends:

I like to think of Will Rogers as flying on. Certainly no material crackup should halt that blithe spirit. Freed of the cloddish body, he must be ascending new heights, scaling new peaks...I have known Rogers for 20 years, intimately

August 17, 1935 front page reporting the deaths of Will Rogers and Wiley Post. *Los Angeles Times*

for 10. We met when I was a brash and fresh-every-hour press agent for Flo Ziegfeld and he was the rope twirling, gum-chewing comedian star of the Frolic Roof...I saw him last February 2 of this year at a small dinner party at the Will Hayes' in the Waldorf. Betty was there, the Joseph J. Kennedys and my wife and I...suddenly, he jumped up, glanced at his wrist watch and said he must be off. He was to speak at a dinner, as I recall, of real estate men. He slouched out, turned in the doorway in that head-tucked-under-the-wing manner of his and called, 'So long, folks!' I did not know, of course, that I would never see him again in this world...So they buried Will Rogers today—that is, his bruised and battered body that was only his shell. His brave spirit goes winging on![289]

In 1938, Rogers' friend, David Randolph Milsten, wrote a poem about him titled, "Howdy Folks." The poem included references to many of Rogers' friends and family members, and was used on a plaque near the entrance of the Will Rogers Museum in Claremore, Oklahoma. It was later designated the official poem of Oklahoma. Odd would be thrilled to know that the last lines of the poem bind the two friends together forever:

"...But I ain't ungrateful, I just can't see
Such a hullabaloo 'bout a cowboy like me.
Well, so long folks, it's time to retire;
I got a date to keep with Odd McIntyre.

20

The Columning Business

I would not trade jobs with anyone. That goes for
the Prince of Wales, the Christmas-tree salesman and
Rudy Vallée. Such enthusiasm is not difficult to
explain. I had my try at many things and my
yesterdays proved a nightmare of imperiled vision
and defeat. All my occupational efforts fizzled until
a freakish destiny catapulted me into the columning
business...my todays are actual play, a happy
succession of new interests, new thrills.[290]

O. O. McIntyre

Through years of trial and error, Odd McIntyre developed a
system of producing his column, and once it started working,
he never deviated from it. He began his workday around noon,
after a breakfast prepared by their French cook. Guests were kept to a
minimum during the day so he could focus on writing, and later, as his
health grew worse, most were kept away completely. Odd preferred to
work at the chrome and glass desk he designed and had built in 1930.

Odd McIntyre working on his column at home in his study. *The Esther Allen Greer Museum at the University of Rio Grande*

It came with a swivel chair, which he rarely used, preferring to sit on a matching six-foot long bench with light-green velvet cushions. On days he was too ill to sit up, he worked in bed—but he kept working. Although he could no longer attend plays and movies, dine out at fine restaurants, or travel around the world, he still somehow got his columns out every week. Information about what was going on in the world came from Maybelle, from his friends, and from the letters he received each week from fans around the world. He wrote more about the past, and shared some of his personal philosophy for life.

Odd typed on plain, inexpensive typewriter paper, single-spaced with a double line between sections. In order to use as little paper as possible, he typed with the smallest margins he could get away with and, occasionally, the letters even ran off the page. All those typing classes back at the Bartlett Business College in Cincinnati paid off, and Odd still typed like a pro. While he wrote, he wanted Maybelle close by. If she left to run an errand or stepped out of the room for more than a few minutes, he began to panic and claimed he couldn't write without her.

Odd McIntyre working on his column. *The Esther Allen Greer Museum at the University of Rio Grande*

Once he was finished with a first draft, he used scissors to cut out paragraphs he didn't like and pasted other copy in its place. During a final round of edits, he made notes in red ink on what he had written. Red arrows pointed to where new words or sentences he had written in by hand should be inserted. Some words were crossed out with new ones written in above them. The finished results more closely resembled a ransom note than the most-read column in the world; but it worked. Odd's goal each day was to create two complete columns. When finished, he would add one completed column to the stack that was sent to Charles Driscoll each week for editing. The other he filed away. Odd's fear of death manifested itself in an obsession with making sure there were always extra copies of the column "should anything happen." During one of his three-month trips to Paris, he created a whole set of daily and Sunday columns and left them with the manager of the Ritz-Carlton to be used in case something happened. None of them was ever used.

According to Driscoll, the way Odd produced "New York Day by Day" was "his editor's cross and a nightmare for printers."[291] Driscoll

A draft of Odd's daily column before he sent it to his editor. *The Bossard Memorial Library* suggested many times that it would be better if Odd would leave a real margin on each side of the paper and double-space, so notes could be clearly made and more easily read. Of course, that would require two pieces of paper for one column, and Odd saw that as a waste.

Once the columns were printed, he couldn't read them for fear he would find a mistake or see something he wished he had written differently. However, he had Maybelle read everything while he watched her face for signs of approval. She later told a friend he would "watch her like a hawk" while she read anything he had written.

Perhaps because it brought back bad memories of all those years he and Maybelle made duplicates of the letter on an old mimeograph machine, Odd refused to make an actual carbon copy of anything, preferring instead to start from scratch should any columns ever get lost in the mail, which they did from time to time.

On Monday morning, Driscoll would receive a week's worth of columns to edit. He would then call Odd or Maybelle to discuss what he thought needed to be changed, deleted, or added.

Odd was usually able to pull enough from those second, unused columns, that he could save one day of writing each month to work on other articles that needed to be written. Even after Ray Long's death, Odd continued writing a monthly column for *Cosmopolitan*, and in early 1938 he was asked to write a story on Joseph Kennedy, who was being featured in a monthly column, "The Cosmopolite of the Month." Possibly through Will Hayes, Odd and Maybelle had become friendly with Kennedy and his wife Rose. In 1938, President Roosevelt appointed Kennedy ambassador to the United Kingdom, and they were to move to London.

In the article, one of the last pieces he wrote for the magazine, Odd provided readers with an early look at a family that would dominate popular culture for generations to come. Odd focused on the traits he found in Kennedy that he had valued most in others throughout his career—hard work, humility, and family. For Odd, it was important to note that "Kennedy's fortune is entirely his own and he built it up through a series of vicissitudes" and, while it was true he seemed to have "the Midas touch," he also "has a shirt-sleeved capacity for work that is often quite depressing to his associates." Odd also noted Kennedy's dedication to his wife and children. He wrote, "Business is always fretting him because it takes him away from the bosom of his family. His wife is

the beautiful and accomplished daughter of a former Boston mayor…
the Kennedy love match is an epic in devotion. Something, indeed, quite
beautiful to behold."[292]

Without knowing it, Odd was writing about the family of a future
president:

> *To the Kennedys have been born nine healthy children—a veritable stair step*
> *of four boys and five girls ranging in age from five to twenty-two. My wife*
> *and I were dining with them at the Colony one evening. Will H. Hayes*
> *and his wife were present also. During the meal, he was notified of a*
> *telephone call from Boston. It was explained that the name of the caller was*
> *not given but that the charges were reversed. 'That would be one of my boys*
> *at Harvard,' beamed Kennedy.*[293]

Dinners like this with friends were rare in the last months of Odd's life,
and he and Maybelle spent almost no time socializing with others. Odd
was nearly impossible to contact. You couldn't even call directly into his
apartment without going through the building's switchboard operator.
She had a very short list of people who could get through to Maybelle,
and for all others, she took a message. In the last few years of his life,
Odd almost always refused to talk on the telephone. He also no longer
drank alcohol or smoked, and in the seven years they had lived at 290
Park, they had never served a single cocktail.

Business requests were sent to Driscoll. Once "New York Day by Day"
was syndicated, Odd had a strict rule that no payment was to be received
from anyone who was included in the column, and although there were
requests that would have doubled or tripled his yearly income, he never
allowed his image or name to be used in advertising. The technology
of movie and radio production had advanced to the point that it was
then less expensive and relatively easy to create content, especially
with someone like Odd who was now so well known around the world.
However, each time Driscoll brought opportunities for radio shows or
movie shorts, Odd turned them down, telling Driscoll he would just stick
to the letter. In the end, Driscoll finally stopped asking Odd and turned
them down himself. There was talk of a movie about Odd's life, and
some initial contracts were even signed, but the movie was never made.

A chauffeur usually arrived around six as Odd was finishing his day's
work. After his illness had progressed, he was sometimes unable to even

Odd and Maybelle planed to retire to Gatewood, the home they purchased and refurbished in Gallipolis, Ohio.

sit up straight, so he was positioned in the back of the limousine with pillows. A pad of paper and pencil were kept in the side pocket, and he sometimes made notes about things he saw or heard as the chauffeur drove slowly down the streets of New York. If Odd were feeling well enough, he liked to get out and walk slowly along with Nimble and Maybelle, as the car followed, just in case it was needed. Occasionally, for the opening night of a play, Odd would have the chauffeur pass the theater slowly so he could see all the activity going on outside.

Of course, the public knew nothing of the seriousness of Odd's illness. He did acknowledge a change in his lifestyle in articles that he wrote at the time. In February 1938, an article appeared in *Cosmopolitan* titled "The First Fifty Years are the Best," in which he admitted he had grown tired of the role of "professional gadabout," and now only occasionally attended the theater. He even admitted he had grown to loath jazz and swing clubs. He wrote, "My evening clothes, which had been laid out each dusk for years, are used but seldom."[294]

When radio was in its infancy, Odd had been too busy to spend much time listening. Although he had been among the first to interview *Amos 'n' Andy*, he had not listened regularly to the show himself. But by 1938, many of his evenings were spent next to the couple's built-in Atwater-Kent radio, and Odd began looking over the radio program guide as avidly as he used to look for reviews of plays.

In 1933, Odd purchased a home in Gallipolis for Maybelle to commemorate their silver wedding anniversary. The Old Bovie Place, as locals called it, at Seventy-Six State Street had been built in 1786 and needed a great deal of repair and restoration. Fred M. Bovie, a successful grocery merchant, had lived in the house for thirty years before it was purchased by Odd. The two-story, colonial house built of red brick had sentimental value for both Odd and Maybelle, as it originally belonged to Captain James Gatewood, Maybelle's grandfather. As a young boy, Odd's grandmother had even told him about visiting Maybelle's grandmother, Virginia Lowery Gatewood, there in the living room of the house during the Civil War. As a young man, Odd would pass the house on his way to see Maybelle.

In a fitting tribute, they named the house Gatewood. Josephine Mullineaux, Maybelle's cousin who had been living with them in New York, began spending a lot of her time in Gallipolis helping with the restoration and decorating, while Maybelle supervised from New York. She sent truckloads of furniture and accessories to the house, some of it coming from an old French château that was torn down in Long Island. Although Odd never actually returned to Gallipolis to see the house before his death, it was decorated as though he lived there, and Maybelle made sure the owner of Gatewood would be clear to even a casual visitor. There were personal photos like the one of him and Billy in the music room and a large portrait of Odd over the mantle. The initials "OOM" could be found everywhere from the doormat out front to the headboard in the master bedroom. Eventually, many of the items they picked up in their travels made their way to Gatewood making it seem as though Odd and Maybelle would walk through the door at any minute.

Owning a house in Gallipolis that he and Maybelle were decorating together gave Odd great pleasure. Helping Maybelle pick out furniture also inspired him to visit the Metropolitan Museum of Art for the first time in 1936, after which he became a frequent visitor until his declining health made leaving the apartment too difficult.

Maybelle later told friends that Odd was planning to retire in 1940, move to Gatewood, and write a novel. Sadly, when Odd finally made it home to Gatewood, it was in a casket. Maybelle had known the end was near, so when she negotiated Odd's last contract, her heart was clearly not in it. She later told friends she knew there was no way he would live long enough for it to matter.

21

The End

To the average healthy human being, Death is always far away. Turning westward into brilliantly lighted Broadway, with its eager hunger for life and gaiety, the thought of Death seemed as much folly as the pleasures all about.[295]

O. O. McIntyre

One day, around the time Odd was depressed over Christopher Morley's public accusations of plagiarism, Charles Driscoll joined Odd and Maybelle in their evening limousine ride around Manhattan. Odd sat quietly looking out the window, holding Nimble, while Driscoll and Maybelle talked. He only began paying attention to the conversation in the limo when he heard Driscoll suggest that he write Odd's biography.

"Not of defense, but of declaration...that will recognize your part in shaping American journalism as it is today," Driscoll was saying. Odd was embarrassed and began to protest, but Maybelle thought it was a good idea, so he became quiet again. After a few minutes staring out the window, he spoke up, "That's a nice thought, Charlie, but who'd want to read anything about me?"[296]

Odd and Maybelle were planning a party for Friday, February 18, 1938 to celebrate both his fifty-fourth birthday and their thirtieth wedding anniversary. However, Maybelle was considering calling the party off because Odd was as bad as she had ever seen him. It was so bad, she even asked Odd if she could call a doctor, but he wouldn't let her. On the weekend of his death, Odd was unable to get out of bed, so he lay there occasionally trying to make some notes for his next column. Nimble was curled up next to him.

Late Sunday night, he seemed to be slipping away. Maybelle sat on her twin bed and read to him for a while, and then they listened to the radio. Finally, she turned over facing the wall, hoping to take a little nap. Odd looked over at his wife, who had done so much to create the career in which he had been so successful, and said, "Turn your face toward me so I can see you." Fittingly, his last words to his wife were spoken on Valentine's Day.

On February 14, 1938, his body was first taken to the Frank E. Campbell Funeral Parlor at Broadway and Sixty-Sixth Street in Manhattan, where Valentino had created such a riot years earlier. Maybelle selected a blue suit with a red tie and a red and black dressing gown to bury him in, and then began making phone calls.

Later, after his body had been taken away, they looked at the pad on which he had been writing. Although the handwriting was weak and difficult to read, one of the things he had written was, "Came up one of those sudden spooky blacknesses and the dog whimpered and I was affrighted myself a bit, everybody being away, so I pretended to talk to Mrs. Quigley, the telephone lady, and engage her about this and that until the clouds lifted."[297]

Of course, Odd's death was a big shock for most people. Few even knew how ill he really was. By mid-morning, newspapers featured headlines like, "Loyal Boston Bull Guards Deathbed of Odd McIntyre," "O. O. McIntyre, Noted Columnist, Dies Suddenly in 54th Year," and "Broadway and Main Street Pour Out Sorrow Tributes to Columnist."

Odd would have appreciated his *New York Times* obituary, that included:

A fanciful figure who left a small town more than a quarter-century ago to rise to the top of his profession, Mr. McIntyre never completely grew up. His greatest stock-in-trade for his column, syndicated to 380 newspapers

(top) Many of the residents of Gallipolis outside Gatewood on the day of Odd's visitation. (bottom) Odd's funeral service at Mound Hill Cemetery in Gallipolis. (seated left to right) Dr. E. M. Martindale, James Gatewood, Maybelle McIntyre, Josephine Mullineaux, Mrs. Martindale. *Edna Pierce Whiteley*

Editorial cartoon by John Knox Jr. that appeared in the Memphis paper following Odd's death.
The Commercial Appeal

throughout the world, was his incarnate rapture at the glories of a New York recognizable to none but himself. To him the towers of Manhattan were studded with minarets and the neon lights of Broadway flickered like jewels.[298]

Telegrams poured in from around the world. Condolences were sent to Maybelle from William Randolph Hearst, Irving Berlin, Roy Howard, Joseph Kennedy, Marion Davies, Cecil B. DeMille, Lillian Gish, Jack Dempsey, Irvin Cobb, Will Hayes, Will Rogers' wife Betty, the Hogg family and hundreds of others.

Maybelle began making plans to get Odd's body back home to Gallipolis for the funeral and burial. Knowing Odd would not have wanted a fuss made, she asked friends in New York and California not to make the trip to Ohio.

Maybelle walked into Gatewood for the first time when she arrived to prepare the house for Odd's visitation. She thought some members of the community might want to drop by to pay their respects. She was not, however, expecting the more than two thousand people who filed

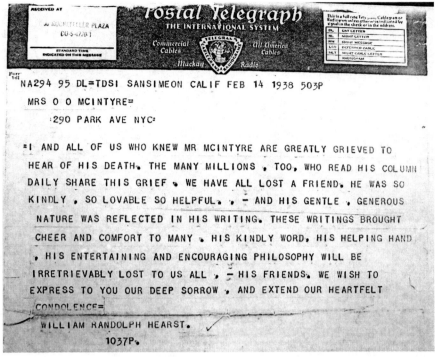

NA294 95 DL=TDS1 SANSIMEON CALIF FEB 14 1938 503P

MRS O O MCINTYRE=

:290 PARK AVE NYC=

=I AND ALL OF US WHO KNEW MR MCINTYRE ARE GREATLY GRIEVED TO HEAR OF HIS DEATH. THE MANY MILLIONS , TOO, WHO READ HIS COLUMN DAILY SHARE THIS GRIEF . WE HAVE ALL LOST A FRIEND. HE WAS SO KINDLY , SO LOVABLE SO HELPFUL. , - AND HIS GENTLE , GENEROUS NATURE WAS REFLECTED IN HIS WRITING. THESE WRITINGS BROUGHT CHEER AND COMFORT TO MANY . HIS KINDLY WORD, HIS HELPING HAND , HIS ENTERTAINING AND ENCOURAGING PHILOSOPHY WILL BE IRRETRIEVABLY LOST TO US ALL , - HIS FRIENDS. WE WISH TO EXPRESS TO YOU OUR DEEP SORROW , AND EXTEND OUR HEARTFELT CONDOLENCE=

WILLIAM RANDOLPH HEARST.

1037P.

Telegram sent to Maybelle from William Randolph Hearst shortly after Odd's death. *The Bossard County Library*

past his body the next day. For a small town not used to managing large crowds, Gallipolis responded quickly and remarkably well. The police, Rotary Club, Legionnaires Club, and Boy Scouts worked together to protect Gatewood and keep order among those who were filing through the house.

Gene Buck, Odd's friend from the *Ziegfeld Follies* days, made the trip to Gallipolis, as did editor Charles Driscoll, and Odd's old friend Will Hayes. Will Hogg's sister and brothers chartered a plane and arrived to pay their respects on behalf of the Hogg family and their late brother, Will.

Ministers from four denominations conducted final rites in a modest service that was over in half an hour. As the hearse slowly made its way up the steep incline at the Mound Hill Cemetery, members of the community silently lined the drive with heads bowed in respect. Odd had not wanted an expensive monument so Maybelle initially had a simple rectangle marked with his initials. But when so many visitors began visiting Mound

Hill from all over the world to pay their respects, she placed a stone bench with the inscription, "O. O. McIntyre, Beloved of a Nation" at Odd's grave. It overlooks the river and the city about which he so often wrote. In the days following his death, tributes to Odd appeared in newspapers around the nation. John Knox Jr., cartoonist for *The Commercial Appeal* in Memphis, and whose work usually appeared next to Odd's columns, wrote, "We'll be missing you in that column next door."

Charles Driscoll's biography of Odd was quickly excerpted in a series in *Cosmopolitan*, and it was announced by McNaught that Driscoll would replace Odd in writing his own version of "New York Day by Day." Odd would have been pleased to know that people did want to read about him. When *The Life of O. O. McIntyre* was released in book form, it made it to *The New York Times* best-seller list.

Especially since Odd wrote so many words in his career, and had such a unique way of sharing his thoughts on so many subjects, it's only fitting that he should have the last word here. In October 1928, after sitting with a friend who was about to have an operation, Odd wrote an article about his own last day. He shared:

Had I one more day to live, I reflected, and the courage to carry on without whimpering, there were many of whom I should like to ask forgiveness for intentional and unintentional hurts. The nature of mankind is to seek forgiveness in final hours. It was the last despairing cry of the Master. And it is probably that only on the brink of eternity most of us become conscious how silly and useless hate is. On my last day I should like to clasp the hand of every person who has helped me over the rough spots. In the hurry of every-day life there is a rude casualness in our attitude toward genuine friendship. I should like to recall the many little acts of selfishness toward those so near and dear to me. I should like to blot out useless falsehoods that brought me only misery. What a priceless sense of peace, as the shadows fall, to be conscious of having tried to give the world as much happiness as it had given me! To feel I had never taken the slightest advantage of a friend or foe and that my life had been an open book that all might read. Such idealistic thoughts perhaps sound mawkish to those in the full bloom of excellent health, yet given one day to live I am certain they are the sort that come to us all. Indeed, on the final day I think my greatest regret would be that I had fallen so far short of being the kind of son my mother wished me to be.[299]

Epilogue

In 1971, Max and Phyllis Shively were visiting friends in West Virginia when they met Maybelle McIntyre who, at eighty-seven, was still very active. They were all attending the same lecture, so they decided to have a quick lunch together. Max Shively had never even heard of O. O. McIntyre, but was intrigued by this elderly lady and the stories she began telling about her husband, a famous newspaper reporter who had died decades earlier. In fact, he became so interested in the lives of Odd and Maybelle, when it came time to write his doctoral dissertation at Ohio University in 1980, he chose O. O. McIntyre as his topic.

While working on his dissertation, Shively interviewed Maybelle about her life in New York. Surrounded by the autographed portraits of many celebrities who were then long gone, she began telling her story. With Odd looking down from the portrait over the mantle, she told of George Gershwin's playing the piano all night at parties they threw at the Ritz-Carlton, and then of later receiving a postcard from Gershwin who was in Charleston beginning work on *Porgy and Bess*. She described Carl Sandburg as "charming and entertaining," while Sinclair Lewis could be "rude and unpleasant." She spoke about their days in Paris with F. Scott Fitzgerald and other members of the Lost Generation, and got a little emotional as she remembered her old friend Will Hogg and their last trip through Europe. She had been there at the birth of silent films, and was happy to claim many of those early stars as friends. She told Shively about having lunch with Herbert Hoover at the White House, and shared memories of all the good times she and Odd had with many of the most well-known politicians, entertainers, and writers of the early twentieth century.

The world hadn't forgotten about Odd right away. In 1952, NBC radio's *The Big Show* produced a tribute in which bandleader Paul Whiteman directed his orchestra in a performance of Meredith Willson's *O. O. McIntyre Suite*. As the orchestra performed "Thoughts While Strolling," actress Tallulah Bankhead's deep, husky voice could be heard reading a portion of Odd's column about the death of Junior. For a few years, "Thoughts While Strolling" was played on the radio on the anniversary of Odd's death, and no matter where she was in the world,

In 2011, Gatewood was purchased by the Holzer Health System, which had it completely restored.

Maybelle would listen for it. After one anniversary, Willson received a postcard from her from India, where she had listened to it by shortwave radio.

The column about Junior was also featured in a scene on a 1954 episode of the television show *Dragnet* titled "The Big Dog." A character, trying to explain his sadness over the death of his own dog, picks up a book and reads a lengthy portion of Odd's article to Sergeant Joe Friday.

After Odd's funeral, Maybelle left Gatewood in the care of her friends and family and returned to her apartment at 290 Park

The home in which Odd grew up in Gallipolis is noted by a historic marker.

253

Maybelle McIntyre later in life.

Avenue. She remained there until she was forced to sell it in 1960 because the building was being torn down. A generic glass office building was built in its place. She moved to an apartment at the St. Regis Hotel, where she spent the first part of each year enjoying concerts, plays, and museum openings in New York. She would then spend her summers at Gatewood in Gallipolis, and then travel in the fall to Paris, where she always stayed at the Hotel Ritz. In addition to shopping for the latest clothing and accessories, Maybelle collected Art Nouveau and Parisian furniture and especially loved collecting mirrors in huge, hand-carved frames. In 1975, she returned to Gallipolis and Gatewood became her permanent home. Because it became impossible to find anyone who was able to service it, she traded in her last Rolls for a 1966 Lincoln Continental, but still depended on the services of a chauffeur. She later moved into the Point Pleasant Nursing Home in Point Pleasant, West Virginia, where she spent the last five years of her life. Maybelle McIntyre died in April 1985 at 101 years old.

Although Odd and Maybelle McIntyre have largely been forgotten by most of the world, their presence can still be found in Gallipolis, Ohio. The Ariel Opera House, where Odd worked as a boy, still stands tall. Thanks to executive director, Lora Lynn Snow, in 2017 it was the venue for a rare performance of Willson's *O. O. McIntyre Suite*. Randall Fulks and the other librarians at Gallia County's Bossard Memorial Library will gladly show off the O. O. McIntyre Reading Room, that was funded by donations from some of the town's leading citizens. Locked bookcases in the room hold Odd and Maybelle's collection of first edition books, many of them autographed by the authors. In front of Odd's boyhood home is a large plaque, placed by the Chamber of Commerce, letting those who happen to pass by know that it was the home of the "famous newspaperman and author of 'New York Day by Day.'" The Gallia County Historical Society has an assortment of artifacts and documents from Odd and Maybelle's life and career, while the Esther Allen Greer Museum at the University of Rio Grande, about ten miles from Gallipolis, archives a collection of artifacts originally collected and then donated by Maybelle's cousin, Laura E. Kratz. There are several places around town where a copy of Edna Whiteley's 1994 documentary about Odd and Maybelle can still be purchased. And Gatewood is still there, looking even better than it did when Maybelle closed the door for the last time in 1980. In 1986, it was entered into the National Register of Historic Places and, in a bit of irony, in 2011 the house was purchased by the Holzer Health System, which had it completely restored. Gatewood is currently used as a guest house for visiting physicians.

Although neither of them had been to college, Odd and Maybelle had a great appreciation for higher learning. Maybelle gave Odd's swivel chair, bench, and chrome and glass desk to Dr. Earl F. English, Dean of the University of Missouri's School of Journalism. English was a huge fan of Odd McIntyre and had become a collector of McIntyre memorabilia. In Maybelle's will, she provided funds for the journalism school to establish the O. O. McIntyre Postgraduate Writing Fellowship for aspiring writers, and the O. O. McIntyre Professorship to recognize outstanding educators.

If you are in Gallipolis today, you can enjoy the beautiful park that is still the heart of the town. The park's bandstand is the same one from which a young Odd and Maybelle heard performances more than a hundred years ago. Maybelle felt such a connection to the park and the town of Gallipolis, she donated the many park benches that are still being used there today.

Odd McIntyre didn't write to become rich, and he would certainly be surprised that, at least in Gallipolis, Ohio, he is still a little famous. As he wrote, "I am not writing for posterity nor do I believe anything I write will live for more than a week or so after publication." So why did he write? That's simple. He added, "I have found satisfaction in entertaining people a little every day."[300]

Notes

1. O. O. McIntyre, "Celebrities," *Hearst's International Combined with Cosmopolitan*, October 1931, 72.
2. Rupert Hughes, "O. O. McIntyre," *Hearst's International Combined with Cosmopolitan*, April 1937, 8.
3. "O. O. McIntyre Dead: Columnist was 54: Writer of New York Day by Day," *The New York Times*, Feb. 15, 1938, 25.
4. O. O. McIntyre, "My Dad," *Hearst's International Combined with Cosmopolitan*, April 1925, 88.
5. Jeffrey A. Lockwood, "Voices from the Past: What We Can Learn from the Rocky Mountain Locust," *American Entomologist*, Winter 2001, 208.
6. *A Plague of Locusts — a Nebraska Story*. Produced by Christine Lesiak (2012; Nebraska: NETNebraska), video.
7. Katherine Ott, *Fevered Lives: Tuberculosis in American Culture since 1870* (Cambridge: Harvard University Press, 1996), 14.
8. O. O. McIntyre, "Autobiography," unpublished manuscript, Kratz Collection, Esther Allen Greer Museum, University of Rio Grande, Rio Grande, Ohio, 1.
9. Ibid.
10. Ibid.
11. Charles B. Driscoll, *The Life of O. O. McIntyre* (New York: The Greystone Press, 1938), 106.
12. McIntyre, "Autobiography," 6.
13. "Portrait and Biographical Record of Buchanan and Clinton Counties, Missouri," (Chicago: Chapman Bros, 1893), 565.
14. "O. O. McIntyre's Father Dies," *Kansas City Star*, June 1, 1926.
15. David Greenberg, *Calvin Coolidge: The American Presidents Series: The 30th President, 1923-1929* (New York: Time Books, 2006), 137.
16. Claude M. Fuess, *Calvin Coolidge: The Man from Vermont* (New York: Fuess Press, 1939), 54.
17. O. O. McIntyre, "They're Real Americans," *Hearst's International Combined with Cosmopolitan*, June 1929, 25.
18. Ibid.
19. Wil Verhoeven, *Americomania and the French Revolution Debate in Britain, 1789-1802* (Cambridge: Cambridge University Press, 2013), 117.
20. Harry Graff, *Gallipolis* (Ohio: Work Projects Administration, 1940), 8.
21. Ibid, 14.
22. Laurence J. Kenny, *The Gallipolis Colony* (Washington, D.C.: Catholic University of America Press, 1919), 415.
23. "Consolidated Telephone Agents," *The Gallipolis Journal*, January 1, 1880, 2.
24. "Train Matters," *Journal* (Gallipolis, OH), Jan. 1, 1880, 3.
25. O. O. McIntyre, "My Dad," *Hearst's International Combined with Cosmopolitan*, April 1925, 88.
26. O. O. McIntyre, "Too Many Cynics," *Hearst's International Combined with Cosmopolitan*, September 1929, 67.
27. Max Edward Shively, *The Conte of O. O. McIntyre: An Assessment of His Contribution to Personalized Journalism*, Ph. D. diss., Ohio University, 1980, 20.
28. O. O. McIntyre, "Bicycle Conscious," *Hearst's International Combined with Cosmopolitan*, September 1933, 75.
29. O. O. McIntyre, "Pecks Bad Boy was a Piker," *Hearst's International Combined with Cosmopolitan*, July 1931, 58.
30. O. O. McIntyre, "I was a Problem Child," *Hearst's International Combined with Cosmopolitan*, May 1931, 66–67.
31. Michael A. Kahn and Richard S. West, *What Fools These Mortals Be: The Story of Puck, America's First and Most Influential Magazine of Color Political Cartoons* (San Diego: IDW Publishing, 2014), 2.
32. O. O. McIntyre, personal letter to Annie Adams, undated.
33. Shively, *The Conte of O. O. McIntyre*, 22.

34. O. O. McIntyre, "I was a problem Child," *Cosmopolitan*, 67.
35. Driscoll, *O. O. McIntyre*, 157.
36. O. O. McIntyre, "My Grandmother," *Hearst's International Combined with Cosmopolitan*, December 30, 1930, 69.
37. "Della Fox Sent to Sanitarium," *Evening World* (New York, NY), June 1, 1900, 1.
38. O. O. McIntyre, "A Tear for the Lost Art," *Hearst's International Combined with Cosmopolitan*, November 1929, 64.
39. Ibid.
40. Ibid.
41. Ibid.
42. O. O. McIntyre, "My Wife Never Asks for Money," *Hearst's International Combined with Cosmopolitan*, October 1936, 62.
43. O. O. McIntyre, "My Only Girl," *Hearst's International Combined with Cosmopolitan*, September 1931, 80–81.
44. McIntyre, "A Tear for the Lost Art," 64.
45. O. O. McIntyre, *Twenty-five Selected Stories of O. O. McIntyre* (New York: Cosmopolitan, 1930), 8.
46. Whet Moser, "Yellow Journalism, Arthur Brisbane, and the Sins of the Grandfather," *Chicago Magazine*, May 31, 2011.
47. O. O. McIntyre, "By Himself, About Himself," *The Atlanta Constitution*, October 23, 1921, F7.
48. Edna Pierce Whiteley, *The O. O. McIntyre Story, Chronicle of a Journalist of Note* (Professional Project, College of Communication, March 1995 March, 1995), 9.
49. Ibid, 11.
50. McIntyre, "O. O. McIntyre by Himself, About Himself," F7.
51. "Death of an Editor," *Weekly Register* (Point Pleasant, WV), April 2, 1902.
52. O. O. McIntyre, Coming to New York, Unpublished biography, 10.
53. Whiteley, "McIntyre Story," 11.
54. O. O. McIntyre, "New York Day by Day," *St. Louis Post Dispatch*, Jan. 1, 1928, 13.
55. McIntyre, "My Wife Never Asks me for Money," *Hearst's International Combined with Cosmopolitan*, 62.
56. Whiteley, "McIntyre Story," 13.
57. O. O. McIntyre, "Be Yourself," *Hearst's International Combined with Cosmopolitan*, July 1928, 27.
58. Charles Cist, *The Cincinnati Miscellany or Antiquities of the West, and Pioneer History* (Cincinnati: Caleb Clark Printer, 1845), 171.
59. Bartlett's Business College: Advertisement. *Journal-News* (Hamilton, OH), Sept. 7, 1901, 18.
60. O. O. McIntyre, Coming to New York, Unpublished biography, 12.
61. Ibid, 13.
62. O. O. McIntyre, "Printer's Ink," *Hearst's International Combined with Cosmopolitan*, July 1935, 58.
63. O. O. McIntyre, Coming to New York, Unpublished biography, 15.
64. O. O. McIntyre, Coming to New York, Unpublished biography, second installment, 1.
65. "Dayton Boys Solve Problem," *Dayton Herald*, December 18, 1903, page unknown.
66. O. O. McIntyre, Coming to New York, Unpublished biography, second installment, 6.
67. O. O. McIntyre, *Twenty-Five Selected Stories*, 7.
68. Ray Long, "This Man Irritates Me But I Like Him," unidentified magazine clipping from Gallipolis Historical Society.
69. O. O. McIntyre, Coming to New York, Unpublished biography, second installment, 8.
70. Congressional Record, Proceedings and Debates of the United States Congress, Volume 99, Part 9, A-864.
71. O. O. McIntyre, "Memories of Cincinnati," *The Cincinnati Post*, 1930, 32.
72. "Who's Who—And Why," *The Saturday Evening Post*, January 16, 1912, 23.
73. O. O. McIntyre, Coming to New York, Unpublished biography, second installment, 7.
74. O. O. McIntyre, "A Story of Days that are Dead and Gone," *Hearst's International Combined with Cosmopolitan*, November 1925, 99.
75. Ibid.
76. O. O. McIntyre, "Printer's Ink," *Hearst's International Combined with Cosmopolitan*, July 1935, 58.

77. *They Built a City; 150 years of Industrial Cincinnati* (Cincinnati: The Wiesen-Hart Press, 1938), 249.

78. Perry J. Ashley, *Dictionary of Literary Biography, Volume 25* (Detroit: Gale Research Company, 1984), 258.

79. A. J. Liebling, *The Telephone Booth Indian* (San Francisco: North Point Press, 1990), 105.

80. John Tebbel, *The History of the American Newspaper* (New York: Hawthorn Books, Inc., 1969), 231–232.

81. Duane C. S. Stoltzfus, *Freedom from Advertising: E. W. Scripps's Chicago Experiment* (Urbana and Chicago: University of Illinois Press, 2007), 45.

82. Edmond D. Coblentz, *Newsmen Speak: Journalists on Their Craft* (Berkeley and Los Angeles: University of California Press, 1954), 136.

83. Walter DeCamp, "The Complete Revolution," (Cincinnati, 1910) unpaged.

84. Ibid.

85. O. O. McIntyre, *The Big Town* (New York: Dodd, Mead & Company, 1935), 86.

86. *Cincinnati, a Guide to the Queen City and Its Neighbors* (Ohio: The Ohio State Archaeological and Historical Society), 121.

87. Henry Collier Wright, *Bossism in Cincinnati* (Cincinnati: Ohio Anti-Saloon League, 1905), 63.

88. O. O. McIntyre, "A Story of Days that are Dead and Gone," *Hearst's International Combined with Cosmopolitan*, November 1925, 99.

89. Lincoln Steffens, *The Struggle for Self-government* (New York: McClure, Phillips & Co, 1906), 202.

90. Lincoln Steffens, "Ohio: A Tale of Two Cities," *McClure's Magazine*, Volume 25, July 1905, 310.

91. Bruce W. Sanford, *Don't Shoot the Messenger: How Our Growing Hatred of the Media Threatens Free Speech for All of Us* (Lanham, Maryland: Rowman & Littlefield Publishers, 2000), 48-49.

92. O. O. McIntyre, "My Wife Never Asks Me for Money," *Hearst's International Combined with Cosmopolitan*, October 1936, 62.

93. Will Irwin, "Cox—The Last of the Bosses," *Colliers*, January 13, 1912, 13.

94. O. O. McIntyre, Coming to New York, Unpublished biography, second installment, 13.

95. United Press, "Fought His Way up from Lowly Desk of 'Cub' Reporter," *Newcastle Herald*, April 11, 1908, 3.

96. "Segal Expires at Age 84," *Cincinnati Enquirer*, March 5, 1968, 21.

97. O. O. McIntyre, "The Simple Rich," *Hearst's International Combined with Cosmopolitan*, November 1924, 78.

98. "Motors for Fifth Avenue," *The New York Times*, August 21, 1897, 12.

99. "The New Fifth Avenue," *New York Times*, June 27, 1909, 37.

100. O. O. McIntyre, Coming to New York, Unpublished biography, 1 – 2.

101. O. O. McIntyre, *The Big Town* (New York: Dodd, Mead & Company, 1935), 69.

102. "Heat's Scyth Mows Down 56 on Fifth Day," *New York Tribune*, July 7, 1911, 1.

103. "Recluse Dies from Heat," *New York Tribune*, July 7, 1911, 2.

104. O. O. McIntyre, Coming to New York, Unpublished biography, 3.

105. O. O. McIntyre, "New York Day by Day," *The Tennessean*, June 10, 1924, 4.

106. "Who's Who—And Wherefore," *Printers' Ink*, January 9, 1907, Volumes 58-59, 11.

107. Frank Luther Mott, *A History of American Magazines* (Cambridge: Harvard University Press, 1968), 147.

108. Ibid, 148.

109. Robert E. Peary, "The Discovery of the North Pole," *Hampton's Magazine*, January 1910, 3.

110. Lyle Dick, "Robert Peary's North Polar Narratives and the Making of an American Icon." Article presented to the annual conference of the Canadian Historical Association in Toronto, May 27, 2002.

111. Driscoll, *The Life of O. O. McIntyre*, 221.

112. Peary, "The Discovery of the North Pole," cover.

113. Robert E. Peary, "The Discovery of the North Pole," 51.

114. Driscoll, *The Life of O. O. McIntyre*, 222.

115. Warren E. Leary, "Who Reached the North Pole First? A Researcher Lays Claim to Solving the Mystery," *The New York Times*, February. 17,1997.
116. McIntyre, Coming to New York, Unpublished biography, 16.
117. Theodore Dreiser, *Twelve Men*, (New York: Boni and Liveright), 216.
118. Ibid, 217.
119. O. O. McIntyre, "New York Day by Day," *The Palm Beach Post*, September 1, 1925, 4.
120. "Writer of Short Stories and Poems Won Renown," *Sedalia Democrat*, December 19, 1927, 8.
121. Zoë Lyon, "Harris Merton Lyon," *American Literary Realism, 1870-1910*, 3, no. 1, 1970, 36-40.
122. McIntyre, Coming to New York, Unpublished biography, 7.
123. O. O. McIntyre, "New York Day by Day," News-Palladium, December 17, 1937, 2.
124. McIntyre, Coming to New York, unpublished biography, 10.
125. "Mail and Express," Skyscraper.com, accessed May 2016: http://skyscraper.org/exhibitions/paper_spires/nw11_maexp.php
126. McIntyre, Coming to New York, Unpublished biography, 10.
127. Ibid, 16.
128. Roy Peter Clark, "How the New York Times invented disaster coverage with Titanic sinking," Poynter.org, accessed May 2016: http://www.poynter.org/how-tos/writing/169316/how-the-new-york-times-invented-disaster-coverage-with-the-titanic-sinking/
129. "Titanic sinking was a news story before it was a movie," Associated Press, April 9, 2012, 1.
130. "Watchers Angered by Carpathia's Silence," *New York Evening Mail*, April 19, 1912, 1.
131. Ibid.
132. Ibid.
133. Ibid.
134. McIntyre, Coming to New York, unpublished biography, 17.
135. Ibid, 11.
136. "Average Man," *Time*, November 26, 1945, 25.
137. O. O. McIntyre, "New York Day by Day," *The Evening News* (Harrisburg, Pennsylvania), July 29, 1931.
138. Henry Havens Windsor, "A Western Trio in New York," *Cartoons Magazine*, Volume 7, 798.
139. Laura E. Kratz, *The Odd Book* (Gallipolis, Ohio: The Gallia County Historical Society, 1990), 43.
140. Michael M. Greenburg, *Peaches & Daddy* (New York: The Overlook Press, 2008).
141. Irvin Cobb, "O! O! McIntyre," *Delineator*, date unknown, 40.
142. O. O. McIntyre, Unpublished autobiography, fourth installment, 14.
143. O. O. McIntyre, "On the Great White Way," *Washington Herald*, July 22, 1914, 5.
144. O. O. McIntyre, "Day by Day in New York," *Evening Review*, Jan. 30, 1915, 4.
145. Ibid.
146. O. O. McIntyre, *The Big Town* (New York: Dodd, Mead & Company, 1935), 20.
147. Jay Warner, *How to Have Your Hit Song Published* (Winona, Minnesota: Hal Leonard Corporation, 2006), 3.
148. O. O. McIntyre, "Tin Pan Avenue," *Hearst's International Combined with Cosmopolitan*, October 1922, 88.
149. McIntyre, *Coming to New York*, unpublished biography, 9.
150. "Woman in Black Mask in the Papers at Last," *Judge*, Date Unknown.
151. Charles L. Edson, "Flashlight Frightened Madame's Pet Leopard," unidentified clipping.
152. O. O. McIntyre, "Home—at Last," *Hearst's International Combined with Cosmopolitan*, May 1931, 72.
153. "Taxicab 'Bandits' Steal Bridegroom," *New York Herald*, March 4, 1917.
154. McIntyre, "Home—at Last," 72.
155. O. O. McIntyre, "I've Always Had a Ringside Seat," *Hearst's International Combined with Cosmopolitan*, September 1933, 69.
156. "Some Little Talk Awhile," *Brooklyn Life*, December 25, 1910, 14.

157. Will Rogers, "Will Performs Among Alligators," *Lincoln Star*, February 14, 1926, 24.
158. Sarah Churchwell, *Careless People: Murder, Mayhem, and the Invention of the Great Gatsby* (New York: Penguin Books, 2013), 173.
159. McIntyre, Coming to New York, unpublished biography, 17.
160. O. O. McIntyre, "Z is for Ziegfeld," *Hearst's International Combined with Cosmopolitan*, March 1936, 70.
161. McIntyre, "Z is for Ziegfeld," 72.
162. "Sport: Death of Sandow," *Time*, October 26, 1925, 34.
163. McIntyre, "Z is for Ziegfeld," 72.
164. "The Midnight Frolic," *Brooklyn Life*, October 7, 1916, 11.
165. McIntyre, *Coming to New York*, unpublished biography, 17.
166. O. O. McIntyre, "Ziggy," *Hearst's International Combined with Cosmopolitan*, July 1922, 97.
167. O. O. McIntyre, "New York Day by Day," *Evening News*, April 9, 1928, 10.
168. McIntyre, *Coming to New York*, unpublished biography, 8.
169. McIntyre, "Z is for Ziegfeld," 72.
170. McIntyre, *Coming to New York*, unpublished biography, 17.
171. O. O. McIntyre, "New York Letter" *The Review* (East Liverpool, OH), November 23, 1918, 4.
172. Frederick Lewis Allen, *Only Yesterday* (New York and London: Harper & Brothers Publishers, 1931), 188.
173. O. O. McIntyre, "New York Day by Day," *The Indianapolis Star*, November 4, 1921, 6.
174. O. O. McIntyre, "New York Day by Day," *The Indianapolis Star*, September 17, 1921, 6.
175. O. O. McIntyre, "New York Day by Day," *The Indianapolis Star*, May 10, 1921, 6.
176. O. O. McIntyre, "New York Day by Day," *The Indianapolis Star*, February 10, 1921, 6.
177. O. O. McIntyre, "New York Day by Day," *The Indianapolis Star*, January 1, 1923, 6.
178. Robert Van Gelder, "Mr. McIntyre's Notes on the Big Town," *The New York Times*, June 30, 1935, BR11.
179. O. O. McIntyre, "New York Day by Day," *The Indianapolis Star*, August 18, 1921, 6.
180. O. O. McIntyre, "New York Day by Day," *The Wilmington, Delaware Morning News*, October 10, 1928, 4.
181. O. O. McIntyre, "New York Day by Day," *The Wilmington, Delaware Morning News*, November 10, 1925, 4.
182. O. O. McIntyre, "New York Day by Day," *The Indianapolis Star*, January 5, 1922, 6.
183. Laura E. Kratz, *Maybelle* (Gallipolis, Ohio: French City Press, 1996), 7.
184. McIntyre, Coming to New York, unpublished biography, 20.
185. O. O. McIntyre, "Happy Birthday to Cosmopolitan," *Hearst's International Combined with Cosmopolitan*, April 1936, 17.
186. John McDonough and Karen Egolf, *The Advertising Age Encyclopedia of Advertising* (Chicago: Fitzroy Dearborn Publishers, 2002), 126.
187. "The Cosmopolitan of Ray Long," *Fortune*, March 1931, 49.
188. Ibid, 50.
189. Ibid.
190. J. Bryan III, "Gallipolis Boy Makes Good," *The Saturday Evening Post*, Nov. 20, 1937, 10.
191. O. O. McIntyre, "A Vignette of New York," *Hearst's International Combined with Cosmopolitan*, September 1922, 56.
192. O. O. McIntyre, "The Bowery—I'll Never Go There Anymore," *Hearst's International Combined with Cosmopolitan*, February 1922, 44.
193. O. O. McIntyre, "Kale and Farewell," *Hearst's International Combined with Cosmopolitan*, August 1922, 72.
194. O. O. McIntyre, "The Men Who Dope Out Your Slang," *Hearst's International Combined with Cosmopolitan*, October 1924, 56.
195. McIntyre, "O. O. McIntyre by Himself, About Himself," F7.
196. E. L. Huddleston, "O. O. McIntyre Broadway Populist," *American Studies*, Spring 1974, 79.
197. O. O. McIntyre, "New York Day by Day," *Indianapolis Star*, Feb. 7, 1921, 6.
198. O. O. McIntyre, "They Call Me Odd," *Hearst's International Combined with Cosmopolitan*,

December 1936, 66.

199. Bryan, "Gallipolis Boy Makes Good," 10.

200. "O. O. McIntyre Dead; Columnist was 54," *The New York Times*, Feb. 15, 1938, 25.

201. Driscoll, O. O. McIntyre, 19.

202. Ibid, 18.

203. "The Twenties in Contemporary Commentary: Religion & Science," *America in Class Primary Source Collection*, National Humanities Center, 4.

204. Shively, *The Conte of O. O. McIntyre*, 113.

205. McIntyre, *The Big Town*, 37.

206. O. O. McIntyre, "My Dad," *Hearst's International Combined with Cosmopolitan*, April 1925.

207. M. J. Barry, Letter in the *Clinton County Democrat*, November 20, 1925. page unknown.

208. Phillip M. Lovell, "Care of the Body," *Los Angeles Times*, March 3, 1929, 158.

209 Royal S. Copeland, "Pernicious Anemia Comes on Slowly," *Evening News* (Harrisburg, PA), June 11, 1928, 25.

210. "Nobel Medical Prize Shared by Three Yank Discoverers," *Cincinnati Enquirer*, Oct. 26, 1934, 16.

211. O. O. McIntyre, "I Enjoy Being a Hick," *Hearst's International Combined with Cosmopolitan*, August 1926, 104.

212. O. O. McIntyre, "New York Day by Day," *Evening Review* (East Liverpool, OH), Jan. 29, 1925, 4.

213. Arlen J. Hansen, *Expatriate Paris: A Cultural and Literary Guide to Paris of the 1920s* (New York: Arcade Publishing, 2012), 2.

214. O. O. McIntyre, "Fitzgerald and Lardner are Neighbors," El Paso Herald, April 18, 1923, 15.

215. Mel Watkins, "What Was It About 'Amos 'n' Andy'?" New York Times, July 7, 1991, 26.

216. O. O. McIntyre, "Amos 'n' Andy," Hearst's International Combined with Cosmopolitan, May 1930, 72.

217. Ibid, 73.

218. Benjamin B. Hampton, *A History of the Movies* (New York: Covici, Friede, 1931), 3.

219. "New Strand Theater Opens Saturday," *Brooklyn Daily Eagle*, April 5, 1914, 47.

220. Ibid.

221. Mordaunt Hall, "Vitaphone Stirs as Talking Movie," *The New York Times*, August 7, 1926.

222. Ibid.

223. O. O. McIntyre, "Dress Reform?" *Hearst's International Combined with Cosmopolitan*, December 1929, 58.

224. Ibid.

225. Cobb, "O! O! McIntyre," 40.

226. Rupert Hughes, "The Cosmopolite of the Month," *Hearst's International Combined with Cosmopolitan*, April 1937, 8.

227. O. O. McIntyre, "I Enjoy Being a Hick," *Hearst's International Combined with Cosmopolitan*, August 1926, 104.

228. O. O. McIntyre, "Gothoms Great God Four Flush," *Hearst's International Combined with Cosmopolitan*, July 1924, 71.

229. O. O. McIntyre, "Pardon the Plus Fours," *Hearst's International Combined with Cosmopolitan*, February 1926, 50.

230. O. O. McIntyre, "New York Day by Day," *Evening Review* (East Liverpool, OH), Jan. 29, 1924, 4.

231. O. O. McIntyre, "New York Day by Day," *Evening Review*, May 1, 1924, 4.

232. O. O. McIntyre, "My Friend Gene Tunney," *Hearst's International Combined with Cosmopolitan*, December 1926, 89.

233. O. O. McIntyre, "New York Day by Day," *Altoona* Tribune, Feb. 2, 1933, 4.

234. O. O. McIntyre, "New York Day by Day," *The Palm Beach Post*, January 18, 1930. 12.

235. McIntyre, "Hick," 104.

236. George S. Ulman, *Valentino as I Knew Him*, (New York: A. L. Burt Company, 1926), 7.

237. Ibid, 4.

238 ."Barred Crowds Clamor to View Valentino's Body," *Brooklyn Daily Eagle*, Aug. 26, 1926, 1.

239. Ulman, Valentino, 6.

240. McIntyre, "By Himself," F7.

241. O. O. McIntyre, "Oddities of Celebrities," *Hearst's International Combined with Cosmopolitan*, March 1935, 50.

242. Fred Gus Neuman, *Irvin S. Cobb: His Life and Achievements* (Emmaus, Pennsylvania: Rodale Press, 1938), ix.

243. Ibid.

244. Cobb, O! O!, 134.

245. McIntyre, "Oddities of Celebrities," 51.

246. O. O. McIntyre, "Our Will," *Hearst's International Combined with Cosmopolitan*, October 1931, 82.

247. Ben Yagoda, *Will Rogers* (New York: Alfred A. Knopf, 1993), 276.

248. McIntyre, "Our Will," 83.

249. Steven K. Gragert and M. Jane Johansson, *The Papers of Will Rogers: The Final Years* (Norman, Oklahoma: University of Oklahoma Press, 1995), 226.

250. O. O. McIntyre, "New York Day by Day," *The Evening News*, October 7, 1930, 12.

251. Irvin S. Cobb, *Exit Laughing* (New York: The Bobbs-Merrill Company, 1941), 541.

252. Ibid, 555.

253. McIntyre, "Oddities of Celebrities," 50.

254. Neuman, Irvin S. Cobb, ix.

255. O. O. McIntyre, "New York Day by Day," *The Evening News*, October 7, 1930, 12.

256. O. O. McIntyre, "A Group of Our Serious Young Thinkers," *Hearst's International Combined with Cosmopolitan*, January, 1925, 86.

257. Ibid.

258. Ibid.

259. Driscoll, *The Life of O. O. McIntyre*, 41.

260. O. O. McIntyre, "New York Day by Day," *Daily Messenger*, Oct. 23, 1931, 4.

261. Ring Lardner, "Odd's Bodkins," *The New Yorker*, October 7, 1933, 21.

262. O. O. McIntyre, "Hanging Harps on the Willows," *Indianapolis Sunday Star*, Feb. 6, 1938, 2.

263. John Farrar, "Anonymously-John Farrar," *The Bookman*, April 1928, 171.

264. Ibid.

265. Ibid.

266. O. O. McIntyre, "New York Day by Day," *Valley Morning Star*, Sept. 8, 1936, 4.

267. O. O. McIntyre, "New York Day by Day," *Salt Lake Tribune*, Jan. 4, 1933, 2.

268. O. O. McIntyre, "New York Day by Day," *Lincoln Evening Journal*, Feb. 9, 1933, 5.

269. Lawrence W. Levine, "American Culture and the Great Depression," *The Yale Review* 74, no. 2, 198.

270. O. O. McIntyre, "New York Day by Day," *Gallipolis Daily Tribune*, Aug. 4, 1932.

271. O. O. McIntyre, "A New Grandeur to Living," *Hearst's International Combined with Cosmopolitan*, February 1934, 64.

272. Ibid.

273. O. O. McIntyre, "New York Day by Day," *Gallipolis Daily Tribune*, June 7, 1932.

274. O. O. McIntyre, "New York Day by Day," *Greenville News* (Greenville, SC), Jan. 11, 1933, 4.

275. Deborah Walker Hartwick, "Bowery breadlines, Peruvian bonds and suicides: *O. O. McIntyre's portrayal of the Great Depression, 1929 – 1938*," Thesis, College of Communication, Ohio University, 1998, 66.

276. Bryan, "Gallipolis Boy Makes Good," 11.

277. Neal Gabler, *Winchell: Gossip, Power and the Culture of Celebrity* (New York: Vintage Books, 1994), 171.

278. "The Press: Columnist v. Columnist," *Time*, July 8, 1935, 45.

279. Ibid.

280. Ibid.

281. Driscoll, *The Life of O. O. McIntyre*, 42.

282. O. O. McIntyre, *The Big Town*, 91.

283. O. O. McIntyre, "New York Day by Day," *Courier-Journal* (Louisville, KY), Jan. 20, 1934, 6.

284. *My Favorite Story* (New York: International Magazine Company, 1928), vi.

285. "The Cosmopolitan of Ray Long," *Fortune*, 49.

286. "Ray Long Eulogized at Funeral Service," *The New York Times*, July 12, 1935, 19.

287. Cobb, *Exit Laughing*, 116.

288. O. O. McIntyre, "My Dog," *Hearst's International Combined with Cosmopolitan*, August 1928, 27.

289. O. O. McIntyre, "Tribute to Will Rogers," *Morning News*, Aug. 23, 1935, 15.

290. O. O. McIntyre, "I Wouldn't Trade Jobs with Hoover," *Hearst's International Combined with Cosmopolitan*, April 1930.

291. Driscoll, *The Life of O. O. McIntyre*, 29.

292. O. O. McIntyre, "The Cosmopolite of the Month," *Hearst's International Combined with Cosmopolitan*, April 1938, 8.

293. Ibid.

294. O. O. McIntyre, "The First Fifty Years," *Hearst's International Combined with Cosmopolitan*, February 1938, 59.

295. O. O. McIntyre, "I Wouldn't Trade Jobs with Hoover," *Hearst's International Combined with Cosmopolitan*, April 1930.

296. Driscoll, *The Life of O. O. McIntyre*, 13.

297. Ibid, 316.

298. "O. O. McIntyre Dead," *The New York Times*, 23.

299. O. O. McIntyre, "On My Last Day," *Hearst's International Combined with Cosmopolitan*, October 1926, 21.

300. McIntyre, *Twenty-five Selected Short Stories*, xii.

Bibliography

Books

Allen, Frederick Lewis. *Only Yesterday, An Informal History of the Nineteen-twenties*. New York: Harper & Brothers Printing, 1931.

Ashley, Perry J. *American Newspaper Journalists, 1901 – 1925*. Detroit: Gale Research Company, 1984.

Baughman, Judith S. American Decades, 1920-1929. New York: A Manly, Inc., 1996.

Beard, Patricia. *Newsmaker, Roy W. Howard: The Mastermind Behind the Scripps-Howard News Empire from the Gilded Age to the Atomic Age*. Connecticut: Rowman & Littlefield, 2016.

Belote, Theodore Thomas. *The Scioto Speculation and the French Settlement at Gallipolis*. Cincinnati: University of Ohio Press, 1906.

Bleyer, Willard Grosvenor, Ph.D. *Main Currents in the History of American Journalism*. New York: Houghton Mifflin Company, 1927. Borkowski, Mark. *The Fame Formula*. London: Sidgewick & Jackson, 2008.

Cincinnati: A Guide to the Queen City and Its Neighbors. Cincinnati: The Wiesen-Hart Press, 1943 Charyn, Jerome. *Gangsters and Gold Diggers, Old New York, The Jazz Age, and the Birth of Broadway*. New York: Four Walls Eight Windows, 2003.

Churchwell, Sarah. *Careless People: Murder, Mayhem, and the Invention of the Great Gatsby*. New York: Penguin Books, 2013.

Cist, Charles. *Antiquities of the West and Pioneer History and General and Local Statistics*. Cincinnati: Caleb Clark Printer, 1845.

Cobb, Irvin. *Exit Laughing*. New York: The Bobbs-Merrill Company, 1941.

Coblentz, Edmond. *Newsmen Speak*. Berkeley: University of California Press, 1954.

Condee, William Faricy. *Coal and Culture: Opera Houses in Appalachia*. Athens: Ohio University Press, 2005.

Conover, Frank. *Centennial Portrait and Biographical Record of the City of Dayton*. A. A. Bowen and Company, 1897.

Davis, Joseph Stancliffe. *Essays in the Earlier History of American Corporations*. Clark, New Jersey: The Lawbook Exchange, LTD., 1885.

Douglass, Ann. *Terrible Honesty, Mongrel Manhattan in the 1920s*. New York: The Noonday Press, 1995.

Drewrey, John E. *Post Biographies of Famous Journalists*. Athens: University of Georgia Press, 1942.

Dreiser, Theodore. *Twelve Men*. New York: Bondi and Liveright. 1919.

Driscoll, Charles B. *The Life of O. O. McIntyre*. New York: The Greystone Press, 1938.

Drury, Augustus Waldo. *History of the City of Dayton and Montgomery County, Ohio, Volume 1*. Chicago: The J. J. Clarke Publishing Co., 1909.

Ehmer, Kerstin and Hinderman, Beale. *The School of Sophisticated Drinking*. Vancouver: Greystone Books, 2015.

Fleming, Thomas. *The Story of American Newspapers, Behind the Headlines*. New York: Walker and Company, 1989.

Fitzpatrick, Kevin. *A Journey Into Dorothy Parker's New York, Second Edition*. Berkeley: Roaring Forties Press, 1996.

Fuess, Claude M. *Calvin Coolidge: The Man from Vermont*. New York: Fuess Press, 1939.

Gabler, Neal. *Winchell, Gossip, Power and the Culture of Celebrity*. New York: Vintage Books, 1994.

Gaines, James R. *Wits End, Days and Nights of the Algonquin Round Table*. New York: Harcourt Brace Jovanovich, 1997.

Graff, Harry. *Gallipolis*. Ohio: Works Projects Administration, 1940.

Greenberg, David. *Calvin Coolidge: The American Presidents Series: The 30th President, 1923-1929*. New York: Henry Holt and Company, LLC, 2006.

Greenburg, Michael M. *Peaches & Daddy*. Woodstock & New York: The Overlook Press, 2008.

Hansen, Arlen. Expatriate Paris: A Cultural and Literary Guide. Delaware: Arcade Publishing, 1990.

Henderson, Bruce. *True North: Peary, Cook, and the Race to the Pole*. New York: W. W. Norton. 2005.

Jaker, Bill, Sulek, Frank, and Kanze, Peter. *The Airwaves of New York*. Jefferson, North Carolina, 1998.

Kenny, Laurence J. *The Gallipolis Colony*. Washington: Catholic University of America Press, 1919.

Kratz, Laura E., Ph.D. *Maybelle, Mrs. O. O. McIntyre as We Knew Her*. Gallipolis, Ohio: French City Press, Inc., 1996.

Hines, Stephen W. *Titanic*. Naperville, Illinois: Cumberland House, 2011.

Kahn, Michael A. and West, Richard S. *What Fools These Mortals Be: The Story of Puck, America's First and Most Influential Magazine of Color Political Cartoons*. San Diego: IDW Publishing, 2014.

Ketchum, Richard M. *Will Rogers, His Life and Times*. New York: American heritage Publishing Company, Inc. 1973.

Homberger, Eric. *New York City, A Cultural History*. Northampton, Massachusetts: Interlink Publishing Group, Inc., 2003.

Kratz, Laura E., Ph.D. O. O. McIntyre, *The "Odd" Book*. Jackson, Ohio: Jackson Publishing Co., 1989.

Landers, James. *The Improbable First Century of Cosmopolitan Magazine*. Columbia and London: University of Missouri Press, 2010.

Lawson, Anita. *Irvin S. Cobb*. Bowling Green, Ohio: Bowling Green State University Popular Press, 1984.

Liebling, A. J. *The Telephone Booth Indian*. San Francisco: North Point Press, 1990.

Long, Ray. *My Favorite Story*. New York: International Magazine Company, 1928.

Long, Ray. *My Stories That I Like Best*, New York: International Magazine Company, 1925.

McDonough, John and Egolf, Karen. *The Advertising Age Encyclopedia of Advertising*. Chicago: Fitzroy Dearborn Publishers, 2002.

McIntyre, O. O. *25 Selected Stories of O. O. McIntyre*. New York: International Magazine Company, 1929.

———. *Another "Odd" Book, 25 Selected Stories of O. O. McIntyre*. New York: International Magazine Company, 1932.

———. *The Big Town*. New York: Dodd, Mead & Company, 1935.

———. *White Light Nights*. New York: J. J. Little and Ives Company, 1922.

Miller, Donald L. *Supreme City, How Jazz Age Manhattan Gave Birth to Modern America*. New York: Simon & Schuster, 2014.

Miller, Nathan. T*he 1920s and the Making of Modern America*. Cambridge: Da Capo Press, 2003.

Miller, Zane. *Boss Cox's Cincinnati*. Chicago: The University of Chicago Press, 1968.

Mott, Frank Luther. *A History of American Magazines*. Cambridge: Harvard University Press, 1968.

Nelson, S. B. *History of Cincinnati and Hamilton County, Ohio: Their Past and Present*. Cincinnati: S. B. Nelson and Company, 1894.

Newlin, Keith. *A Theodore Dreiser Encyclopedia*. Connecticut: Greenwood, 2003.

Ohman, Richard. *Selling Culture, Magazines, Markets, and Class at the Turn of the Century*. London: Verso, 1996.

Ott, Katherine. *Fevered Lives*. Cambridge: Harvard University Press, 1996.

Riley, Sam G. *The American Newspaper Columnist*. Westport, Connecticut: Praeger, 1998.

Rutherford, Edward. *New York*. New York: Ballantine Books Trade Paperbacks, 2009.

Sanford, Bruce W. *Don't Shoot the Messenger: How Our Growing Hatred of the Media Threatens Free Speech for All of Us*. New York: Rowan & Littlefield Publishers, Inc. 1999.

Sotos, John G. *The Mary Lincoln Mind-Body Sourcebook: Including a Unifying Diagnosis to Explain Her Public Decay, Manifest Insanity, and Slow Death*. Mt. Vernon, VA: Mount Vernon Book Systems, 2016.

Seckman, Cathy Hester. *East Liverpool*. Charleston, South Carolina: Arcadia Publishing, 2015.

Spencer, David Ralph. *The Yellow Journalism: The Press and America's Emergence as a World Power*. Evanston, Illinois: Northwestern University Press, 2007.

Steffins, Lincoln. *The Struggle for Self-government*. New York: McClure, Phillps & Co, 1906.

Stephens, Mitchell. *A History of News*. New York: Harcourt Brace College Publishers, 1997.

Stoltzfus, Duane C. S. *Freedom from Advertising: E.W. Scripps's Chicago Experiment*. Urbana and Chicago: University of Illinois Press, 2007.

Sullivan, Mark and Rather, Dan. *Our Times, edited with new material by Dan Rather*. New York: Scribner, 2013.

Tebbel, John. *The Compact History of the American Newspaper*. New York: Hawthorn Books, Inc., 1963.

They Built a City, 150 Years of Industrial Cincinnati. Cincinnati: The Cincinnati Post, 1938.

Turner, Hy B. *When Giants Ruled, The Story of Park Row*. New York: Fordham University Press, 1999.

Ulman, George. *Valentino as I Knew Him*. New York: A. L. Burt Company, 1926.

Vandercook, John. *The Complete Revolution*. Madison: The University of Wisconsin, 1910.

Verhoeven, Wil. *Americomania and the French Revolution Debate in Britain, 1789-1802*. Cambridge: Cambridge University Press, 2013.

Warner, Jay. *How to Have Your Hit Song Published*. Winona, Minnesota: Hal Leonard Corporation, 2006.

Webster, H. T. *Webster Unabridged*. New York: American-Straford Press, Inc., 1945.

Yagoda, Ben. *Will Rogers, A Biography*. New York: Alfred A. Knopf, 1993.

Young, William H. with Young, Nancy K. *American Popular Culture Through History, the 1930s*. Westport, Connecticut: Greenwood Press, 2002.

Ziegfeld, Patricia. *The Ziegfeld's Girl*. Boston: Little, Brown and Company, 1964.

Newspapers

The syndicated columns of O. O. McIntyre, 1917-1938.

Asbury Park Press. "Liver Extract Used to Combat Pernicious Anemia." May 13, 1927, 9.

Briggs, Jonathon E. *The Baltimore Sun*. "Wright Brothers Flew Into a Newspaper Fog." December 14, 2003

Bell, Nelson B. "About the Showshops." *The Washington Post*. July 15, 1931, 11.

The Brooklyn Daily Eagle. "Barred Crowds Clamor to View Valentino's Body." August 26, 1926, 1.

———. "Crowds Jam Street to View Valentino's Body Lying in State." August 24, 1926, 1.

The Cincinnati Enquirer. "Author's Widow Dies: Native of Gallipolis." June 19, 1942, 8.

———. "Bullet Victim." July 10, 1935, 1.

———. "'Cincinnatus,' Alfred Segal Dead at 84." March 5, 1968, 21.

———. "Eugene Walter Dies: Authored Many Plays." September 27, 1941, 19.

———. "French are After our Airhips." December 1905, 2.

———. "Ohio Inventors and Their Airship." December 19, 1903, 1.

New Castle Herald. "Fought his way up from Lowly Desk of 'Cub' Reporter." April 11, 1908, 3.

Copeland, Royal S., M. D. "Pernicious Anemia Comes on Slowly." *The Evening News*. June 11, 1928, 25.

Dayton Herald. "Dayton Boys Solve Problem." December 18, 1903.

Democrat and Chronicle. "Ex-War Correspondent Dies." January 17, 1957, 8.

The Evening Mail. "Ismay Tells Probers How he Came to Save Himself." April 19, 1912, 1.

———. "List of Saved Grows as Carpathia Comes in." April 18, 1912, 1.

———. "Bride of Editor Whose Marriage was a Surprise." August 2, 1922, 3.

———. "Della Fox Sent to Sanitarium." June 1, 1900, 1.

Gallipolis Journal, "Married: Small-Gatewood." October 28, 1880, 3.

Grady, Denise. Was Mary Todd Lincoln Driven 'Mad' by a Vitamin Deficiency? *The New York Times*. July 8, 2016.

Harper, Lucius. "Dustin' Off the News: McIntyre was Really 'Odd.'" *The Chicago Defender*. February 26, 1938, 16.

Harrisburg Telegraph. "Herbert H. Weakley." July 31, 1906, 7.

Hubner, Rose E. "O. O. McIntyre Described as O. Henry's Successor." *The Atlanta Journal Constitution*. January 12, 1921. 8.

The Journal (Gallipolis, Ohio). "Consolidated Telephone Agents," January 1, 1880, 2.

Kansas City Star. "O. O. McIntyre's Father Dies. June 1, 1926. n.p.

The Los Angeles Times. Lovell, Philip M. "Care of the Body." March 3, 1929, 158.

The Marion Star. "A Newspaperwoman Weds Magazine Man." September 27, 1910, 1.

Leary, Warren E. "Who Reached the North Pole First?" *The New York Times*. February 7, 1997.

McIntyre, O. O. "Memories of Cincinnati." *The Cincinnati Post*. 1930, 32.

New York Herald Tribune. "Funeral Today for Ray Long will be Private." July 11, 1935, 12.

The New York Times. "Brief Reviews, Valentino." November 14, 1926, BR20.

———. "Charles Driscoll, Columnist, Dead." January 16, 1951. 29.

———. "O. O. McIntyre Dead: Columnist was 54." February 15, 1938. 25.

———. "Ray Long's Ashes Scattered." August 30, 1935, 17.

———. "Ray Long Eulogized at Funeral Service Today." July 12, 1935, 19.

———. "The New Fifth Avenue." June 27, 1909, 37.

———. "Titanic Sinks Four Hours After Hitting Iceberg." April 16, 1912, 1.

The Oneonta Star. "Rudolf Valentino, Film Sheik Dies; Greatest Screen Lover of All Time in Coma at End." August 24, 1926, 1.

Pegler, Westbrook. "Fair Enough." *The Washington Post*. February 26, 1938, X7.

Poughkeepsie Eagle-News. "Rudolph Valentino Loses his Fight Against Death." August 24, 1926. 1.

The Sun. "Carpathia Lets no Secrets of the Titanic's Loss Escape by Wireless as she Draws Near This Port." April 18, 1912.

Tackett, Matthew. "O. O. McIntyre." *The Chicago Defender*. April 7, 1928, A2.

Van Gelder, Robert. "Mr. McIntyre's Notes on the Big Town." *The New York Times*. June 30, 1935, BR11.

Van Paassen, Pierre. "Lights of Paris." *The Atlanta Constitution*. July 9, 1926, 4.

Watkins, Mel. "What was it about 'Amos 'n' Andy'?. *The New York Times*. July 7, 1991, 22.

Xenia Daily Gazette. "Ray Long, Noted Editor and Writer, Is Suicide." July 10, 1935, 1.

Magazines and Journals

The *Hearst's International Combined with Cosmopolitan* articles of O. O. McIntyre, 1922-1938.

Case, Elizabeth. "World of Fiction, Fact and Fancy, An Interesting Account of the Irvin Cobb's Career."
   The Hartford Courant. August 21, 1938, D6.

Cobb, Irvin S. "O! O! McIntyre." *Delineator*. March 1934.

Cooper, Catherine. "Nothing but the Facts: Bootblack, Butcher Boy, Bartender, Boss." *Cincinnati Magazine*, February 1983.

Daugherty, Greg. "Odd McIntyre: The Man Who Taught America About New York." *Smithsonian Magazine*, April 24, 2011.

Dick, Lyle. "Robert Peary's North Polar Narratives and the Making of an American Icon,." *American Studies*, 2004.

The Editor and Publisher. "Cook's Confession. How the North Pole Doctor was Persuaded by a Newspaper Man." December 3, 1910, Vol. 10. No. 23.

Harkins, John. "O. O. McIntyre." *Life*. July 1932, 13.

Farrar, John. "O. O. McIntyre Day by Day." *The Bookman; a Review of Books and Life*. April 1928, 67.

Fortune. "The Cosmopolitan of Ray Long." March 1931. 87.

Howard, Roy. "Such is Life." *Life*. April 26, 1929, 2.

Huddleston, E. L. "O. O. McIntyre Broadway Populist." *American Studies*, Spring 1974, 79.

Hughs, Rupert. "O. O. McIntyre," *Hearst's International Combined with Cosmopolitan*, April 1937, 8.

Irwin, Will. "Cox—the Last of the Bosses." *Colliers*. January 13, 1912. 12 – 13.

Kenny, Lawrence J. "The Gallipolis Colony." *The Catholic Historical Review*, January 1919, 415-451.

Levine, Lawrence W. "American Culture and the Great Depression." *The Yale Review*. January 1885. 196.

Lyon, Zoe. "Harris Merton Lyon." *American Literary Realism* 1879 - 1910,
Lockwood, Jeffrey A. "Voices from the Past: What we can Learn from the Rocky Mountain Locusts." *American Entomologist.* Winter 2001, 208.
The National Magazine. "The Story of Newark." November, 1892, 464 – 477.
Time. "The Press: Columnist v. Columnist. July 8, 1935.
McIntyre, O. O. "The Autobiography of O. O. McIntyre." *New McClure's.* March 1929, 54.
Moser, Whet. "Yellow Journalism, Arthur Brisbane, and the Sins of the Grandfather." *Chicago Magazine,* May 31, 2011. 167.
Rees, Thomas. "Harris Merton Lyon: A Neglected American Master of the Short Story." *The Journal of American Culture.* March 1980. 145 – 148.
The Saturday Evening Post. "Who's Who—And Why." January 16, 1912, 23.
Sotos, J. G. "'What an Affliction': Mary Todd Lincoln's Fatal Pernicious Anemia." *Perspectives in Biology and Medicine*, vol. 58 no. 4, 2015, 419-443.
Starrett, Vincent. "Books Alive." *Random House*, 1940, 132.
Time. "Average Man." November 26, 1945, 25.
Wheeler, Edward J. "George B. Cox, The Last of the American Manchus." *Current Literature.* January 1912.
W. J. P. "O. O. McIntyre has an Off-Day." *Life.* November 17, 1927, 8.

Other Sources

Garfrerick, Beth H. *A History of Weekly Community Newspapers in the United States 1900 to 1980.* Dissertation, The University of Alabama, 2009.
Hartwick, Deborah Walker. *Bowery Bread Lines, Peruvian Bonds and Suicides: O. O. McIntyre's Portrayal of the Great Depression.* Thesis. Ohio University, 1998.
Hayes, Will H. Comments Given at the Twilight Memorial Held in Connection with the Sesqui-Centennial of Gallipolis, Ohio. August 11, 1940.
Lesiak, Christine. *A Plague of Locusts: A Nebraska Story.* NETNebraska, documentary, 2012.
New York Landmarks Preservation Commission. *Upper West Side/Central Park West Historic District Designation Report*, April 24, 1990.
Shively, Max Edward. *The Conte of O. O. McIntyre: An Assessment of his Contribution to Personalized Journalism.* Dissertation. Ohio University, 1980.
Stevens, George E. *From Penny Paper to Post and Times-Star: Mr. Scripps First Link.* Dissertation. University of Minnesota, 1968.
Whitely, Edna Pierce. *The O. O. McIntyre Story, Chronicle of a Journalist of Note.* Thesis. The College of Communication of Ohio University, March 1995.

Index

270

194

About the Type

This book was set in Baskerville. A serif typeface designed in the 1750s by John Baskerville (1706–1775) in Birmingham, England, it's noted for its crisp edges, high contrast, and generous proportions.

Baskerville was a master type-founder and printer who began his career as a servant in a clergyman's home. Although Baskerville was illiterate, he became very interested in calligraphy and taught himself handwriting and inscription.

After making a fortune as a manufacturer of varnished lacquer goods, he created his font as part of an ambitious project to create books of the greatest quality possible. In addition to the typeface, Baskerville's work included experiments with printing technology, development of darker, longer-lasting inks, and the creation of new types of paper.

R. Scott Williams is chief operating officer and senior vice president of sales and marketing at the Newseum in Washington, D.C. Williams earned his degree in journalism from the University of Memphis. He then held positions at several advertising agencies and organizations, including Elvis Presley Enterprises, Inc.

He serves on the board of the Washington D.C. chapter of the American Advertising Federation and on the board of the Historical Society of Washington, D.C.

He currently lives with his wife and two daughters in Arlington, Virginia. Passionate about discovering and sharing forgotten stories from the past, in his spare time he explores the history of the American South, especially around his home in West Tennessee. His first book was *The Forgotten Adventures of Richard Halliburton: from Tennessee to Timbuktu.*

For more about Williams and Odd McIntyre, visit AnOddBook.com.

CPSIA information can be obtained
at www.ICGtesting.com
Printed in the USA
FFOW02n1319130417
34569FF